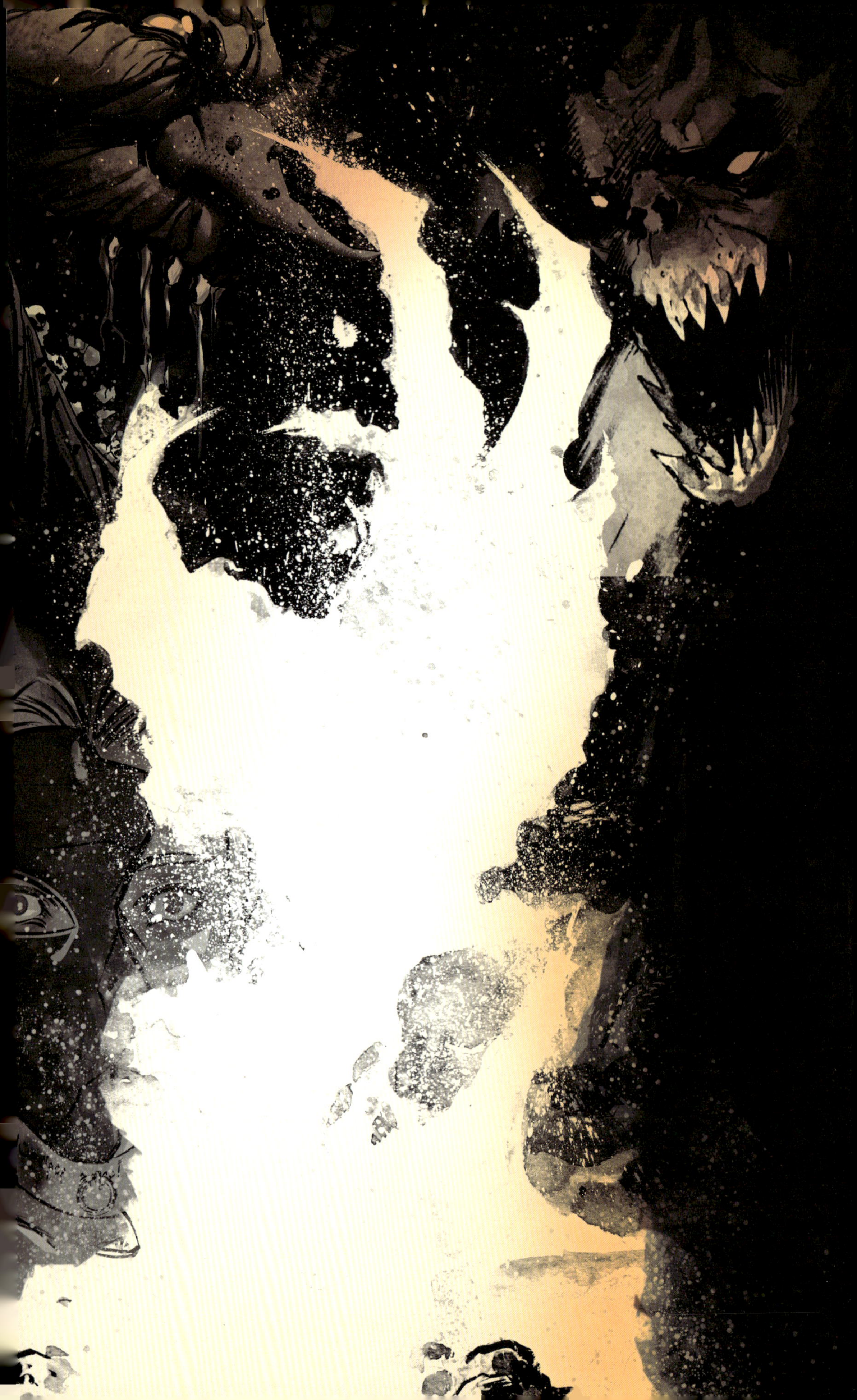

Grimm Tales from the Cave

Soldiers of Fortune

W: Cullen Bunn A: Andrea Mutti
L: Justin Birch E: Chris Fernandez

Pay the Piper

W: Mark London A: Luisa Russo
C: Roman Stevens L: Justin Birch
E: Chris Fernandez

Hello, My Name Is...

W: Nadia Shammas A: Rowan MacColl
L: Micah Myers E: Chris Sanchez

Mother's Thorn

W: Anthony Cleveland A: Shane Connery Volk
C: Luca Romano L: Justin Birch
E: Brian Hawkins

Birds of a Feather

W: Stephanie Phillips A: Maan House
C: Giorgio Spalletta L: Justin Birch
E: Chris Sanchez

Billie and Her Friend Death

W: Che Grayson A: Cecilia Lo Valvo
C: Giorgio Spalletta L: Justin Birch
E: Chris Sanchez

Little Deaths

W: Malissa White A: Rio Burton
L: Micah Myers E: Chris Sanchez

The Girl with Dirty Hands

W: Dalton Deschain A: Ho Seng Hui
C: Joana Lafuente L: Justin Birch
E: Brian Hawkins

No Good Deed

W: Chuck Harp A: Nicolas Faluotico
C: Allison Hu L: Justin Birch
E: Brian Hawkins

Weft

W: Mario Candelaria A: David Escobar
C: Luca Romano L: Justin Birch
E: Brian Hawkins

New Nightmares, Sold Cheap

W: Christopher Sebela A: Val Halvorson
L: Micah Myers E: Chris Sanchez

Laura Chacón	Founder
Mark London	CEO and Chief Creative Officer
Giovanna T. Orozco	VP of Operations
Chris Fernandez	Publisher
Chris Sanchez	Editor-in-Chief
Cecilia Medina	Chief Financial Officer
Manuel Castellanos	Director of Sales & Retailer Relations
Allison Pond	Marketing Director
Miguel Angel Zapata	Design Director/Book Designer
Brian Hawkins	Assistant Editor
Diana Bermúdez	Graphic Designer
David Reyes	Graphic Designer
Adriana T. Orozco	Interactive Media Designer
Nicolás Zea Arias	Audiovisual Production
Frank Silva	Executive Assistant
Stephanie Hidalgo	Executive Assistant

FOR MAD CAVE COMICS, INC. **Grimm Tales from the Cave**™ Published by Mad Cave Studios, Inc. 8838 SW 129 St. Miami, FL 33176. © 2021 Mad Cave Studios, Inc. All rights reserved. All **Grimm Tales from the Cave**™ characters and the distinctive likeness(es) thereof are Trademarks and Copyrights © 2021 Mad Cave Studios, Inc. ALL RIGHTS RESERVED. No portion of this publication may be reproduced or transmitted in any form or by any means, without the express written permission of Mad Cave Studios, Inc. Names, characters, places, and incidents featured in this publication are the product of the author's imaginations or are used fictitiously. Any resemblance to actual persons (living or dead), events, institutions, or locales, without satiric intent, is coincidental. First Printing. Printed in Canada. ISBN: 978-1-952303-24-1

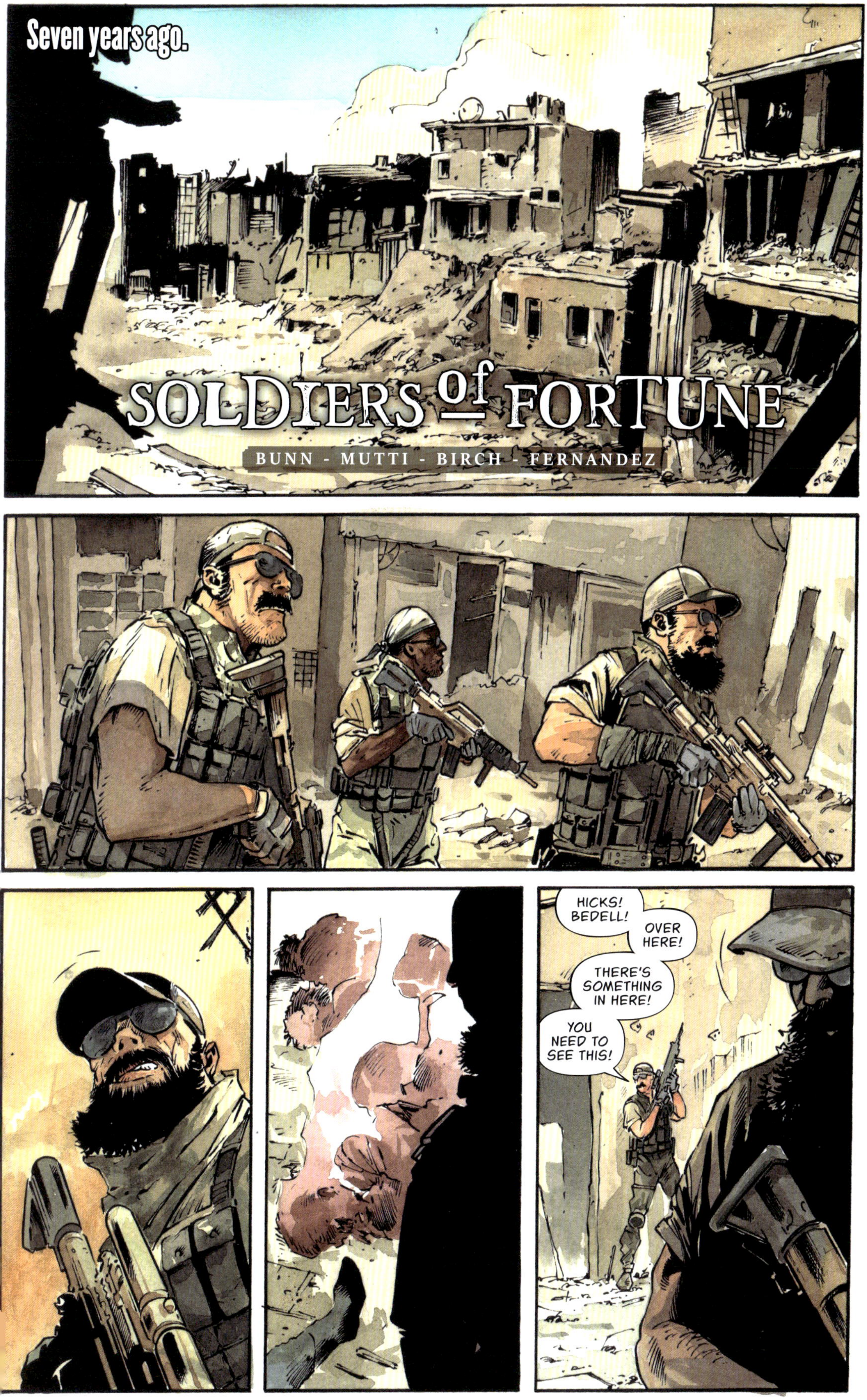
Seven years ago.
SOLDIERS of FORTUNE
BUNN - MUTTI - BIRCH - FERNANDEZ
HICKS! BEDELL!
OVER HERE!
THERE'S SOMETHING IN HERE!
YOU NEED TO SEE THIS!

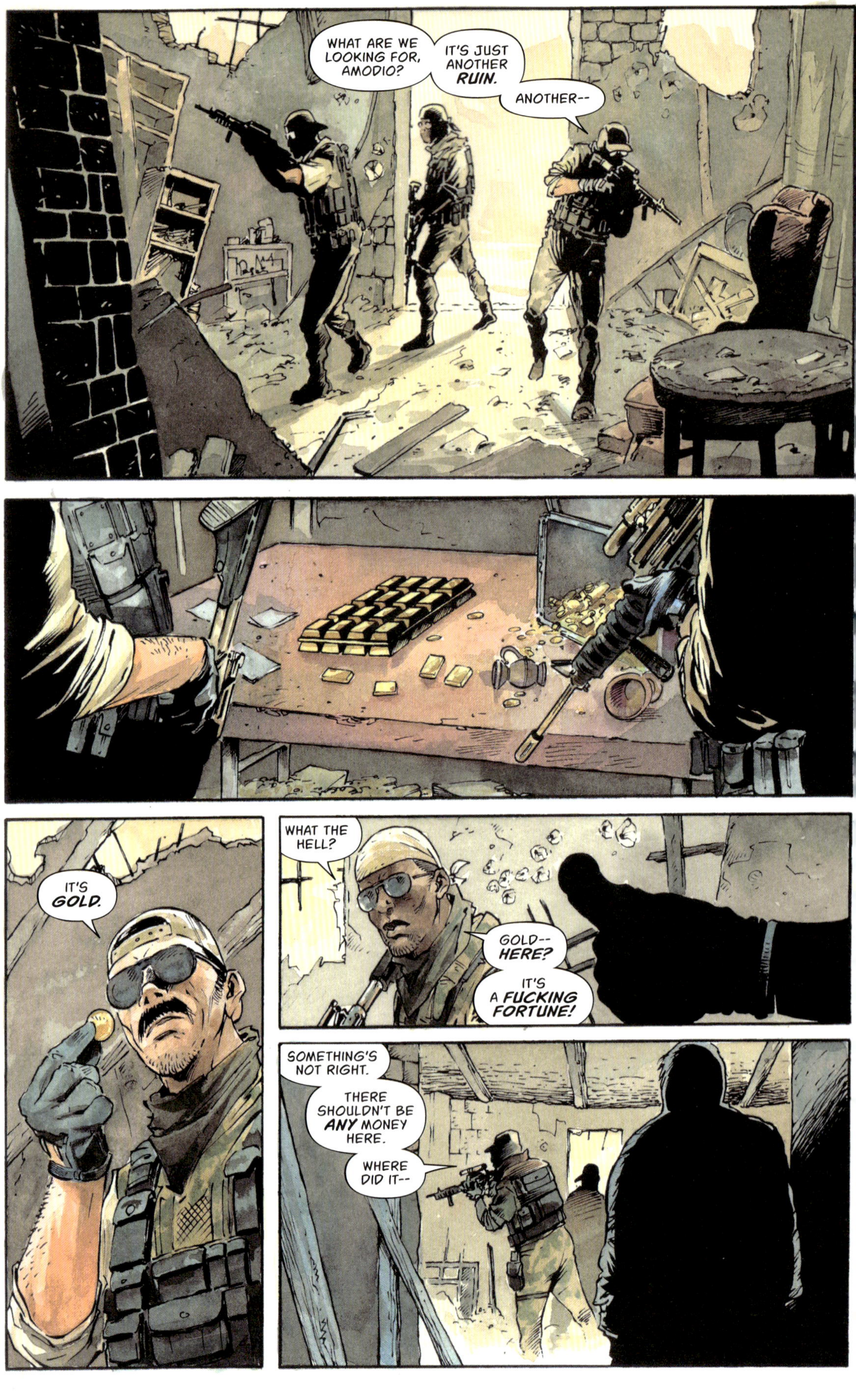
WHAT ARE WE LOOKING FOR, AMODIO?
IT'S JUST ANOTHER RUIN.
ANOTHER--
IT'S GOLD.
WHAT THE HELL?
GOLD-- HERE?
IT'S A FUCKING FORTUNE!
SOMETHING'S NOT RIGHT.
THERE SHOULDN'T BE ANY MONEY HERE.
WHERE DID IT--

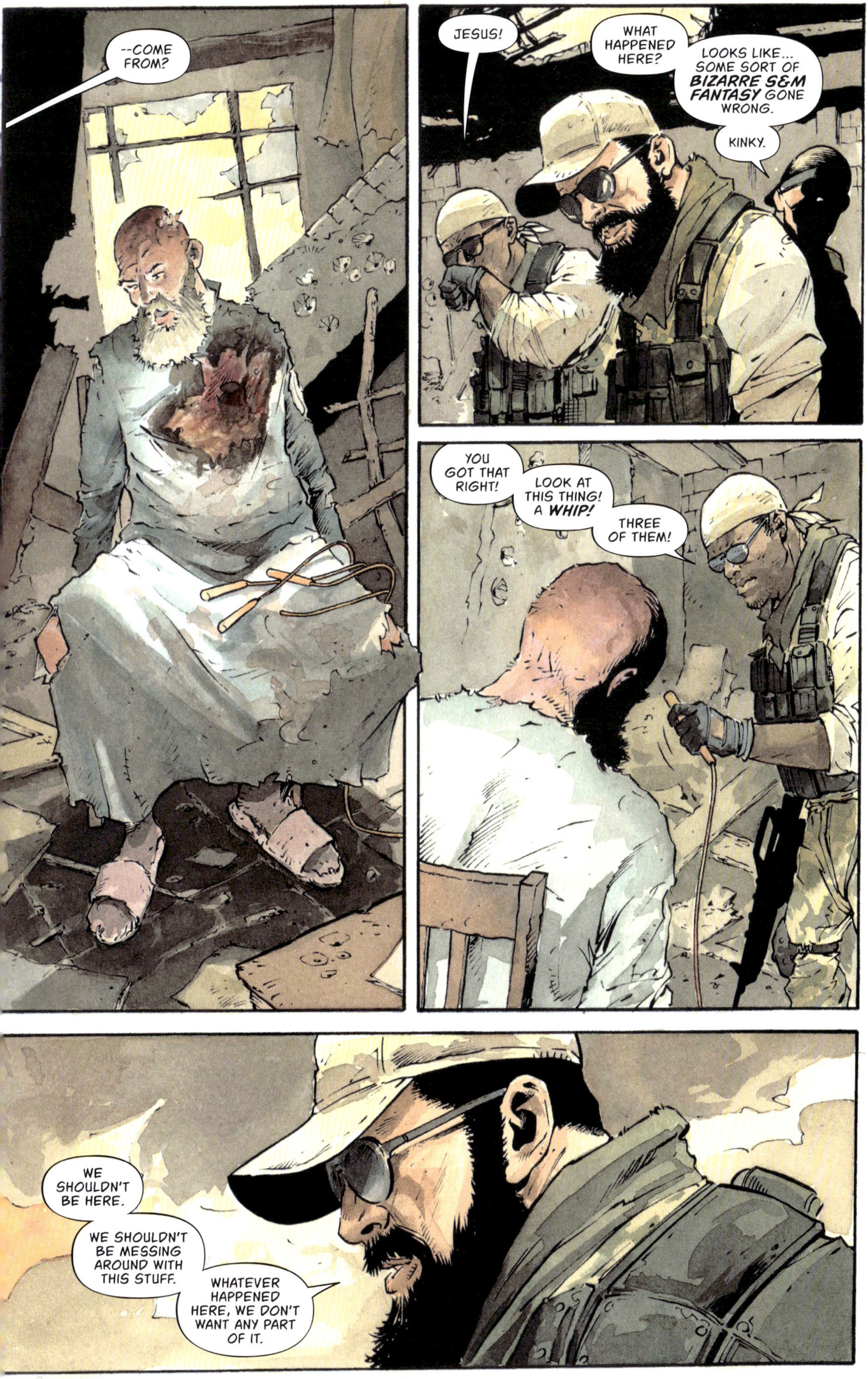
--COME FROM?
JESUS!
WHAT HAPPENED HERE?
LOOKS LIKE... SOME SORT OF **BIZARRE S&M FANTASY** GONE WRONG.
KINKY.
YOU GOT THAT RIGHT!
LOOK AT THIS THING! A ***WHIP!***
THREE OF THEM!
WE SHOULDN'T BE HERE.
WE SHOULDN'T BE MESSING AROUND WITH THIS STUFF.
WHATEVER HAPPENED HERE, WE DON'T WANT ANY PART OF IT.

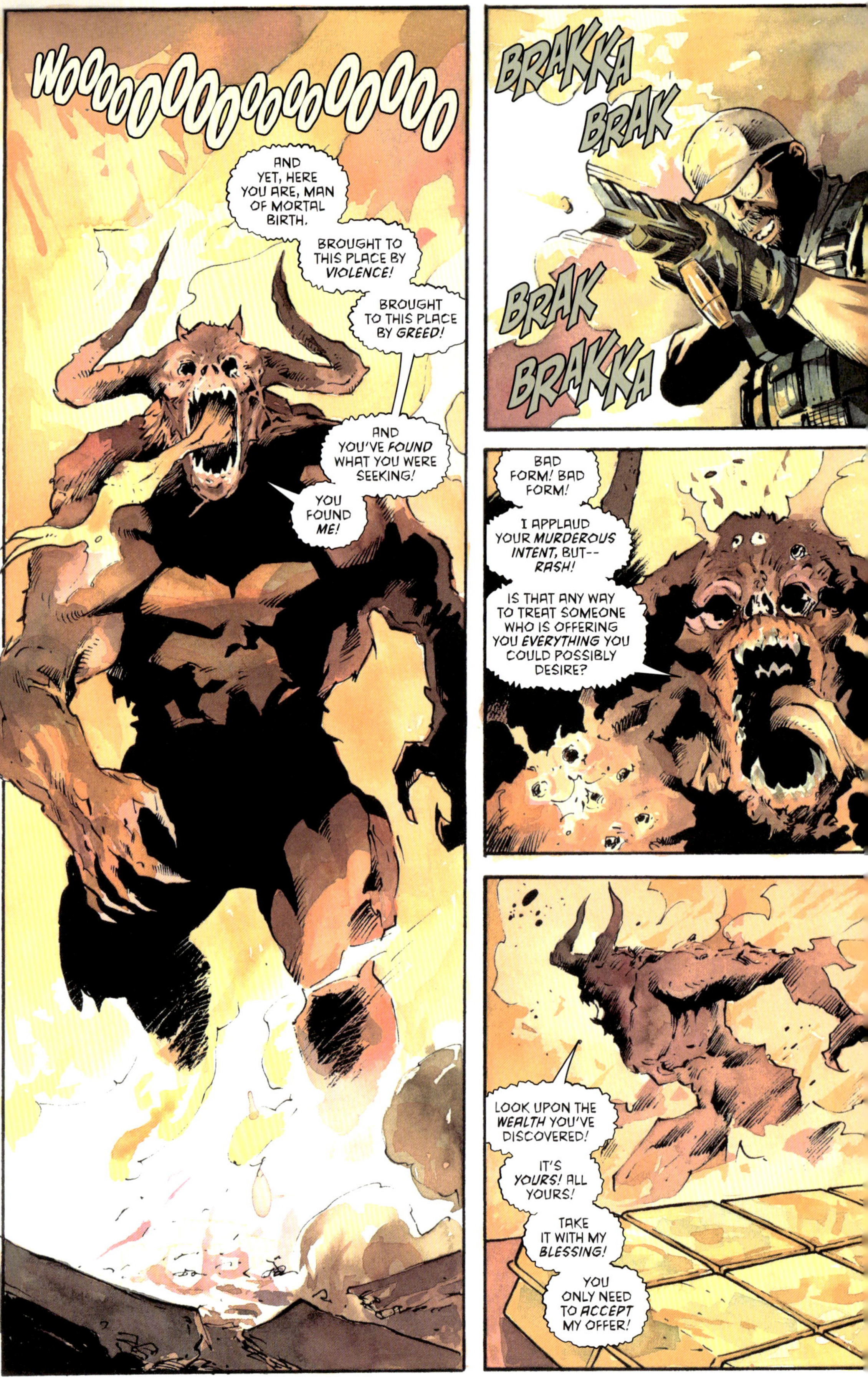
WOOOOOOOOOOOOOOOOOO
AND YET, HERE YOU ARE, MAN OF MORTAL BIRTH.
BROUGHT TO THIS PLACE BY *VIOLENCE!*
BROUGHT TO THIS PLACE BY *GREED!*
AND YOU'VE *FOUND* WHAT YOU WERE SEEKING!
YOU FOUND *ME!*
BRAKKA BRAK
BRAK BRAKKA
BAD FORM! BAD FORM!
I APPLAUD YOUR *MURDEROUS INTENT*, BUT-- *RASH!*
IS THAT ANY WAY TO TREAT SOMEONE WHO IS OFFERING YOU *EVERYTHING* YOU COULD POSSIBLY DESIRE?
LOOK UPON THE *WEALTH* YOU'VE DISCOVERED!
IT'S *YOURS!* ALL YOURS!
TAKE IT WITH MY *BLESSING!*
YOU ONLY NEED TO *ACCEPT* MY OFFER!

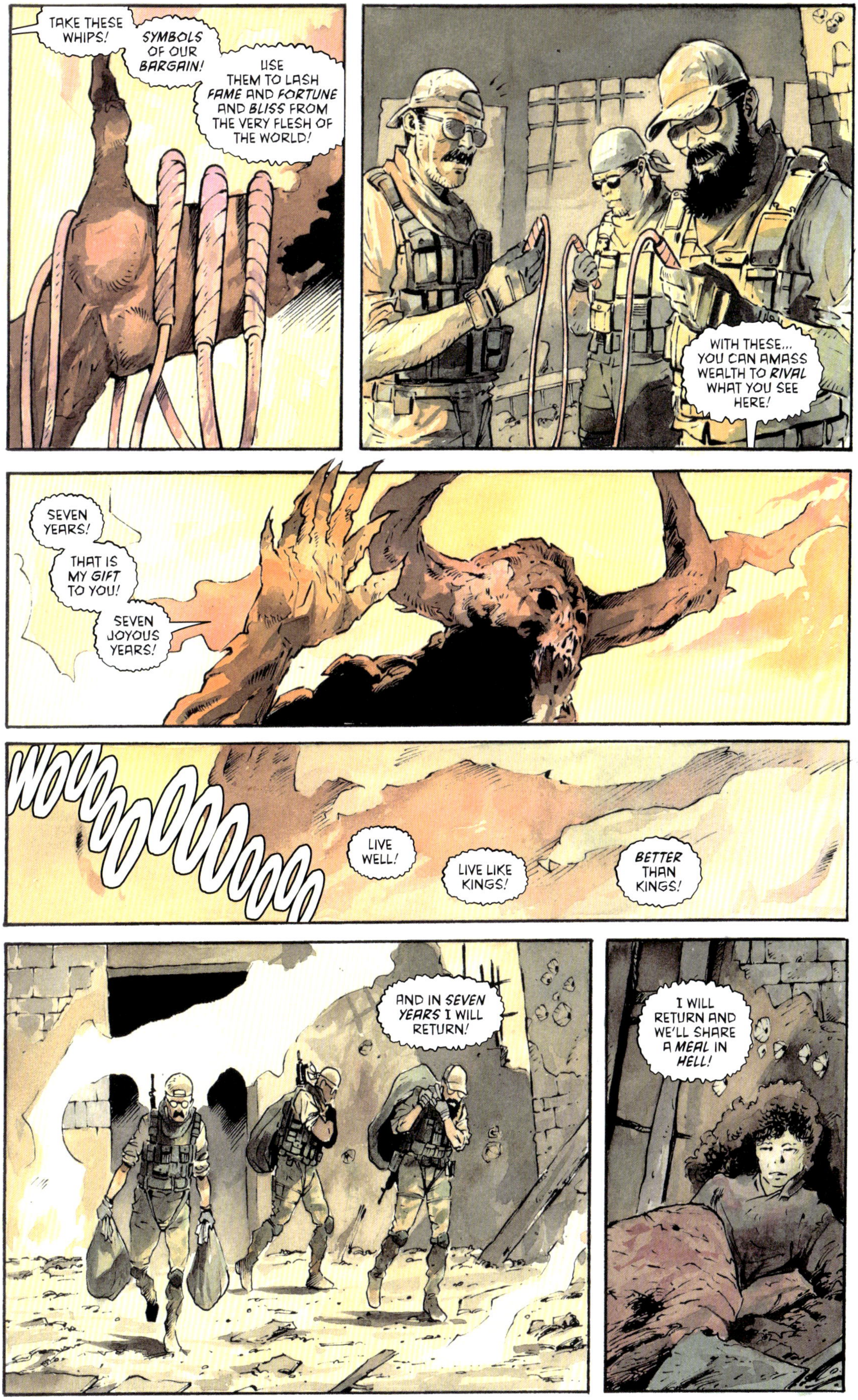
TAKE THESE WHIPS!
SYMBOLS OF OUR BARGAIN!
USE THEM TO LASH FAME AND FORTUNE AND BLISS FROM THE VERY FLESH OF THE WORLD!
WITH THESE... YOU CAN AMASS WEALTH TO RIVAL WHAT YOU SEE HERE!
SEVEN YEARS!
THAT IS MY GIFT TO YOU!
SEVEN JOYOUS YEARS!
WOOOOOOOOOOOOO
LIVE WELL!
LIVE LIKE KINGS!
BETTER THAN KINGS!
AND IN SEVEN YEARS I WILL RETURN!
I WILL RETURN AND WE'LL SHARE A MEAL IN HELL!

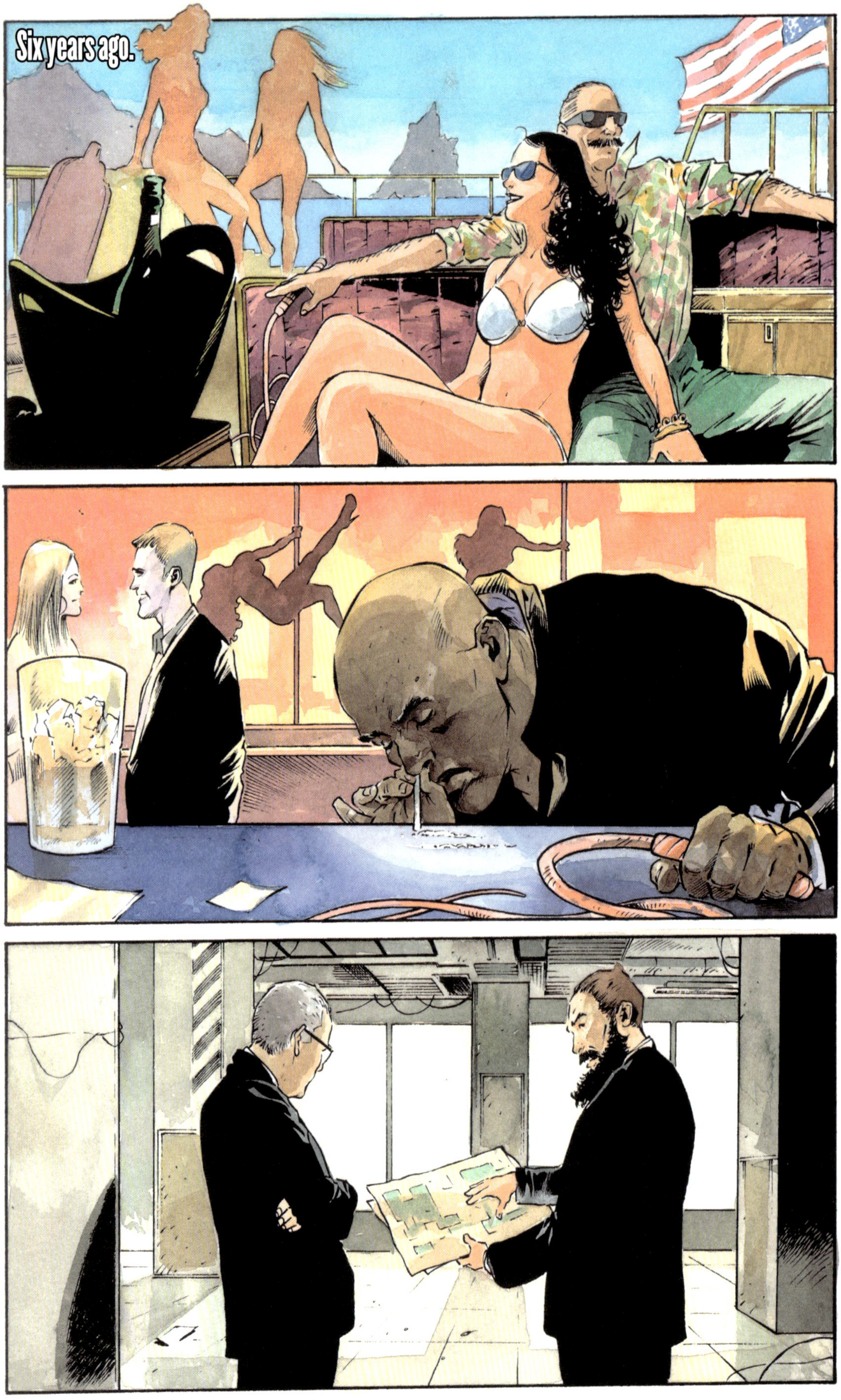
Six years ago.

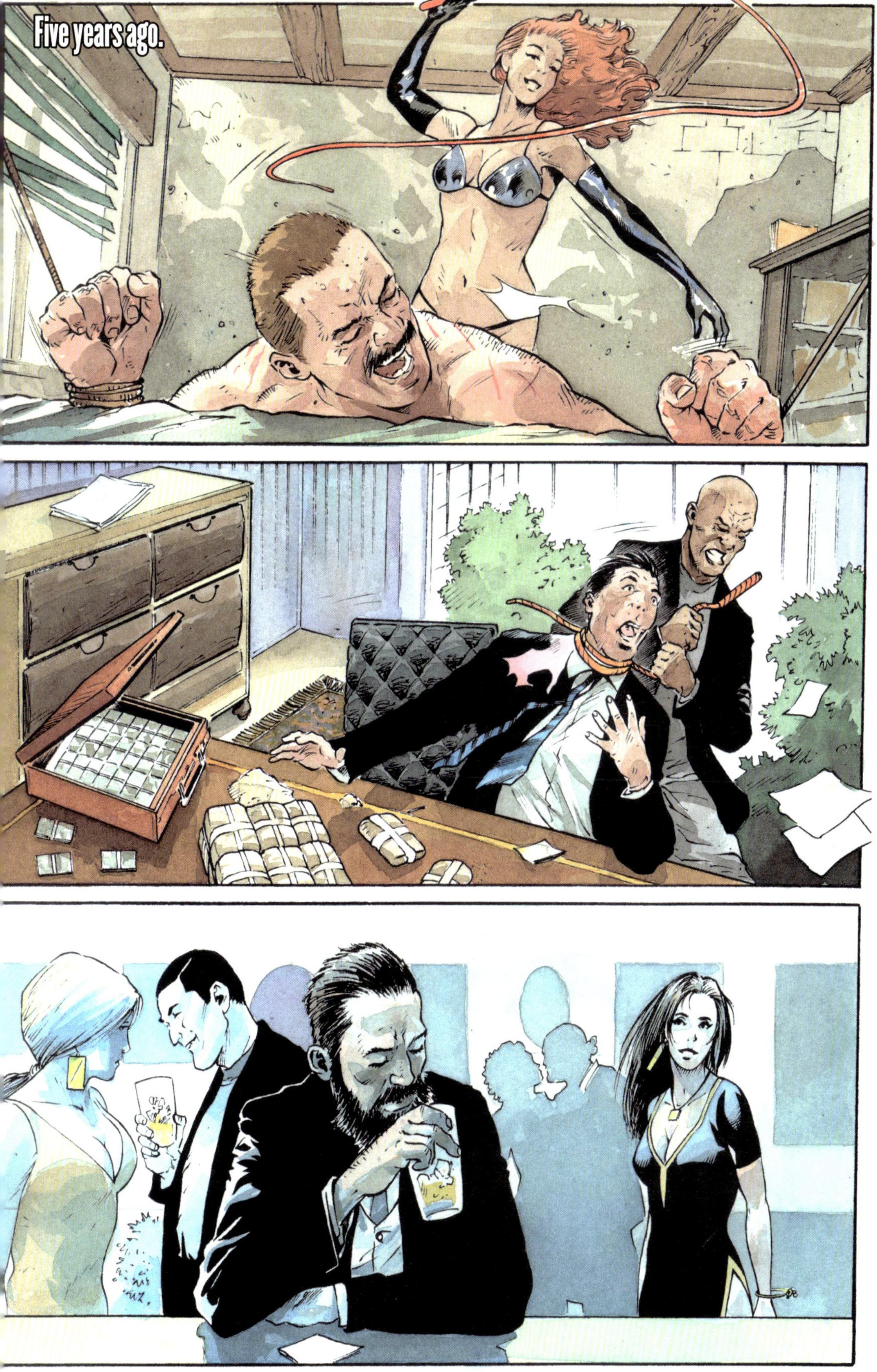
Five years ago.

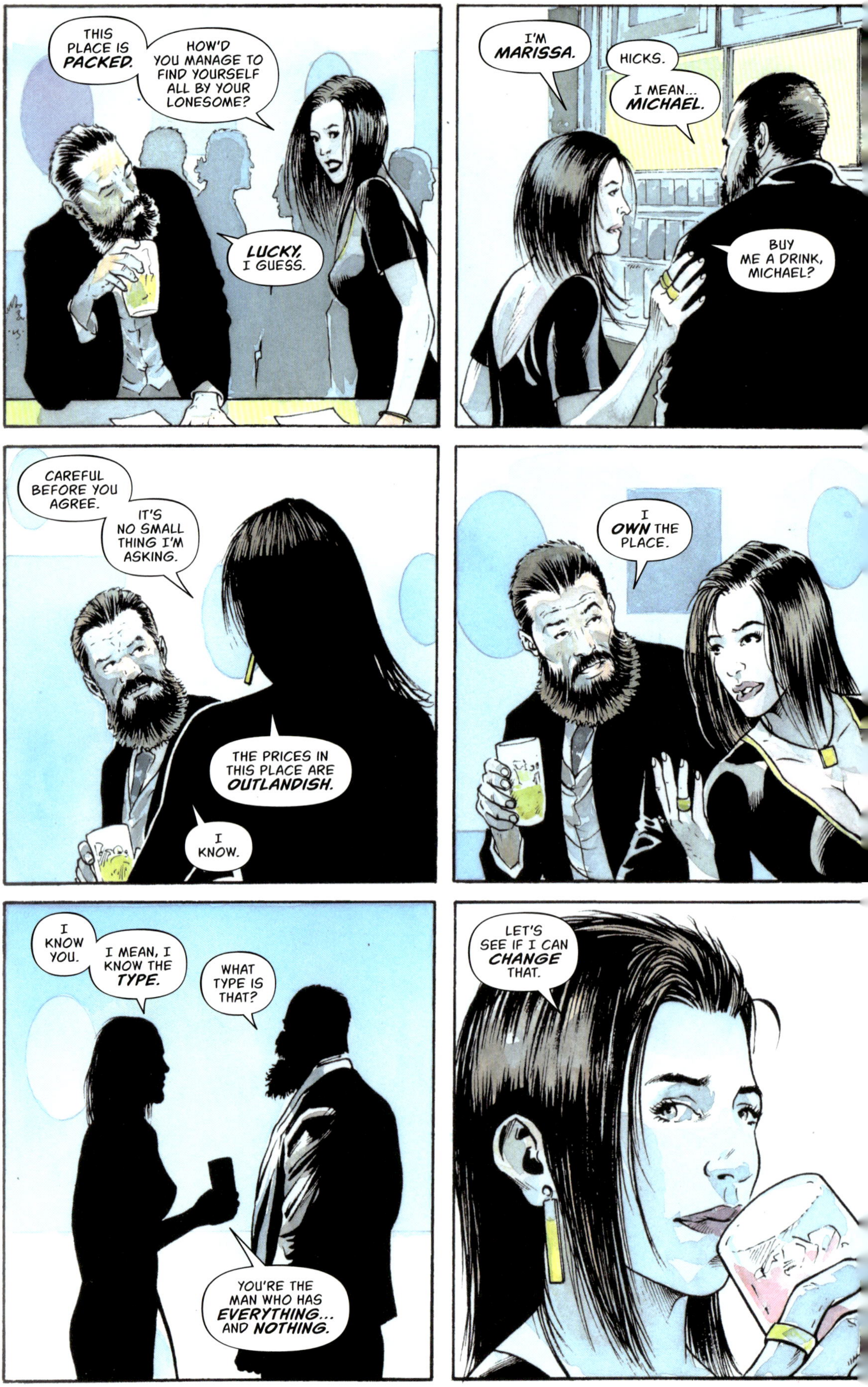
THIS PLACE IS **PACKED.**
HOW'D YOU MANAGE TO FIND YOURSELF ALL BY YOUR LONESOME?
LUCKY, I GUESS.
I'M ***MARISSA.***
HICKS.
I MEAN... ***MICHAEL.***
BUY ME A DRINK, MICHAEL?
CAREFUL BEFORE YOU AGREE.
IT'S NO SMALL THING I'M ASKING.
THE PRICES IN THIS PLACE ARE ***OUTLANDISH.***
I KNOW.
I ***OWN*** THE PLACE.
I KNOW YOU.
I MEAN, I KNOW THE ***TYPE.***
WHAT TYPE IS THAT?
YOU'RE THE MAN WHO HAS ***EVERYTHING...*** AND ***NOTHING.***
LET'S SEE IF I CAN ***CHANGE*** THAT.

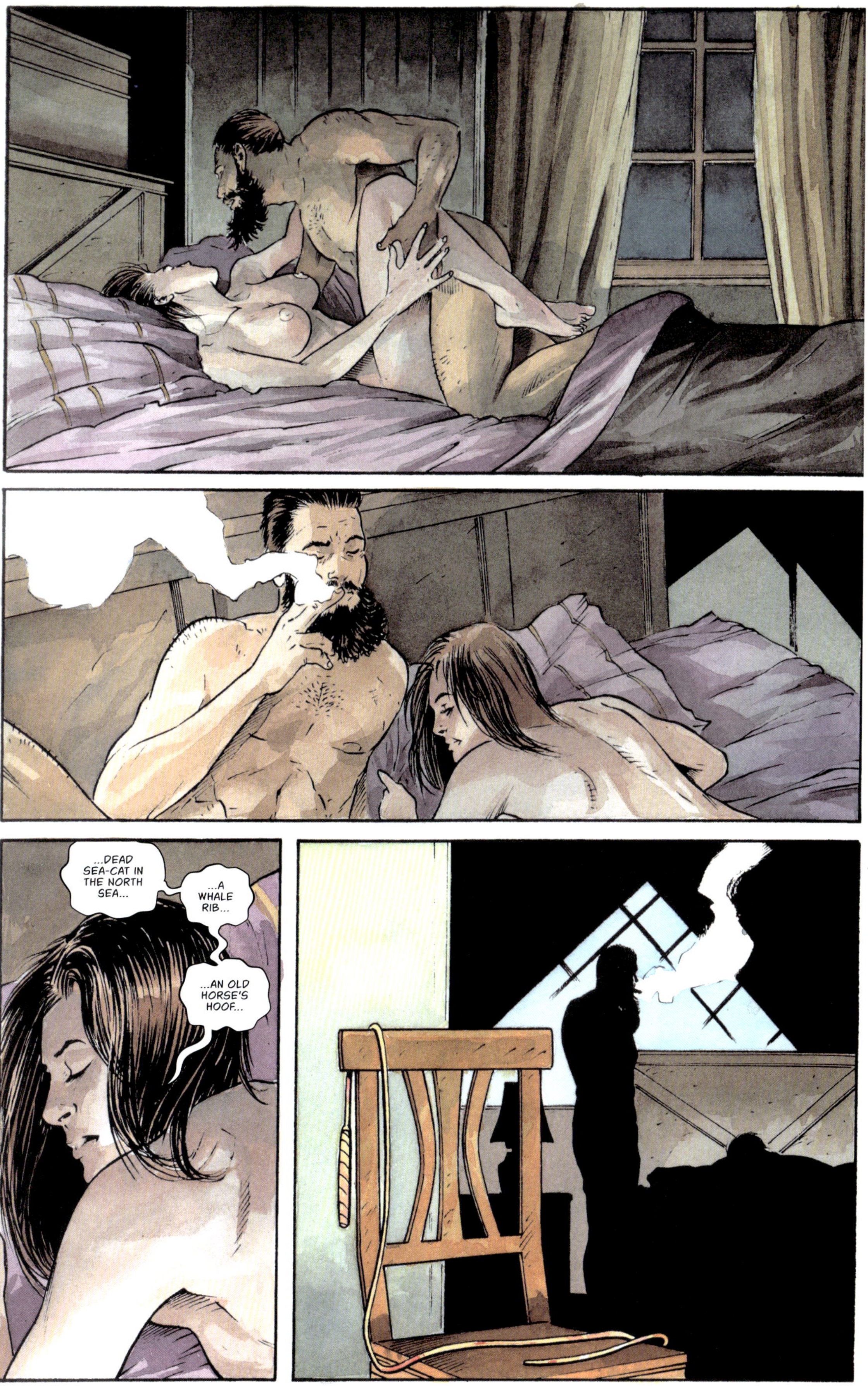
...DEAD SEA-CAT IN THE NORTH SEA...
...A WHALE RIB...
...AN OLD HORSE'S HOOF...

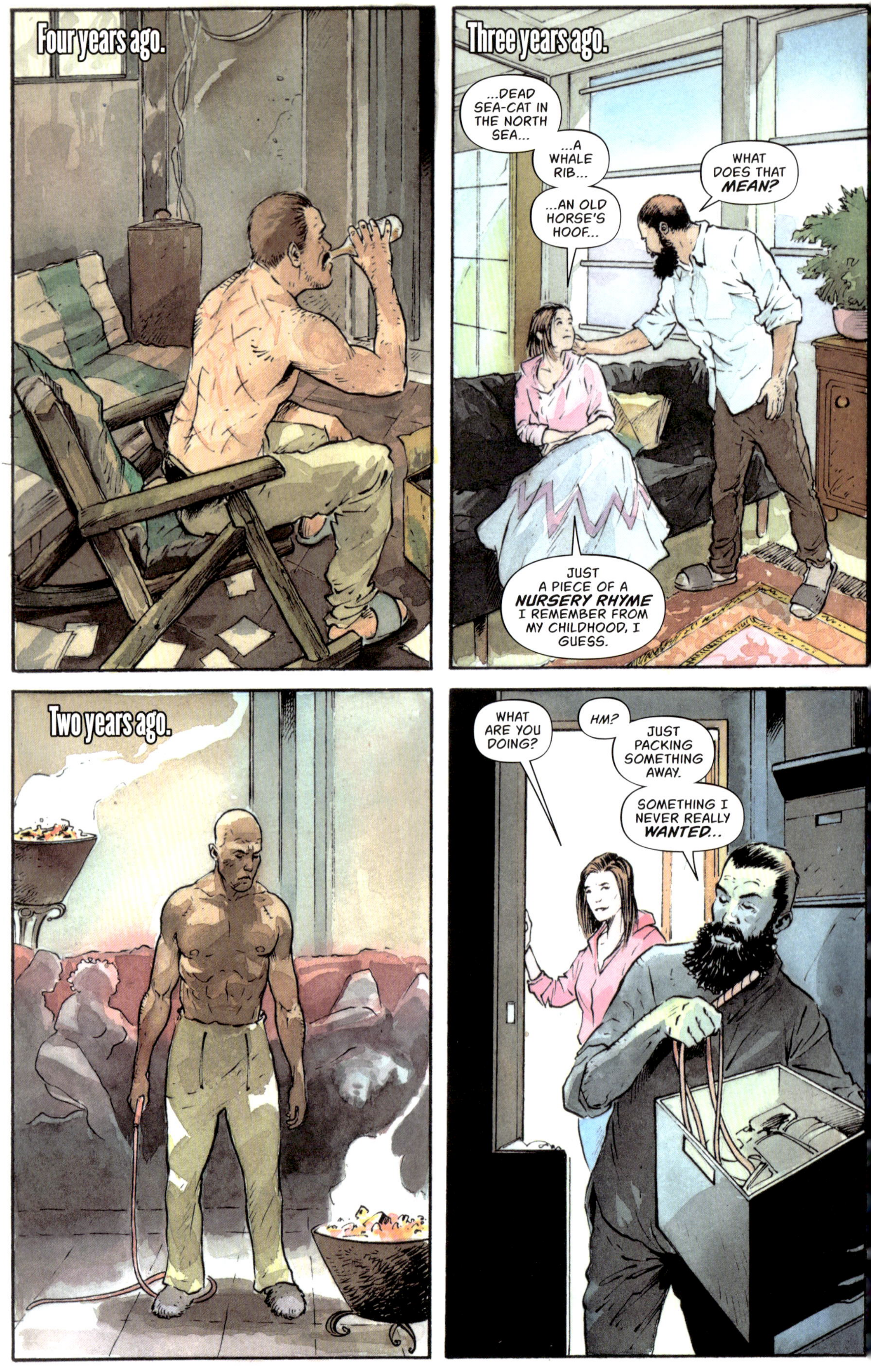
Four years ago.
Three years ago.
...DEAD SEA-CAT IN THE NORTH SEA...
...A WHALE RIB...
...AN OLD HORSE'S HOOF...
WHAT DOES THAT MEAN?
JUST A PIECE OF A NURSERY RHYME I REMEMBER FROM MY CHILDHOOD, I GUESS.
Two years ago.
WHAT ARE YOU DOING?
HM?
JUST PACKING SOMETHING AWAY.
SOMETHING I NEVER REALLY WANTED...

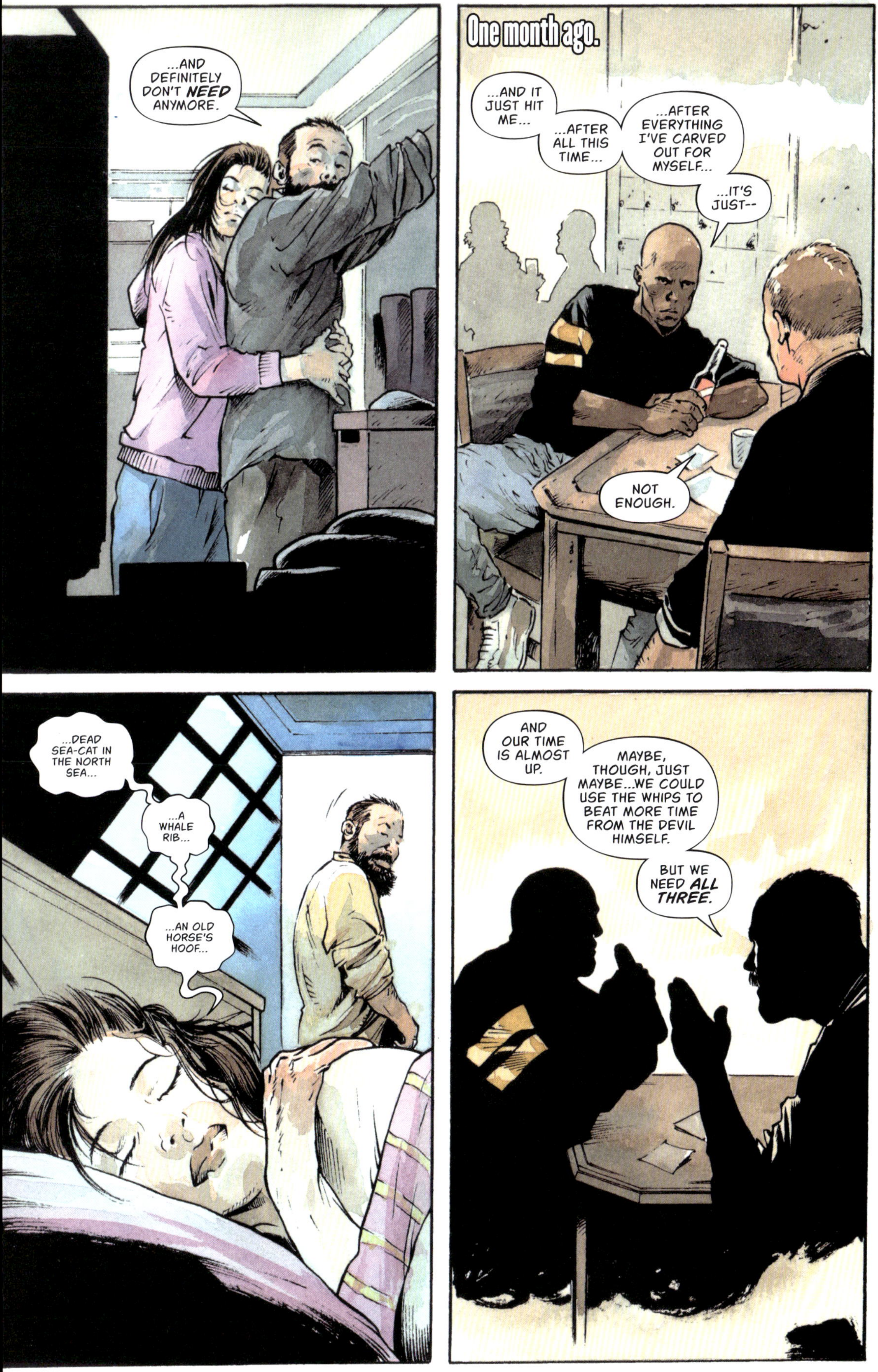
...AND DEFINITELY DON'T NEED ANYMORE.
One month ago.
...AND IT JUST HIT ME...
...AFTER ALL THIS TIME...
...AFTER EVERYTHING I'VE CARVED OUT FOR MYSELF...
...IT'S JUST--
NOT ENOUGH.
...DEAD SEA-CAT IN THE NORTH SEA...
...A WHALE RIB...
...AN OLD HORSE'S HOOF...
AND OUR TIME IS ALMOST UP.
MAYBE, THOUGH, JUST MAYBE...WE COULD USE THE WHIPS TO BEAT MORE TIME FROM THE DEVIL HIMSELF.
BUT WE NEED ALL THREE.

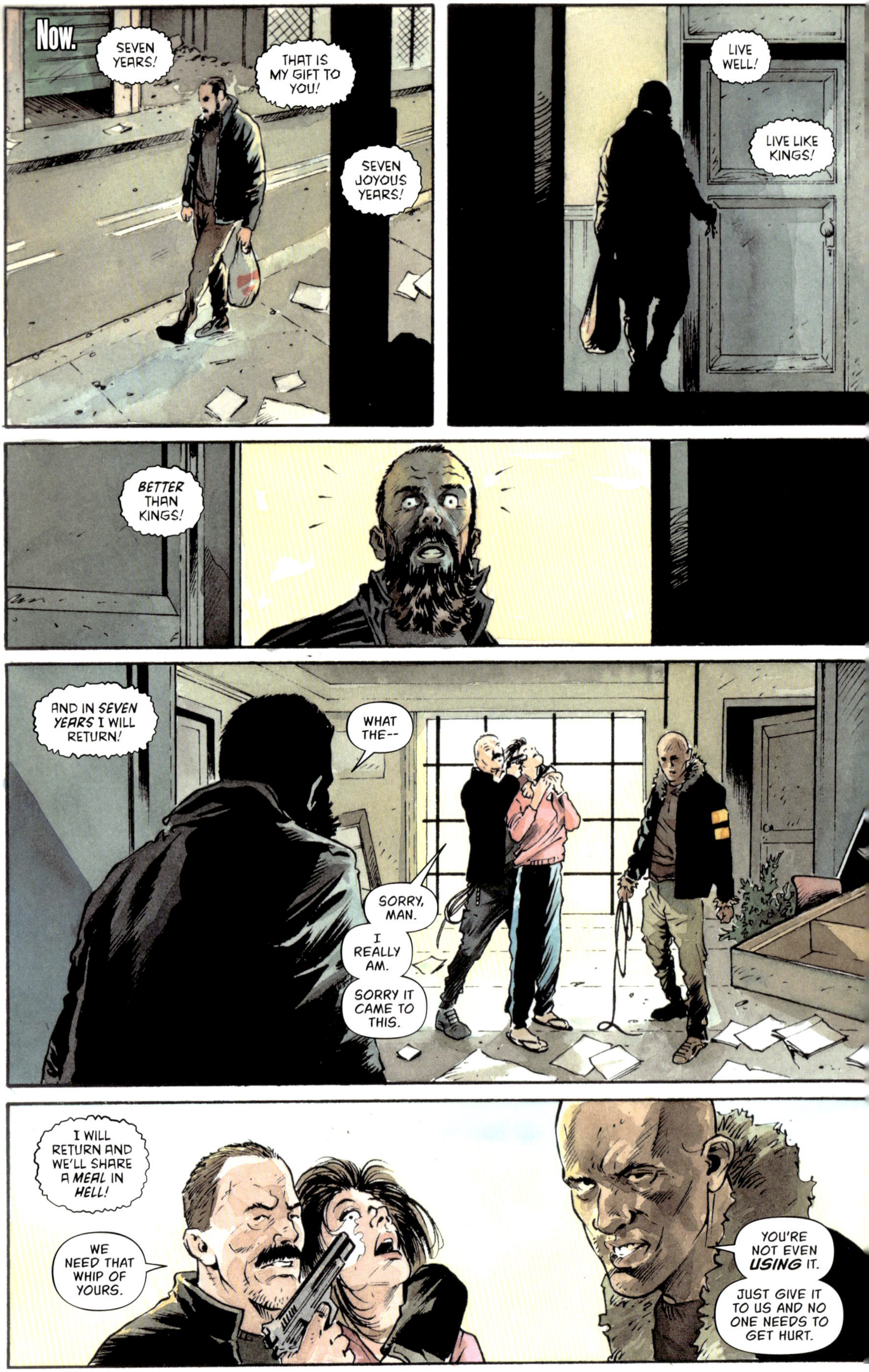
Now.
SEVEN YEARS!
THAT IS MY GIFT TO YOU!
SEVEN JOYOUS YEARS!
LIVE WELL!
LIVE LIKE KINGS!
BETTER THAN KINGS!
AND IN SEVEN YEARS I WILL RETURN!
WHAT THE--
SORRY, MAN.
I REALLY AM.
SORRY IT CAME TO THIS.
I WILL RETURN AND WE'LL SHARE A MEAL IN HELL!
WE NEED THAT WHIP OF YOURS.
YOU'RE NOT EVEN USING IT.
JUST GIVE IT TO US AND NO ONE NEEDS TO GET HURT.

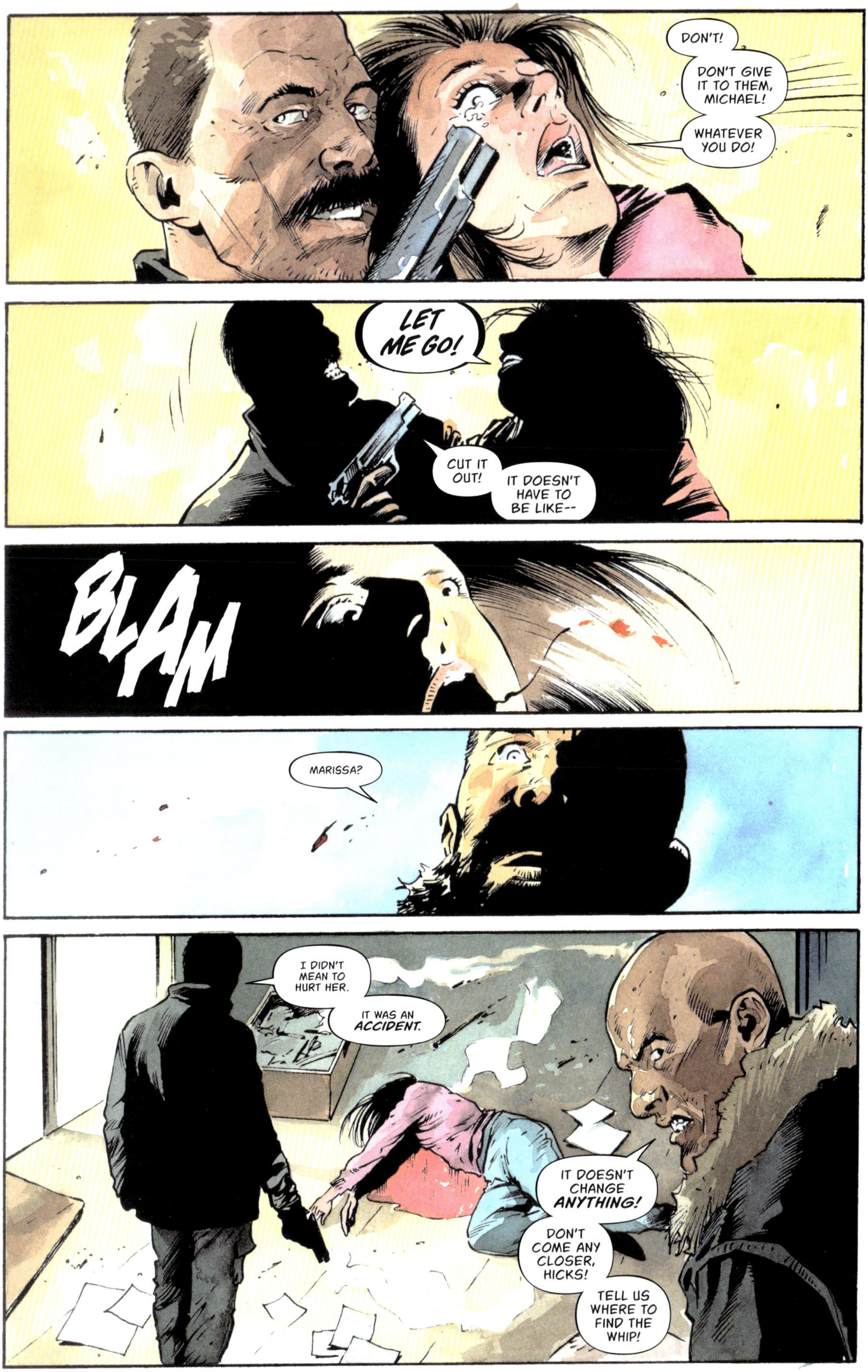
DON'T!
DON'T GIVE IT TO THEM, MICHAEL!
WHATEVER YOU DO!
LET ME GO!
CUT IT OUT!
IT DOESN'T HAVE TO BE LIKE--
BLAM
MARISSA?
I DIDN'T MEAN TO HURT HER.
IT WAS AN ACCIDENT.
IT DOESN'T CHANGE ANYTHING!
DON'T COME ANY CLOSER, HICKS!
TELL US WHERE TO FIND THE WHIP!

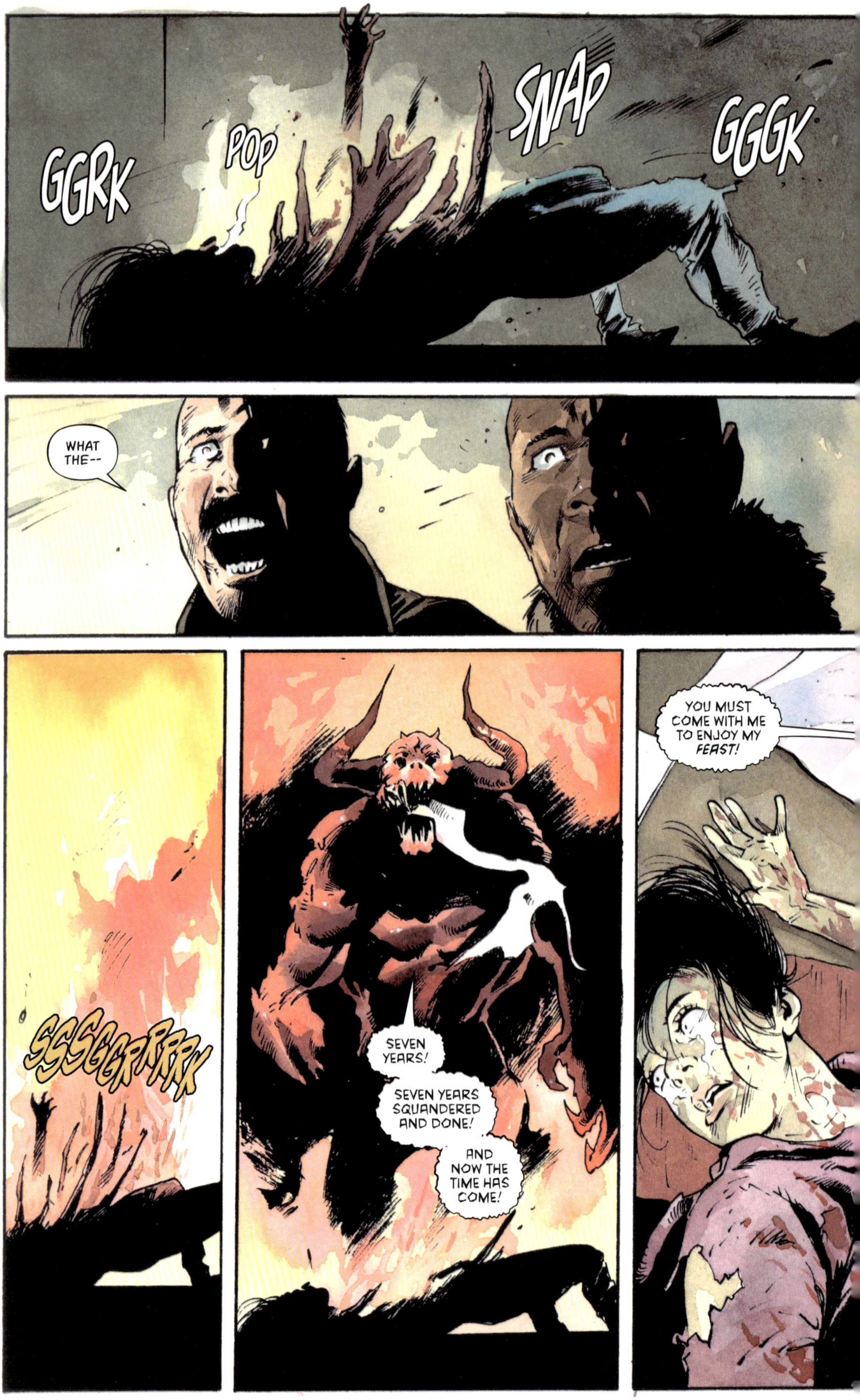
GGRK
POP
SNAP
GGGK
WHAT THE--
SSSGGRRRRK
SEVEN YEARS!
SEVEN YEARS SQUANDERED AND DONE!
AND NOW THE TIME HAS COME!
YOU MUST COME WITH ME TO ENJOY MY FEAST!

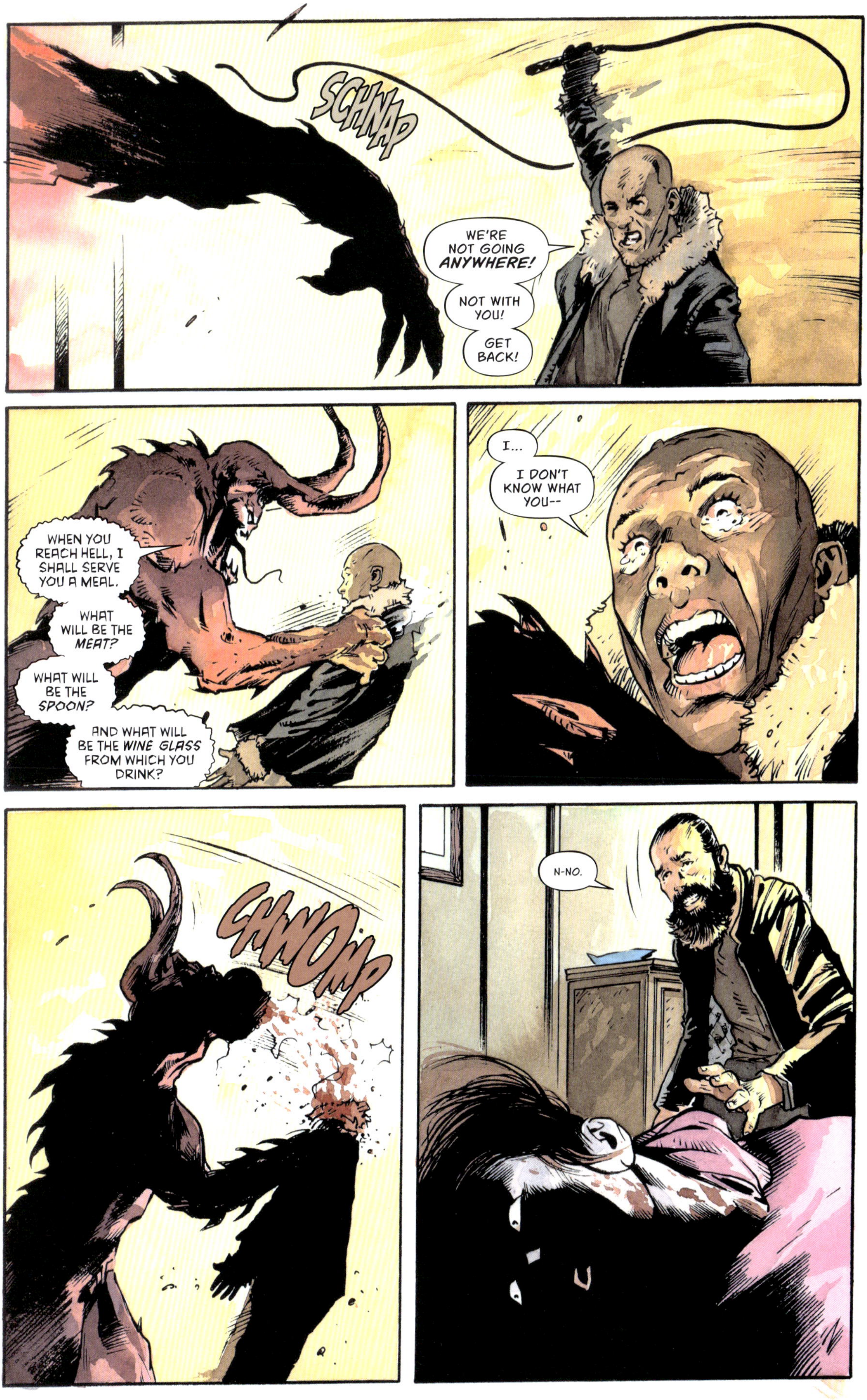
SCHNAP
WE'RE NOT GOING ANYWHERE!
NOT WITH YOU!
GET BACK!
WHEN YOU REACH HELL, I SHALL SERVE YOU A MEAL.
WHAT WILL BE THE MEAT?
WHAT WILL BE THE SPOON?
AND WHAT WILL BE THE WINE GLASS FROM WHICH YOU DRINK?
I...
I DON'T KNOW WHAT YOU--
CHWOMP
N-NO.

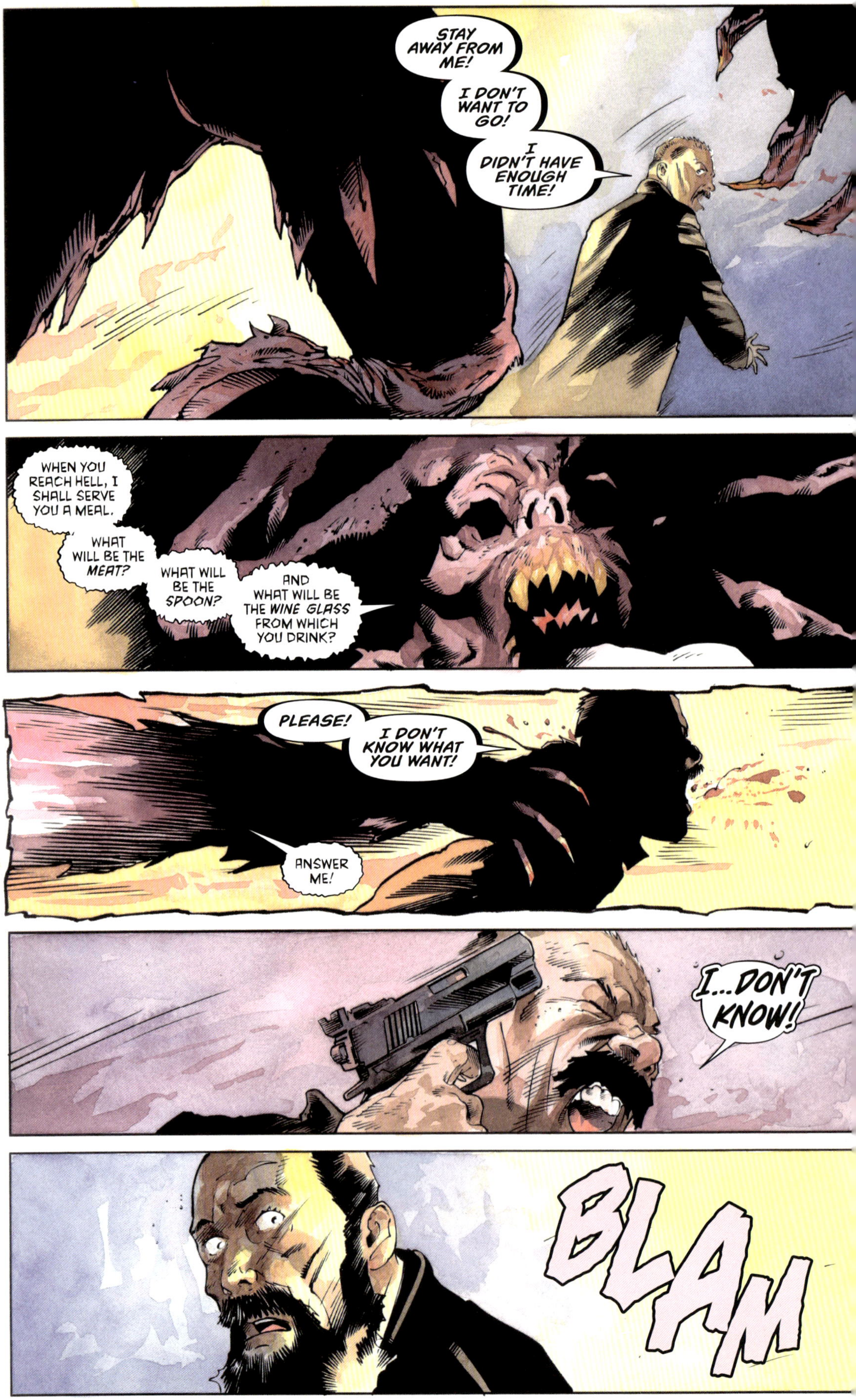
STAY AWAY FROM ME!
I DON'T WANT TO GO!
I DIDN'T HAVE ENOUGH TIME!
WHEN YOU REACH HELL, I SHALL SERVE YOU A MEAL.
WHAT WILL BE THE MEAT?
WHAT WILL BE THE SPOON?
AND WHAT WILL BE THE WINE GLASS FROM WHICH YOU DRINK?
PLEASE!
I DON'T KNOW WHAT YOU WANT!
ANSWER ME!
I...DON'T KNOW!
BLAM

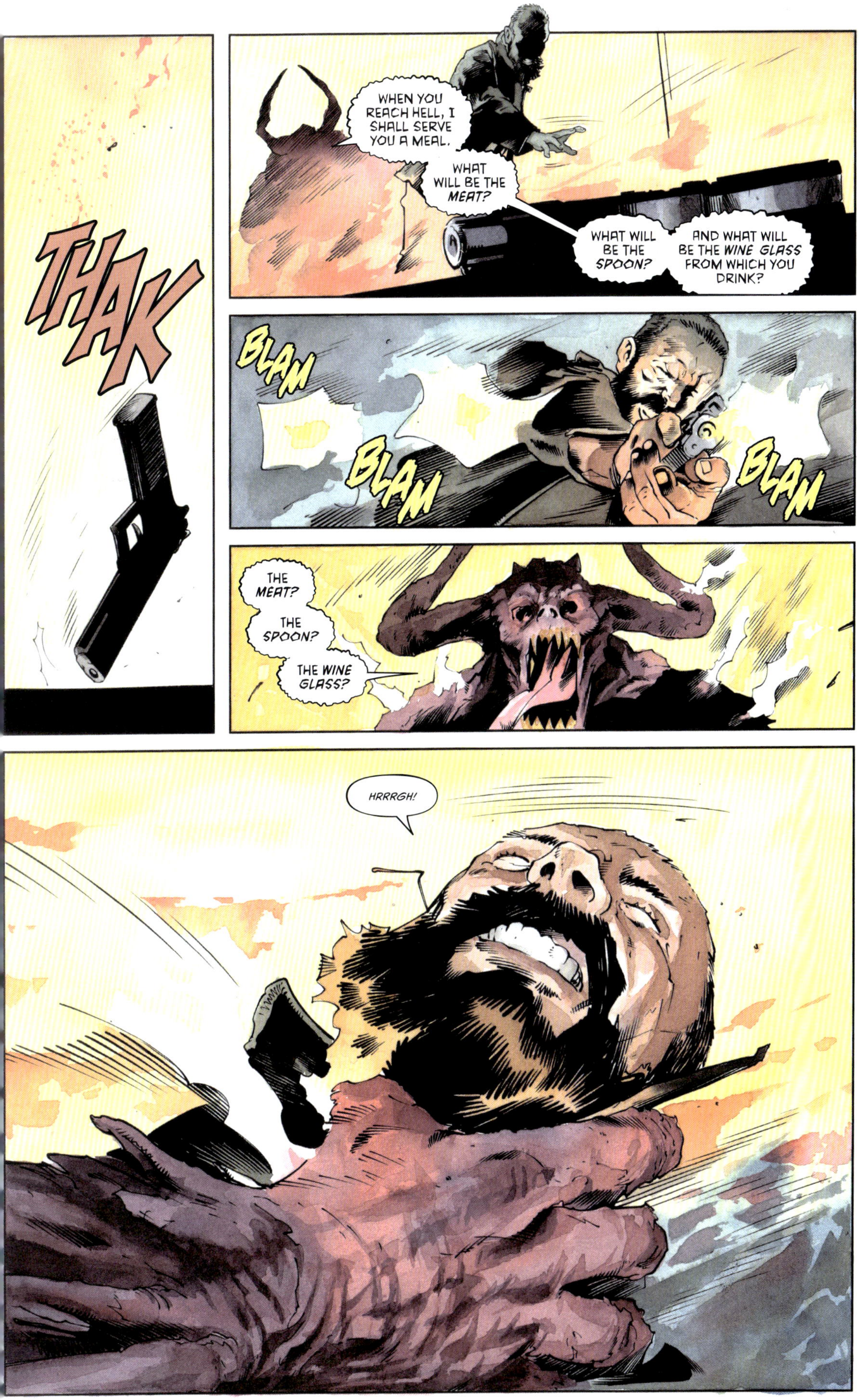
THAK
WHEN YOU REACH HELL, I SHALL SERVE YOU A MEAL.
WHAT WILL BE THE *MEAT?*
WHAT WILL BE THE *SPOON?*
AND WHAT WILL BE THE *WINE GLASS* FROM WHICH YOU DRINK?
BLAM
BLAM
BLAM
THE *MEAT?*
THE *SPOON?*
THE *WINE* GLASS?
HRRRGH!

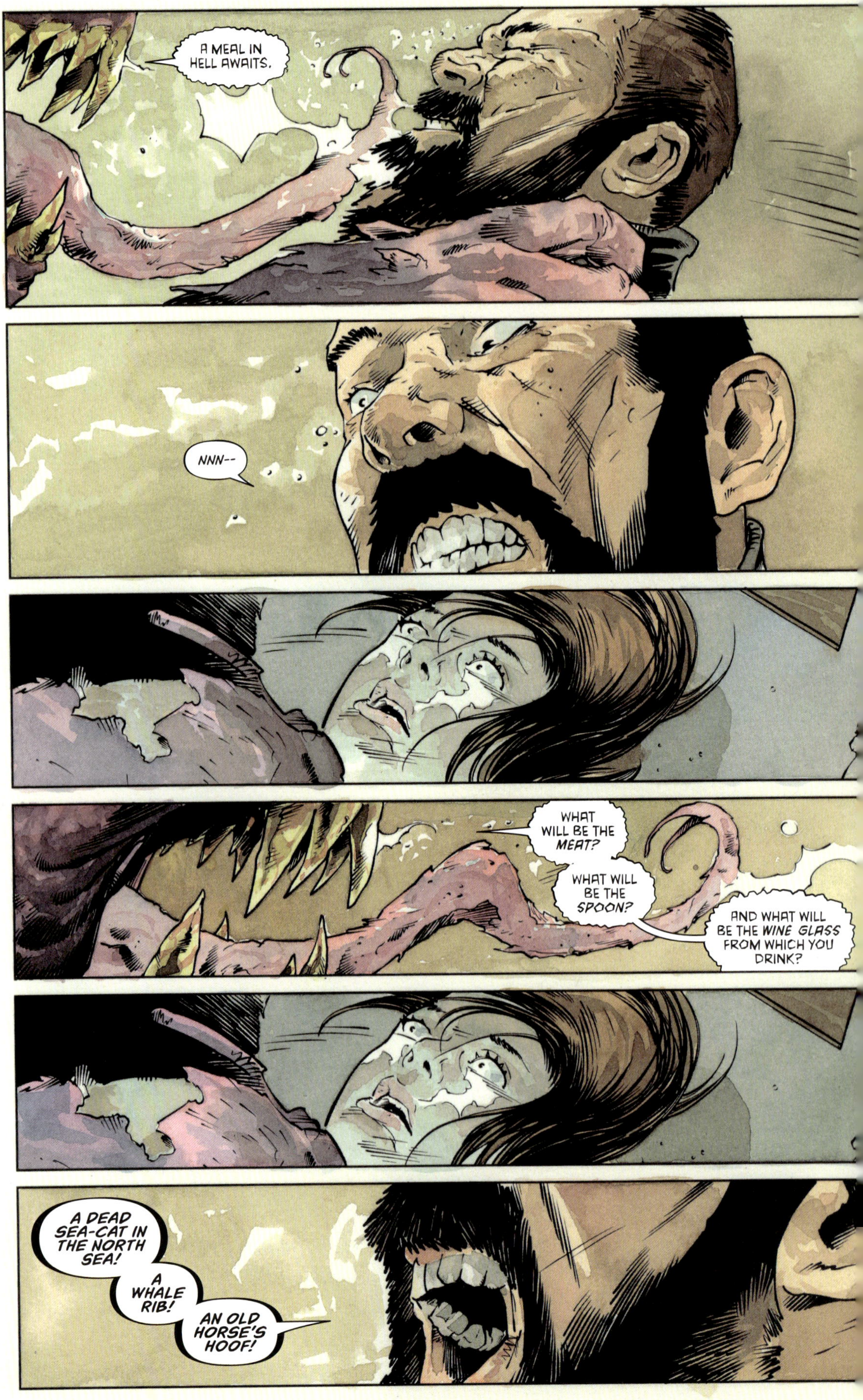

A MEAL IN HELL AWAITS.
NNN--
WHAT WILL BE THE *MEAT?*
WHAT WILL BE THE *SPOON?*
AND WHAT WILL BE THE *WINE GLASS* FROM WHICH YOU DRINK?
A DEAD SEA-CAT IN THE NORTH SEA!
A WHALE RIB!
AN OLD HORSE'S HOOF!

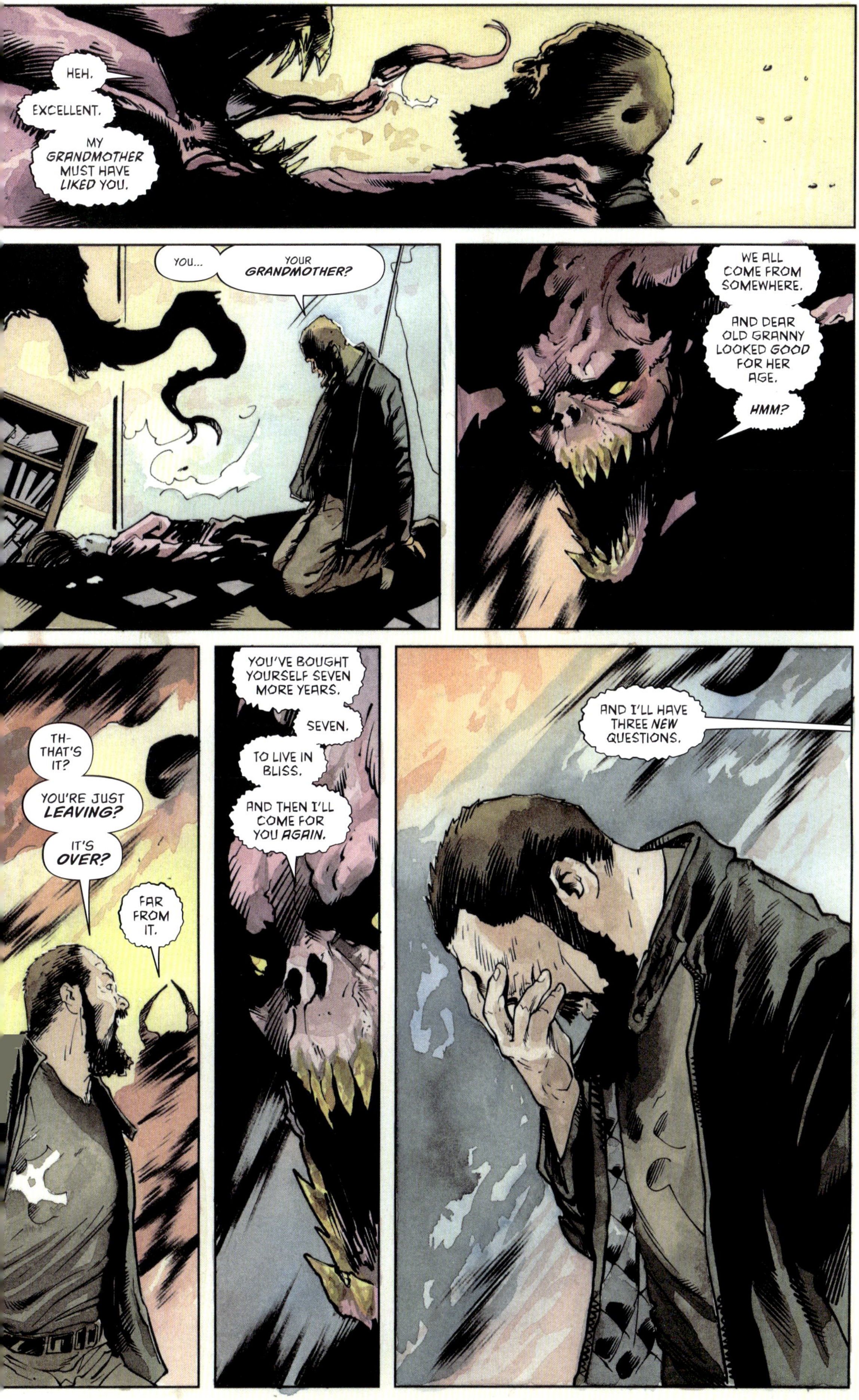

HEH.
EXCELLENT.
MY GRANDMOTHER MUST HAVE LIKED YOU.
YOU...
YOUR GRANDMOTHER?
WE ALL COME FROM SOMEWHERE.
AND DEAR OLD GRANNY LOOKED GOOD FOR HER AGE.
HMM?
TH-THAT'S IT?
YOU'RE JUST LEAVING?
IT'S OVER?
FAR FROM IT.
YOU'VE BOUGHT YOURSELF SEVEN MORE YEARS.
SEVEN.
TO LIVE IN BLISS.
AND THEN I'LL COME FOR YOU AGAIN.
AND I'LL HAVE THREE NEW QUESTIONS.

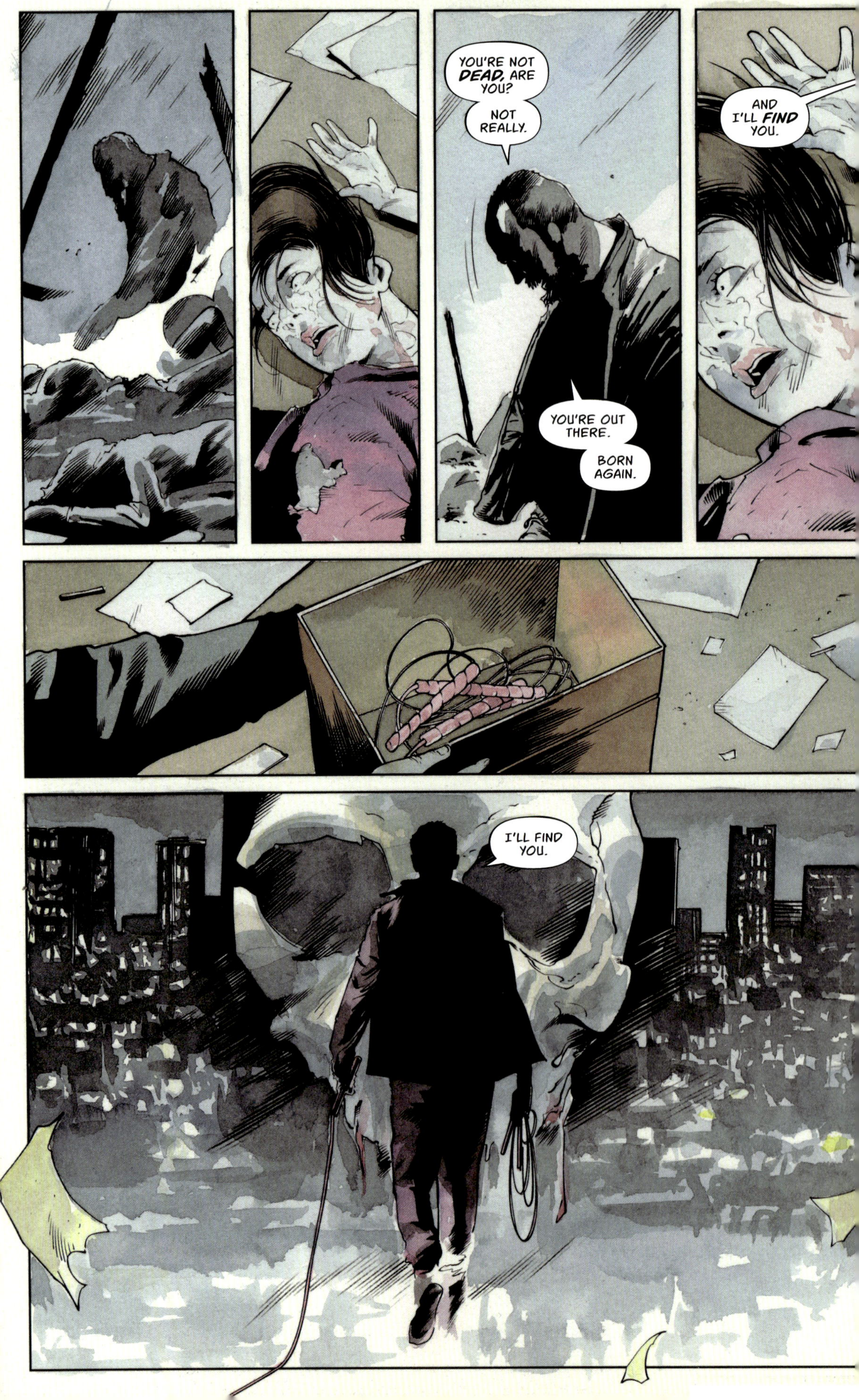
YOU'RE NOT DEAD, ARE YOU?
NOT REALLY.
YOU'RE OUT THERE.
BORN AGAIN.
AND I'LL FIND YOU.
I'LL FIND YOU.

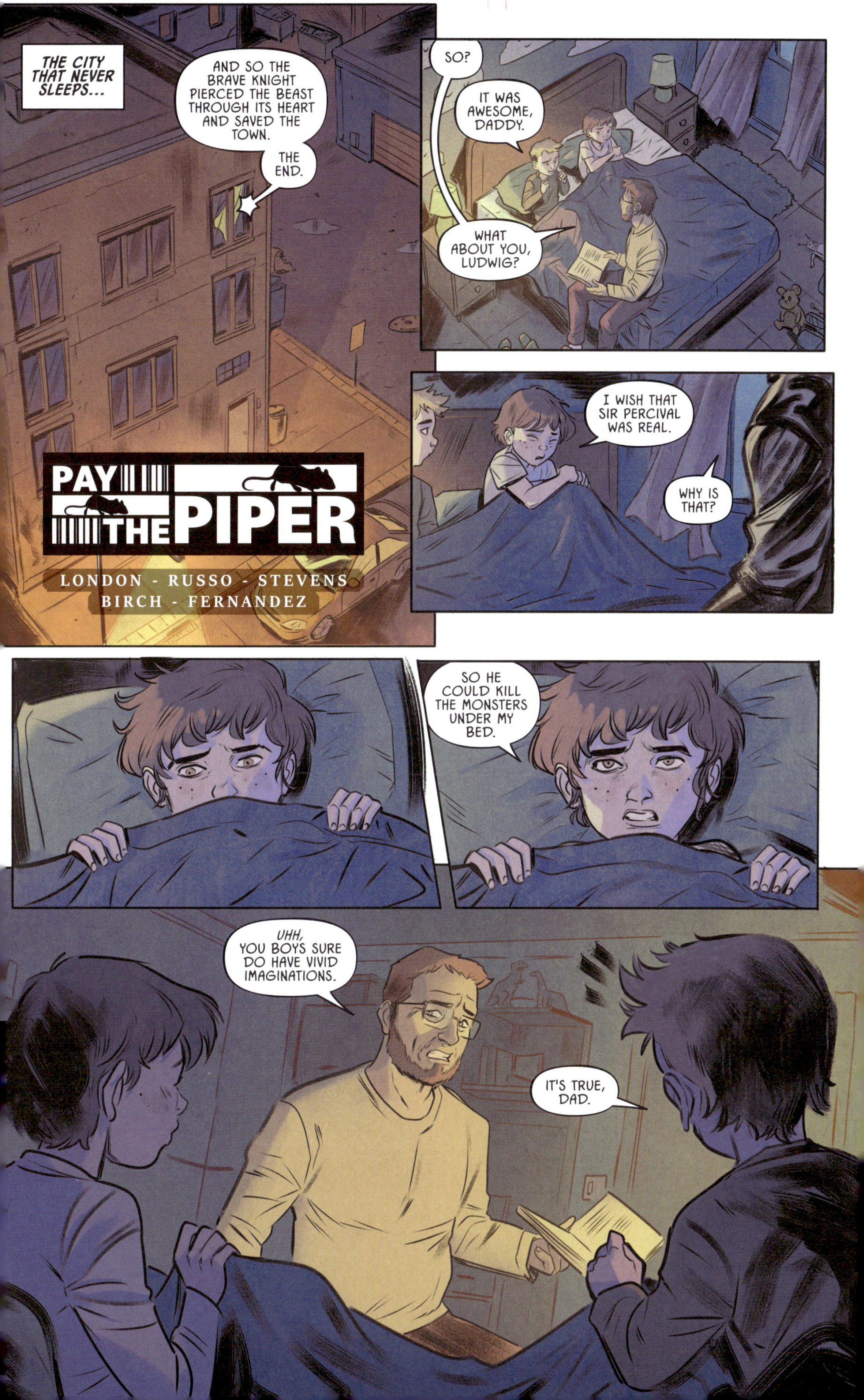
THE CITY THAT NEVER SLEEPS...
AND SO THE BRAVE KNIGHT PIERCED THE BEAST THROUGH ITS HEART AND SAVED THE TOWN.
THE END.
PAY THE PIPER
LONDON - RUSSO - STEVENS
BIRCH - FERNANDEZ
SO?
IT WAS AWESOME, DADDY.
WHAT ABOUT YOU, LUDWIG?
I WISH THAT SIR PERCIVAL WAS REAL.
WHY IS THAT?
SO HE COULD KILL THE MONSTERS UNDER MY BED.
UHH, YOU BOYS SURE DO HAVE VIVID IMAGINATIONS.
IT'S TRUE, DAD.

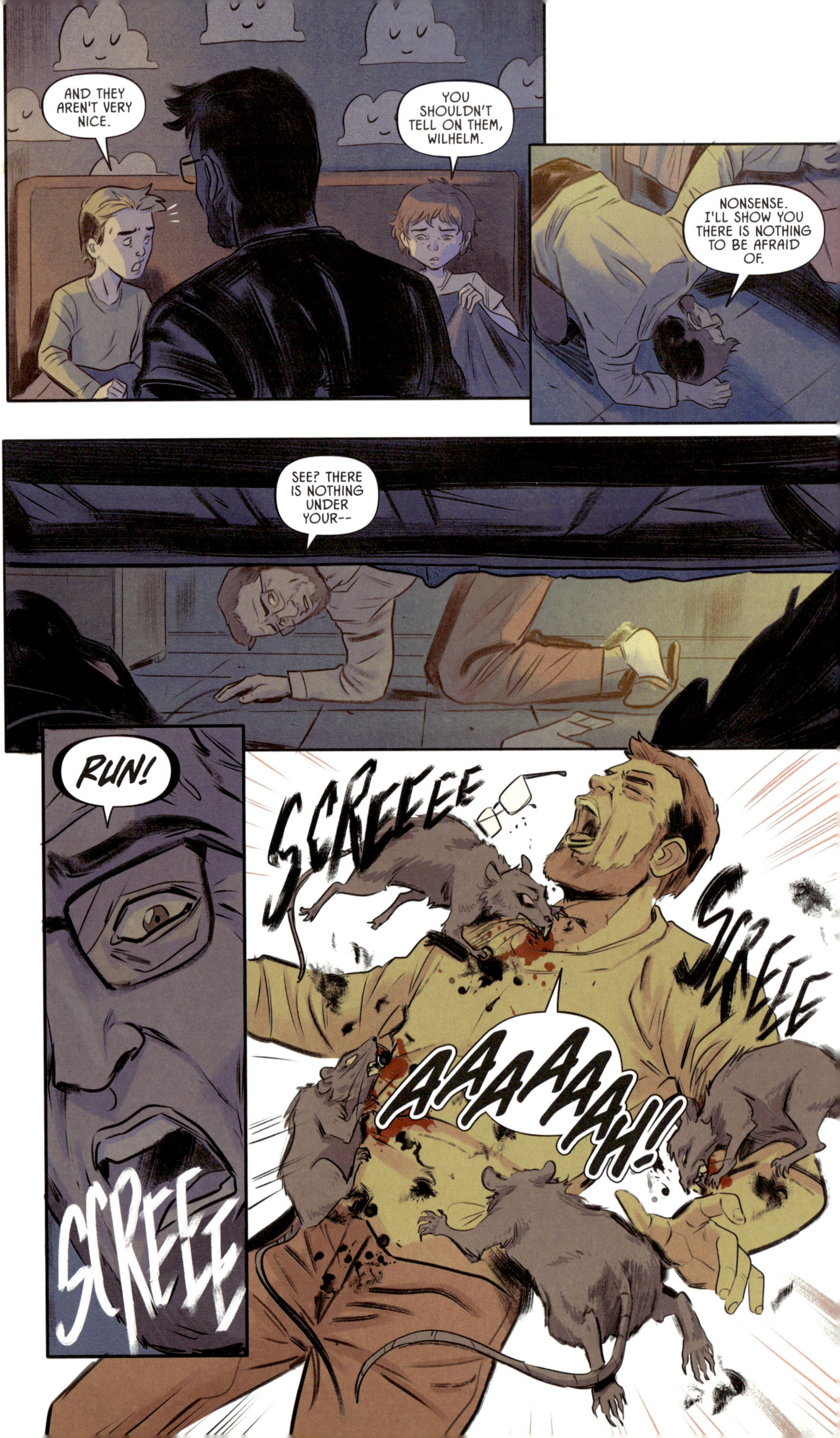
AND THEY AREN'T VERY NICE.
YOU SHOULDN'T TELL ON THEM, WILHELM.
NONSENSE. I'LL SHOW YOU THERE IS NOTHING TO BE AFRAID OF.
SEE? THERE IS NOTHING UNDER YOUR--
RUN!
SCREEEE
SCREEE
SCREEE
AAAAAAH!

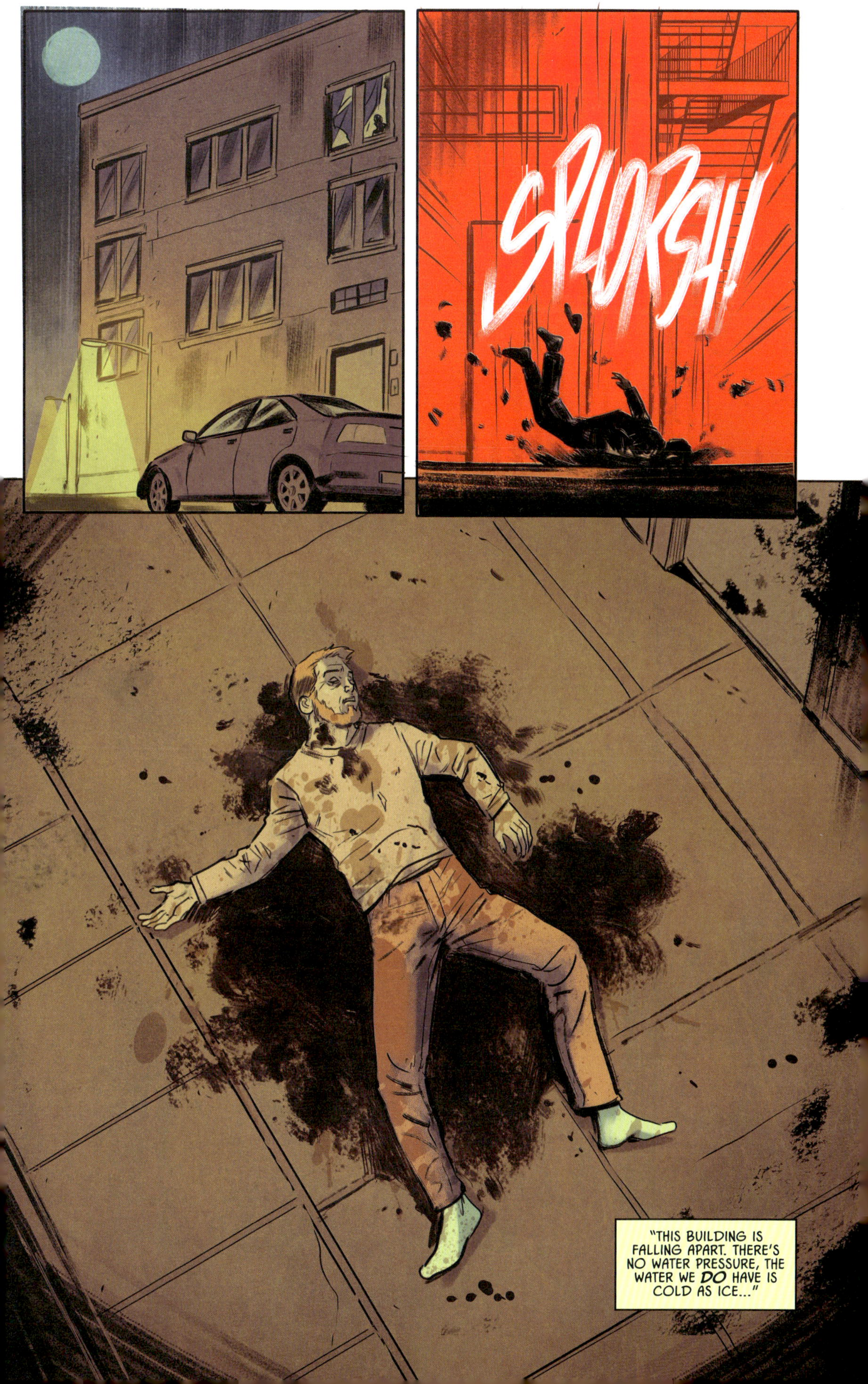
SPLORSH!
"THIS BUILDING IS FALLING APART. THERE'S NO WATER PRESSURE, THE WATER WE DO HAVE IS COLD AS ICE..."

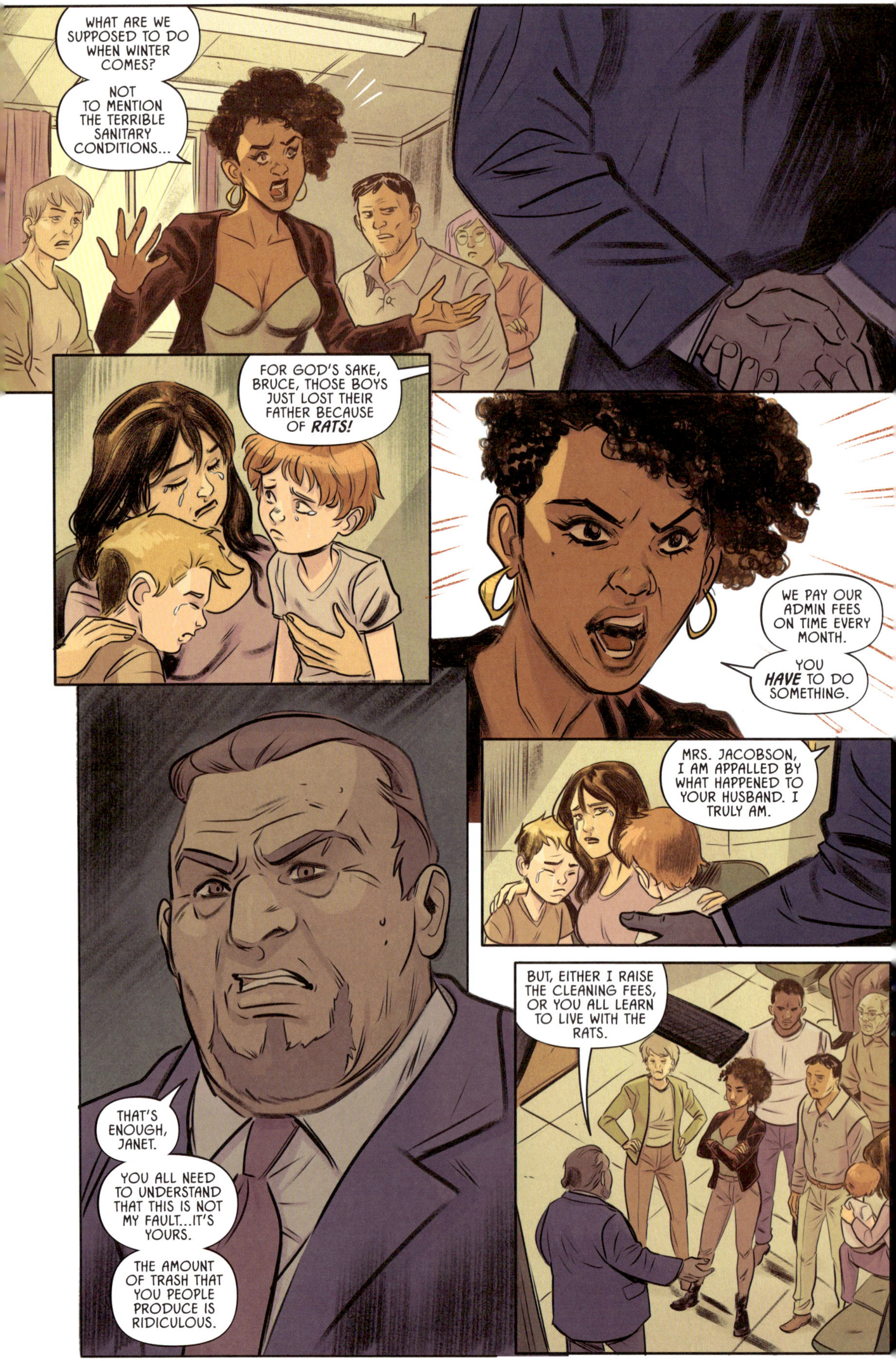
WHAT ARE WE SUPPOSED TO DO WHEN WINTER COMES?
NOT TO MENTION THE TERRIBLE SANITARY CONDITIONS...
FOR GOD'S SAKE, BRUCE, THOSE BOYS JUST LOST THEIR FATHER BECAUSE OF *RATS!*
WE PAY OUR ADMIN FEES ON TIME EVERY MONTH.
YOU *HAVE* TO DO SOMETHING.
THAT'S ENOUGH, JANET.
YOU ALL NEED TO UNDERSTAND THAT THIS IS NOT MY FAULT...IT'S YOURS.
THE AMOUNT OF TRASH THAT YOU PEOPLE PRODUCE IS RIDICULOUS.
MRS. JACOBSON, I AM APPALLED BY WHAT HAPPENED TO YOUR HUSBAND. I TRULY AM.
BUT, EITHER I RAISE THE CLEANING FEES, OR YOU ALL LEARN TO LIVE WITH THE RATS.

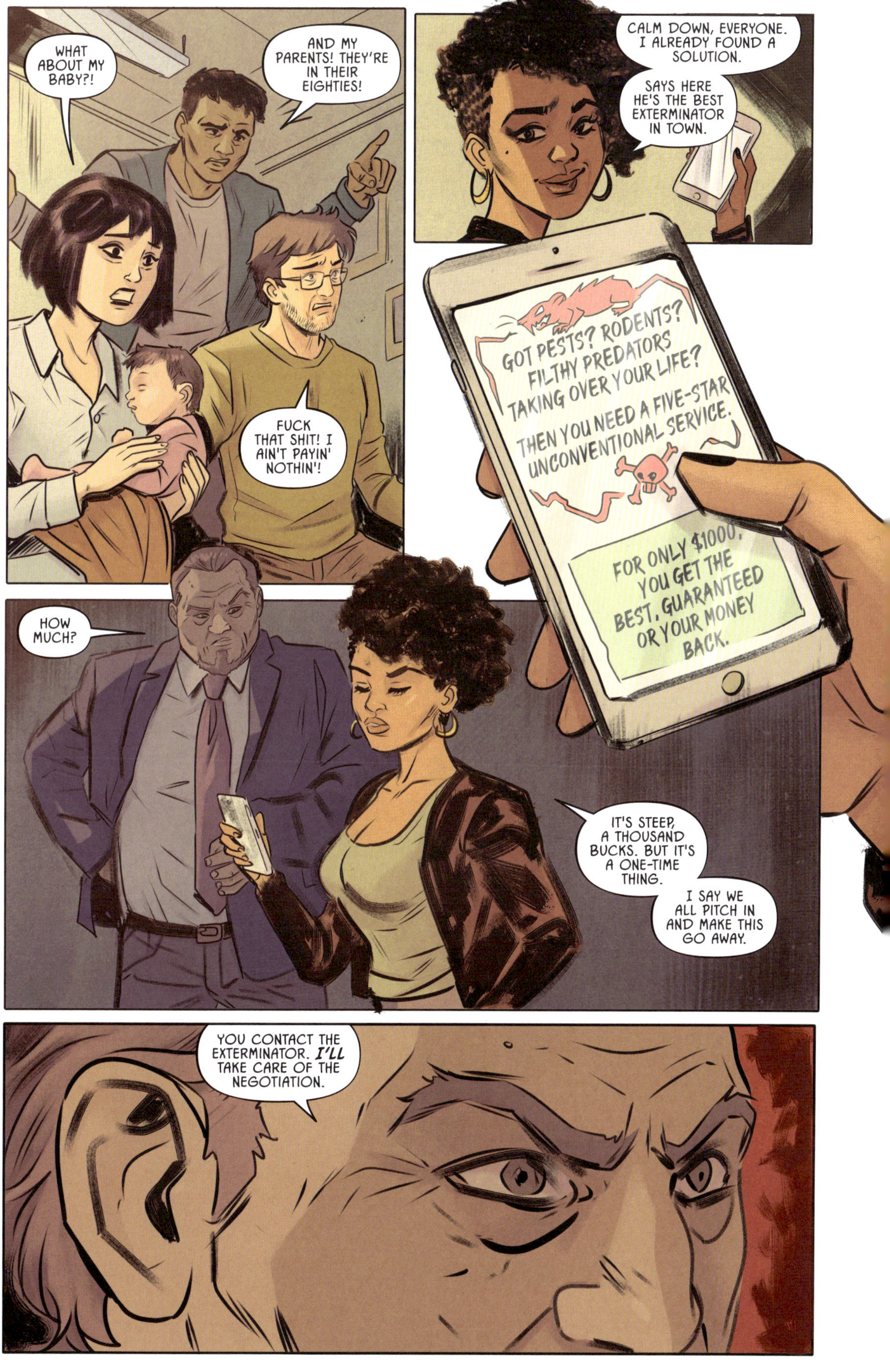
WHAT ABOUT MY BABY?!
AND MY PARENTS! THEY'RE IN THEIR EIGHTIES!
FUCK THAT SHIT! I AIN'T PAYIN' NOTHIN'!
CALM DOWN, EVERYONE. I ALREADY FOUND A SOLUTION.
SAYS HERE HE'S THE BEST EXTERMINATOR IN TOWN.
GOT PESTS? RODENTS? FILTHY PREDATORS TAKING OVER YOUR LIFE?
THEN YOU NEED A FIVE-STAR UNCONVENTIONAL SERVICE.
FOR ONLY $1000, YOU GET THE BEST, GUARANTEED OR YOUR MONEY BACK.
HOW MUCH?
IT'S STEEP, A THOUSAND BUCKS. BUT IT'S A ONE-TIME THING.
I SAY WE ALL PITCH IN AND MAKE THIS GO AWAY.
YOU CONTACT THE EXTERMINATOR. I'LL TAKE CARE OF THE NEGOTIATION.

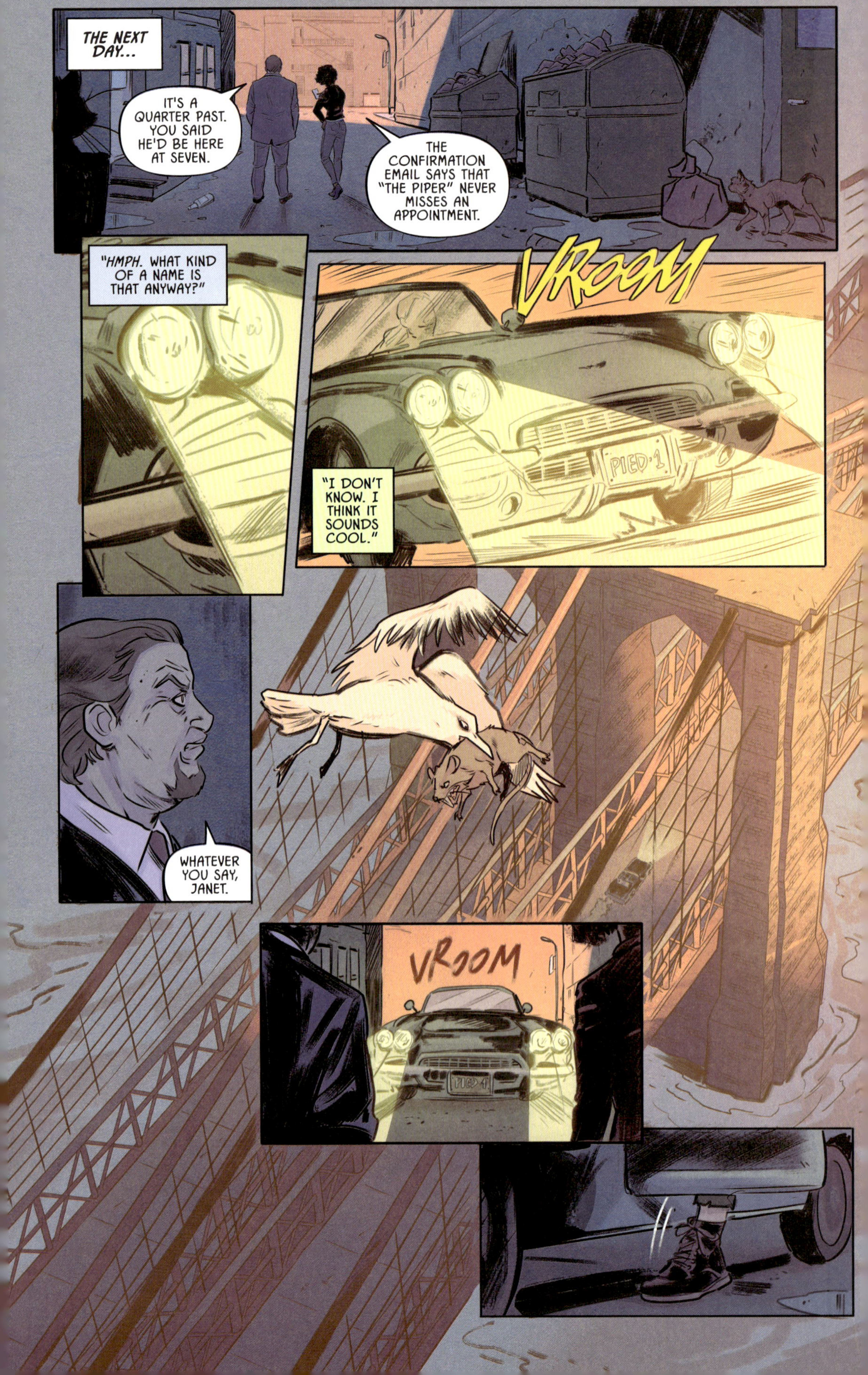
THE NEXT DAY...
IT'S A QUARTER PAST. YOU SAID HE'D BE HERE AT SEVEN.
THE CONFIRMATION EMAIL SAYS THAT "THE PIPER" NEVER MISSES AN APPOINTMENT.
"HMPH. WHAT KIND OF A NAME IS THAT ANYWAY?"
VROOM
PIED·1
"I DON'T KNOW. I THINK IT SOUNDS COOL."
WHATEVER YOU SAY, JANET.
VROOM

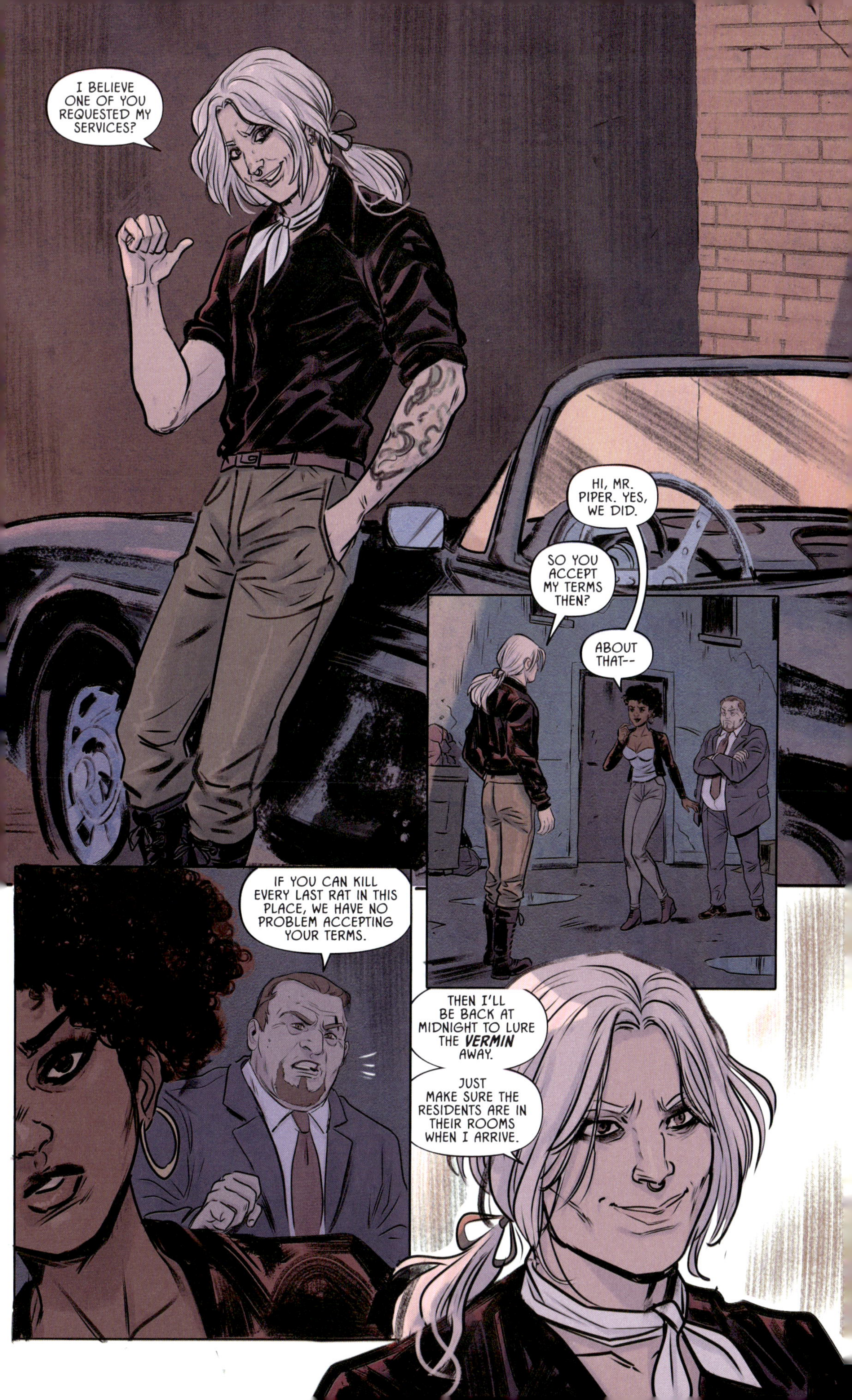
I BELIEVE ONE OF YOU REQUESTED MY SERVICES?
HI, MR. PIPER. YES, WE DID.
SO YOU ACCEPT MY TERMS THEN?
ABOUT THAT--
IF YOU CAN KILL EVERY LAST RAT IN THIS PLACE, WE HAVE NO PROBLEM ACCEPTING YOUR TERMS.
THEN I'LL BE BACK AT MIDNIGHT TO LURE THE ***VERMIN*** AWAY.
JUST MAKE SURE THE RESIDENTS ARE IN THEIR ROOMS WHEN I ARRIVE.

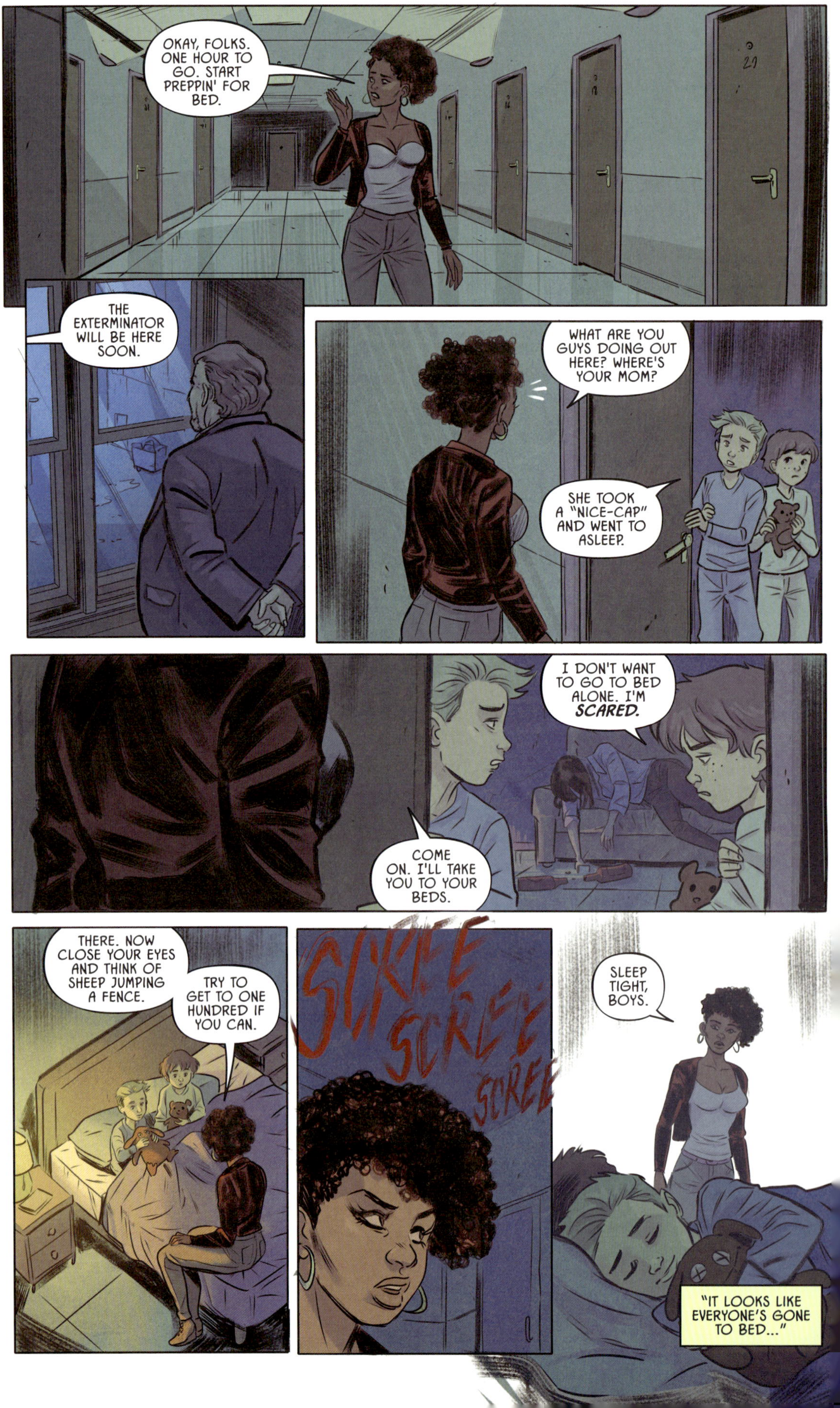
OKAY, FOLKS. ONE HOUR TO GO. START PREPPIN' FOR BED.
THE EXTERMINATOR WILL BE HERE SOON.
WHAT ARE YOU GUYS DOING OUT HERE? WHERE'S YOUR MOM?
SHE TOOK A "NICE-CAP" AND WENT TO ASLEEP.
I DON'T WANT TO GO TO BED ALONE. I'M *SCARED.*
COME ON. I'LL TAKE YOU TO YOUR BEDS.
THERE. NOW CLOSE YOUR EYES AND THINK OF SHEEP JUMPING A FENCE.
TRY TO GET TO ONE HUNDRED IF YOU CAN.
SCREE
SCREE
SCREE
SLEEP TIGHT, BOYS.
"IT LOOKS LIKE EVERYONE'S GONE TO BED..."

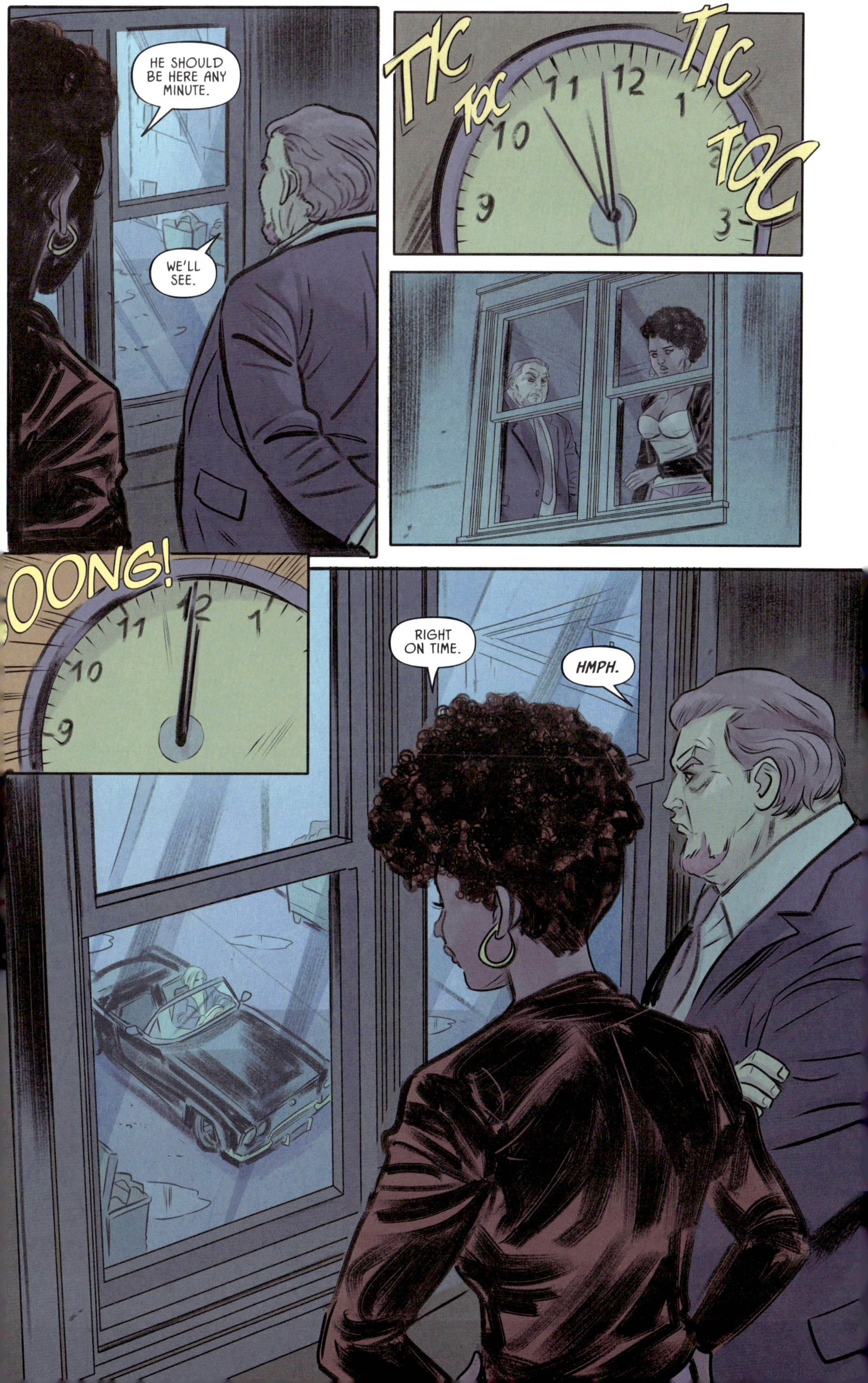
HE SHOULD BE HERE ANY MINUTE.
WE'LL SEE.
TIC
TOC
TIC
TOC
OONG!
RIGHT ON TIME.
HMPH.

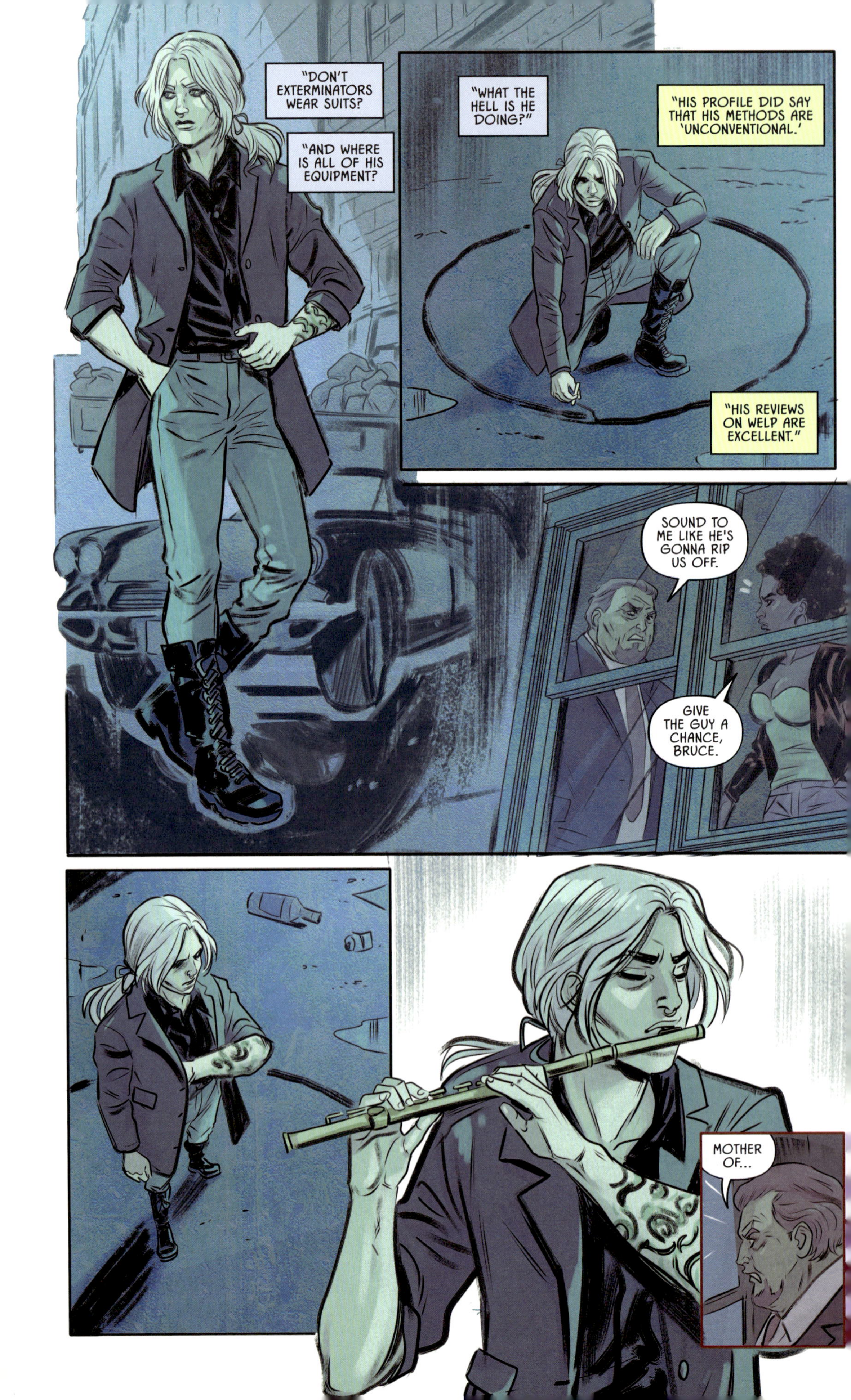
"DON'T EXTERMINATORS WEAR SUITS?
"AND WHERE IS ALL OF HIS EQUIPMENT?
"WHAT THE HELL IS HE DOING?"
"HIS PROFILE DID SAY THAT HIS METHODS ARE 'UNCONVENTIONAL.'
"HIS REVIEWS ON WELP ARE EXCELLENT."
SOUND TO ME LIKE HE'S GONNA RIP US OFF.
GIVE THE GUY A CHANCE, BRUCE.
MOTHER OF...

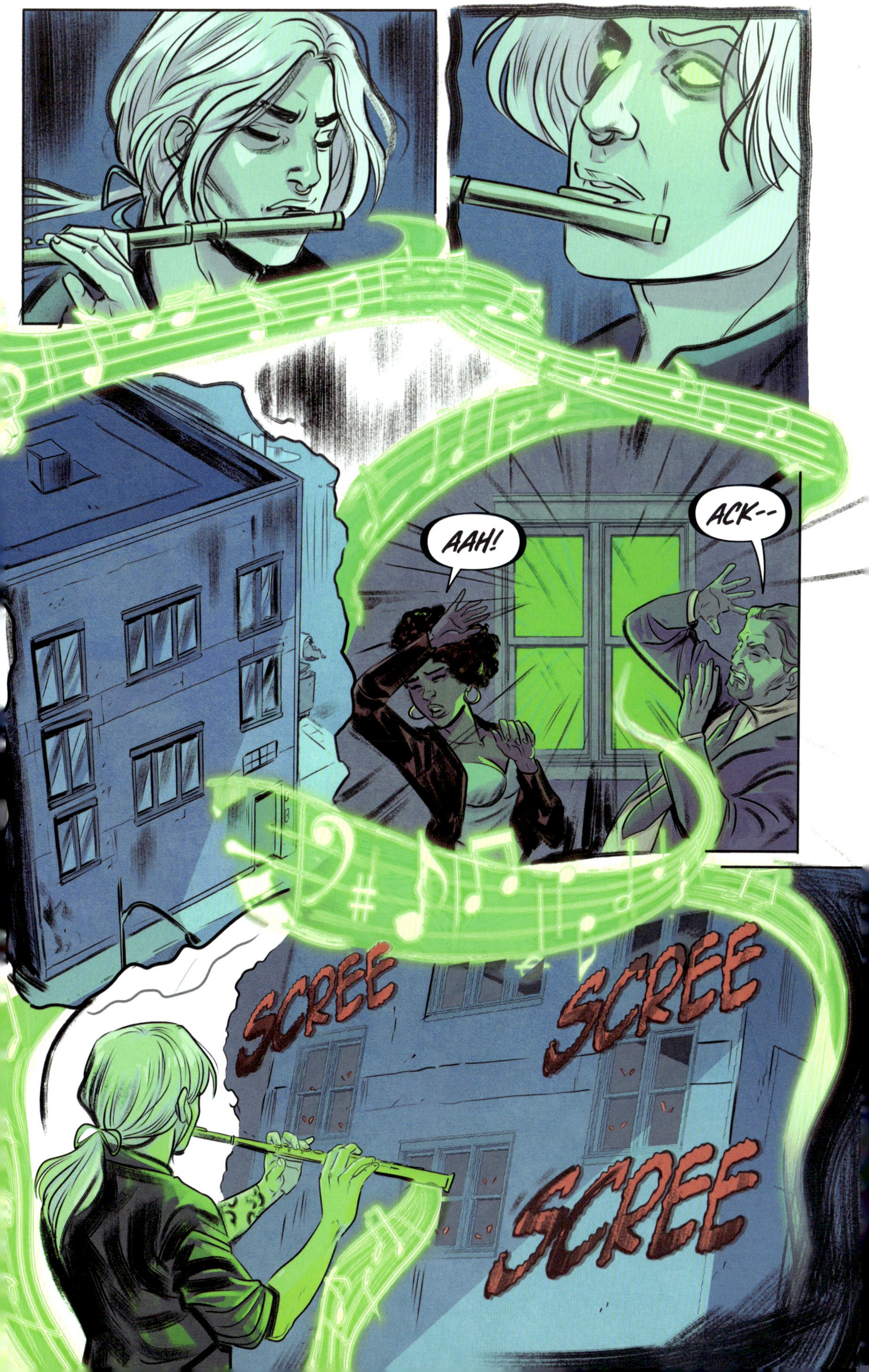
AAH!
ACK--
SCREE
SCREE
SCREE

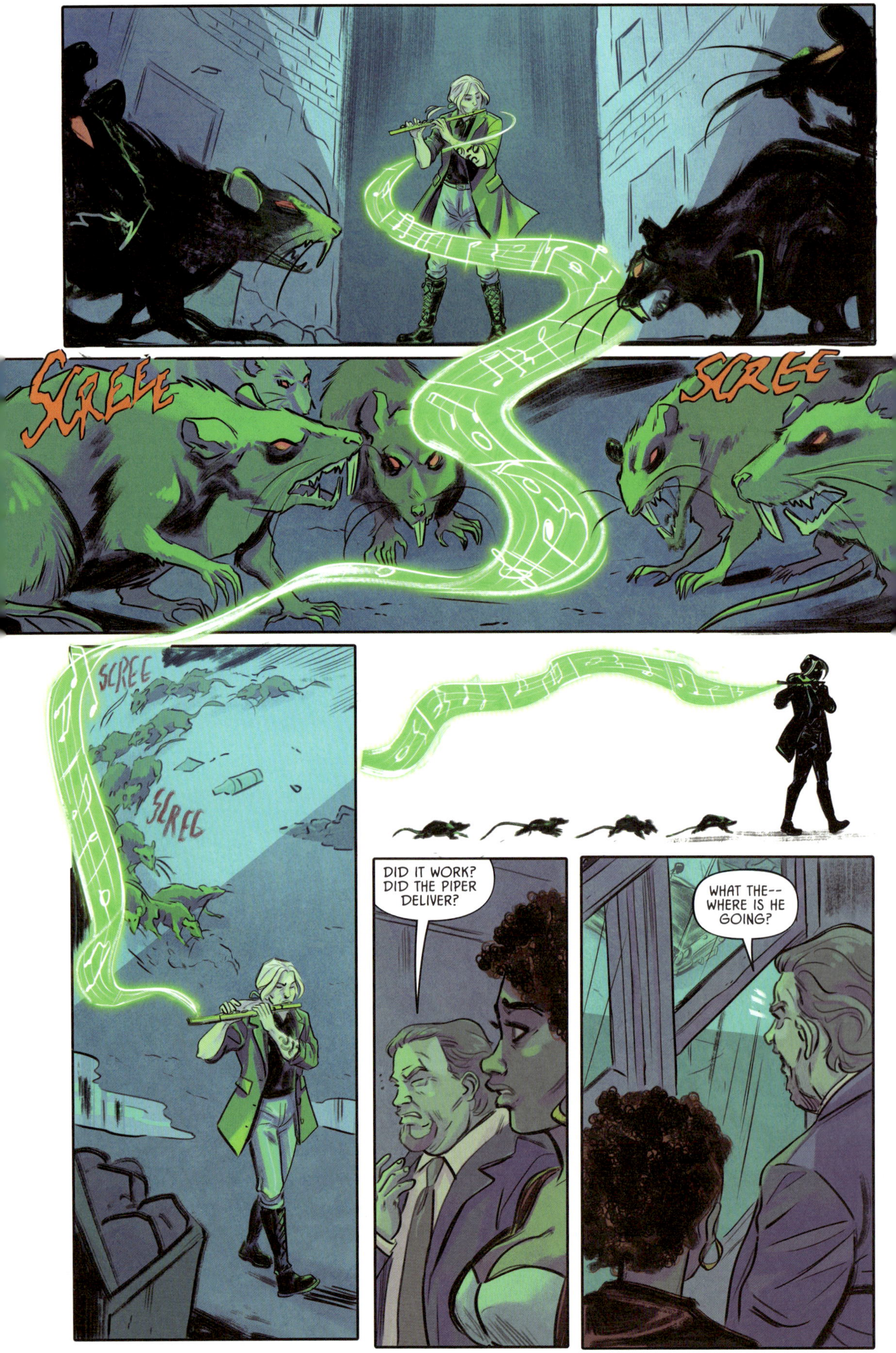
SCREEE
SCREEE
SCREE
SCREG
DID IT WORK? DID THE PIPER DELIVER?
WHAT THE-- WHERE IS HE GOING?

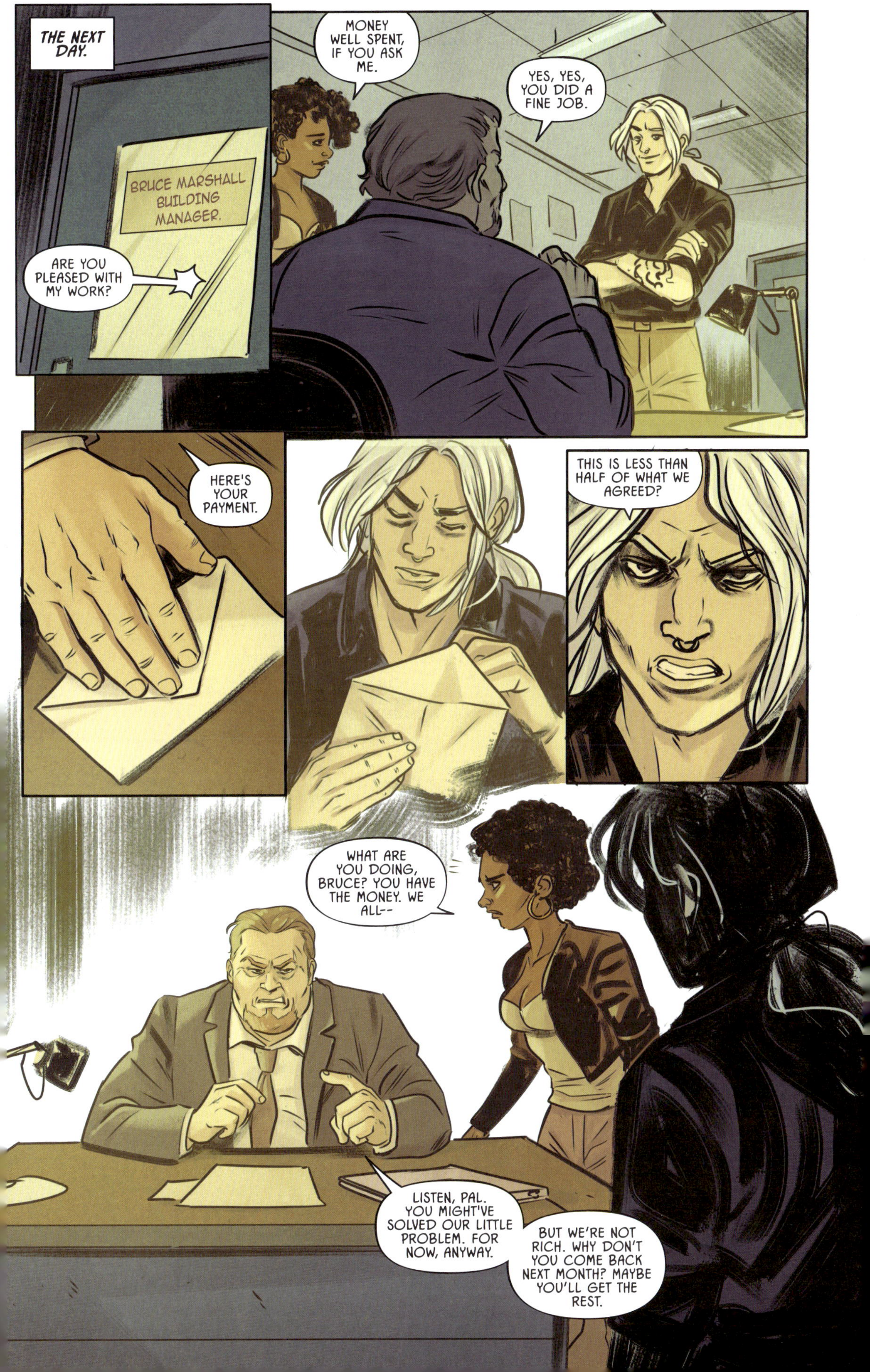

THE NEXT DAY.
BRUCE MARSHALL BUILDING MANAGER.
ARE YOU PLEASED WITH MY WORK?
MONEY WELL SPENT, IF YOU ASK ME.
YES, YES, YOU DID A FINE JOB.
HERE'S YOUR PAYMENT.
THIS IS LESS THAN HALF OF WHAT WE AGREED?
WHAT ARE YOU DOING, BRUCE? YOU HAVE THE MONEY. WE ALL--
LISTEN, PAL. YOU MIGHT'VE SOLVED OUR LITTLE PROBLEM. FOR NOW, ANYWAY.
BUT WE'RE NOT RICH. WHY DON'T YOU COME BACK NEXT MONTH? MAYBE YOU'LL GET THE REST.

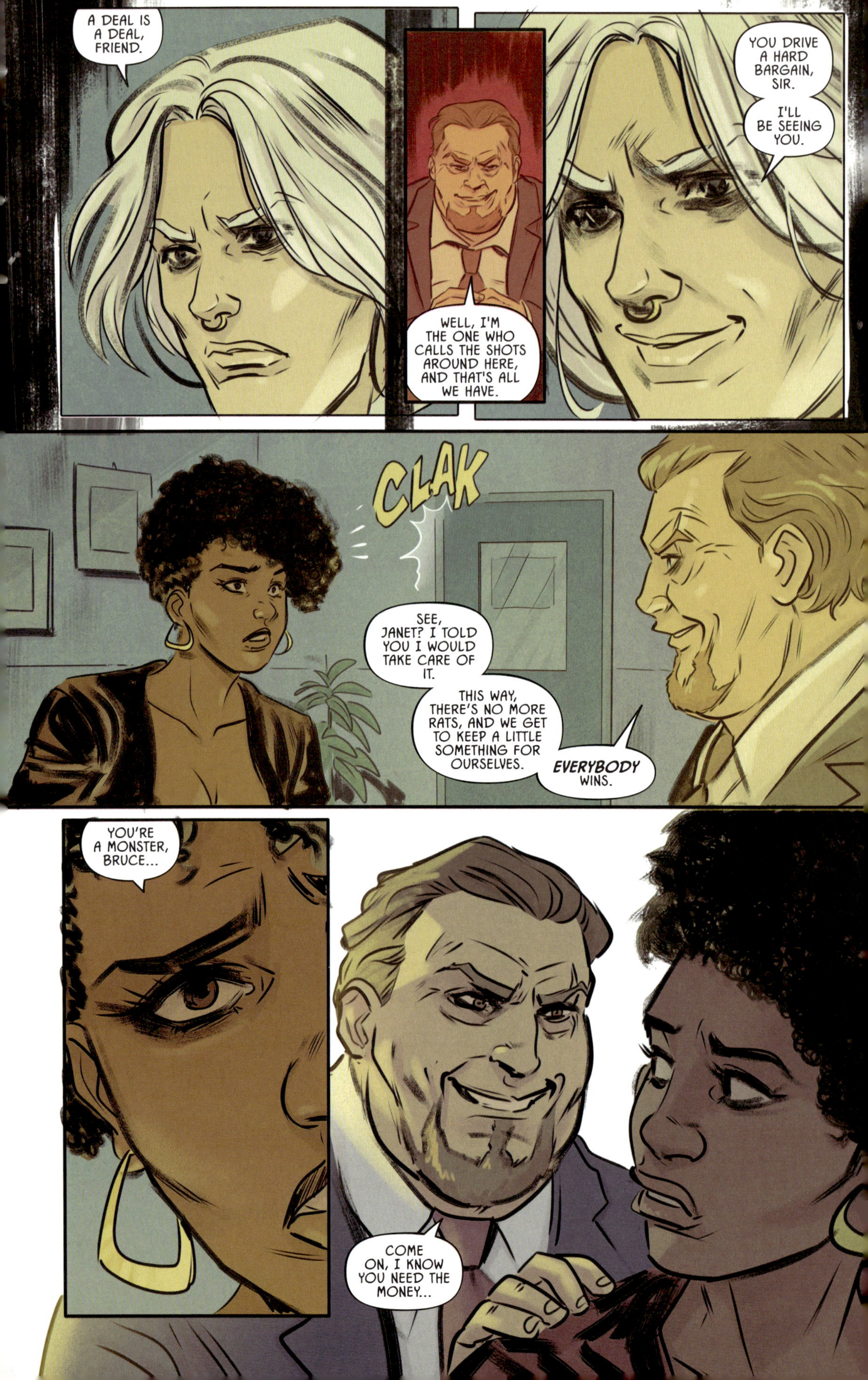
A DEAL IS A DEAL, FRIEND.
WELL, I'M THE ONE WHO CALLS THE SHOTS AROUND HERE, AND THAT'S ALL WE HAVE.
YOU DRIVE A HARD BARGAIN, SIR.
I'LL BE SEEING YOU.
CLAK
SEE, JANET? I TOLD YOU I WOULD TAKE CARE OF IT.
THIS WAY, THERE'S NO MORE RATS, AND WE GET TO KEEP A LITTLE SOMETHING FOR OURSELVES.
EVERYBODY WINS.
YOU'RE A MONSTER, BRUCE...
COME ON, I KNOW YOU NEED THE MONEY...

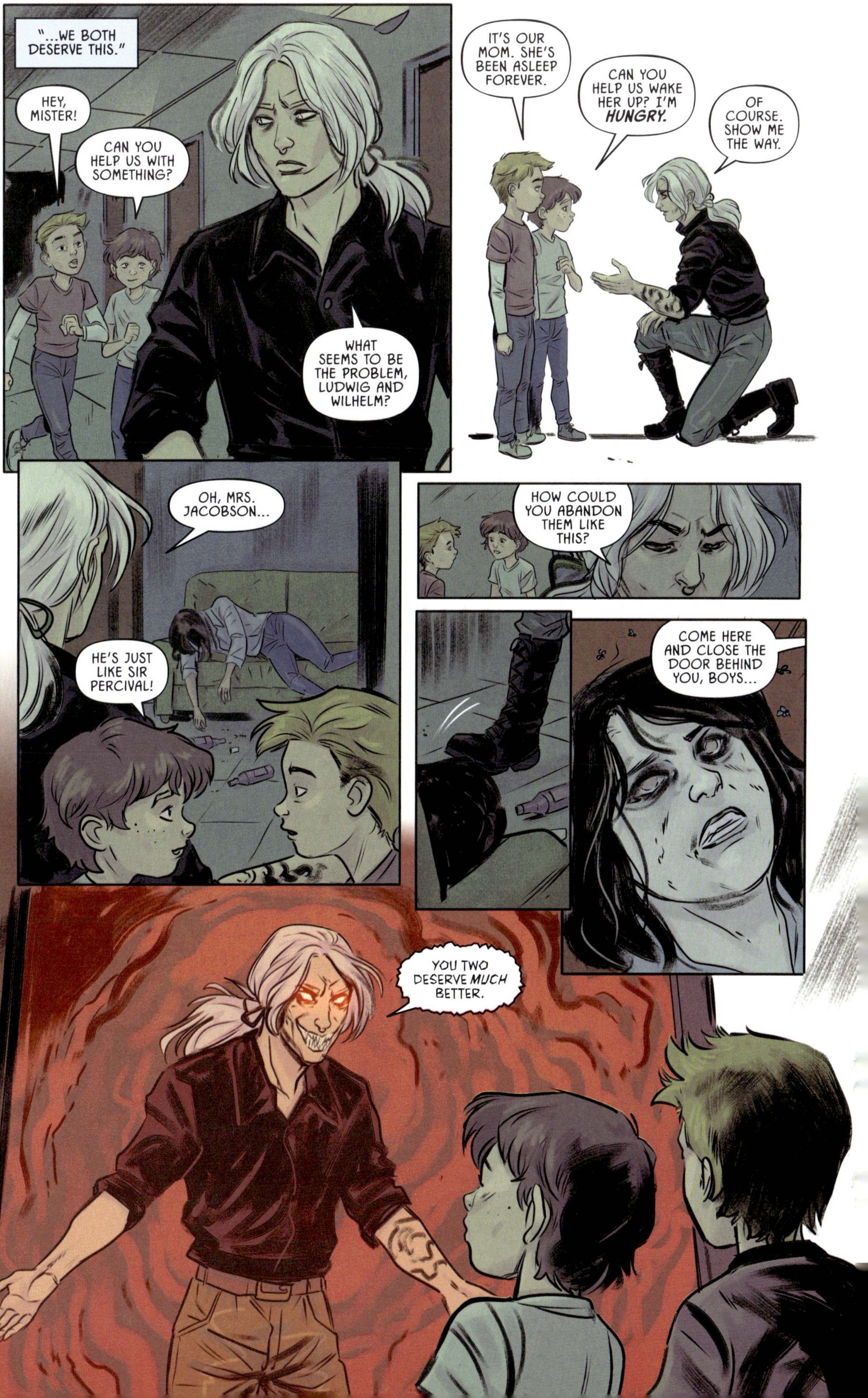
"...WE BOTH DESERVE THIS."
HEY, MISTER!
CAN YOU HELP US WITH SOMETHING?
WHAT SEEMS TO BE THE PROBLEM, LUDWIG AND WILHELM?
IT'S OUR MOM. SHE'S BEEN ASLEEP FOREVER.
CAN YOU HELP US WAKE HER UP? I'M *HUNGRY.*
OF COURSE. SHOW ME THE WAY.
OH, MRS. JACOBSON...
HE'S JUST LIKE SIR PERCIVAL!
HOW COULD YOU ABANDON THEM LIKE THIS?
COME HERE AND CLOSE THE DOOR BEHIND YOU, BOYS...
YOU TWO DESERVE *MUCH* BETTER.

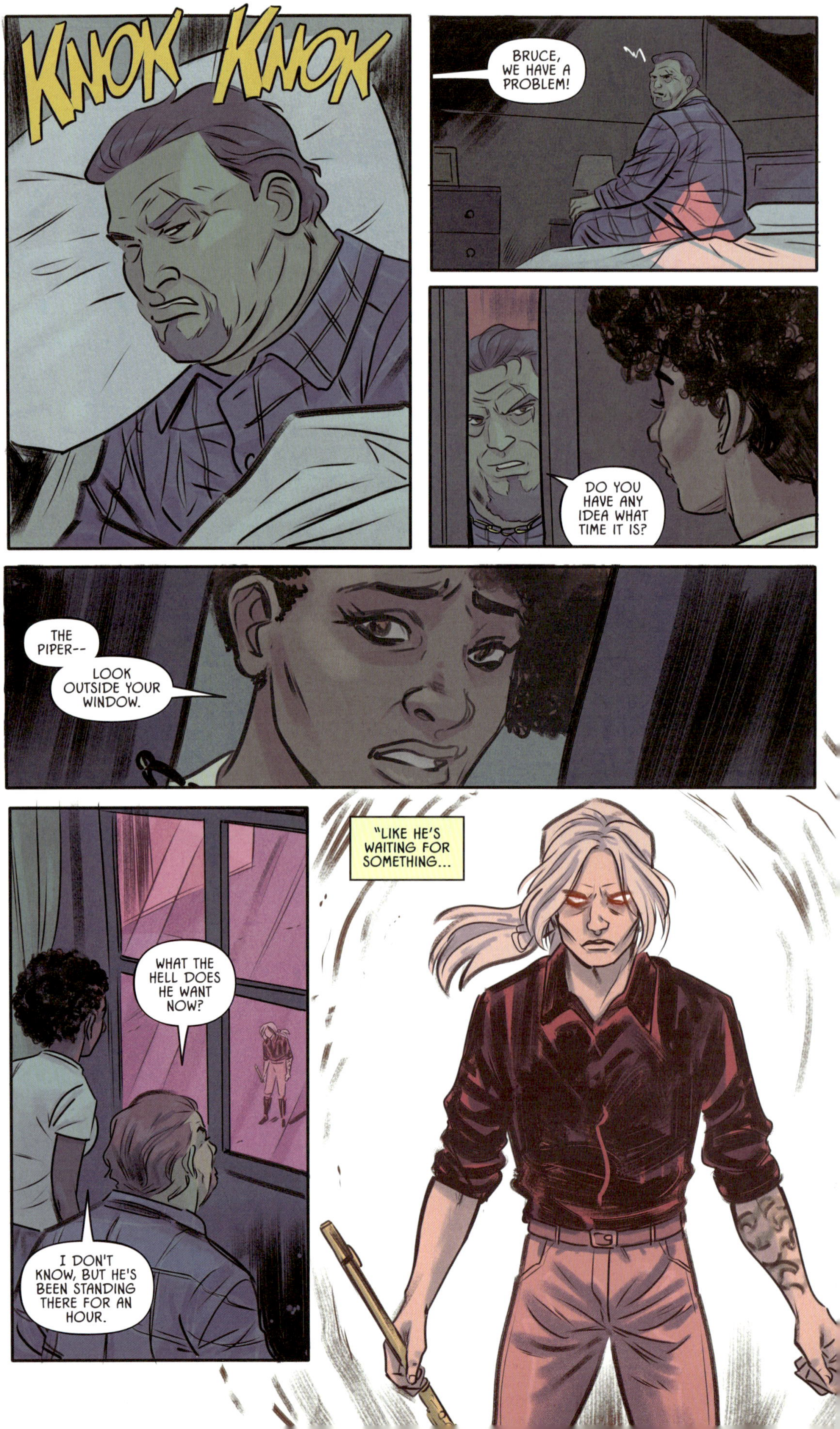
KNOK KNOK
BRUCE, WE HAVE A PROBLEM!
DO YOU HAVE ANY IDEA WHAT TIME IT IS?
THE PIPER--
LOOK OUTSIDE YOUR WINDOW.
WHAT THE HELL DOES HE WANT NOW?
I DON'T KNOW, BUT HE'S BEEN STANDING THERE FOR AN HOUR.
"LIKE HE'S WAITING FOR SOMETHING...

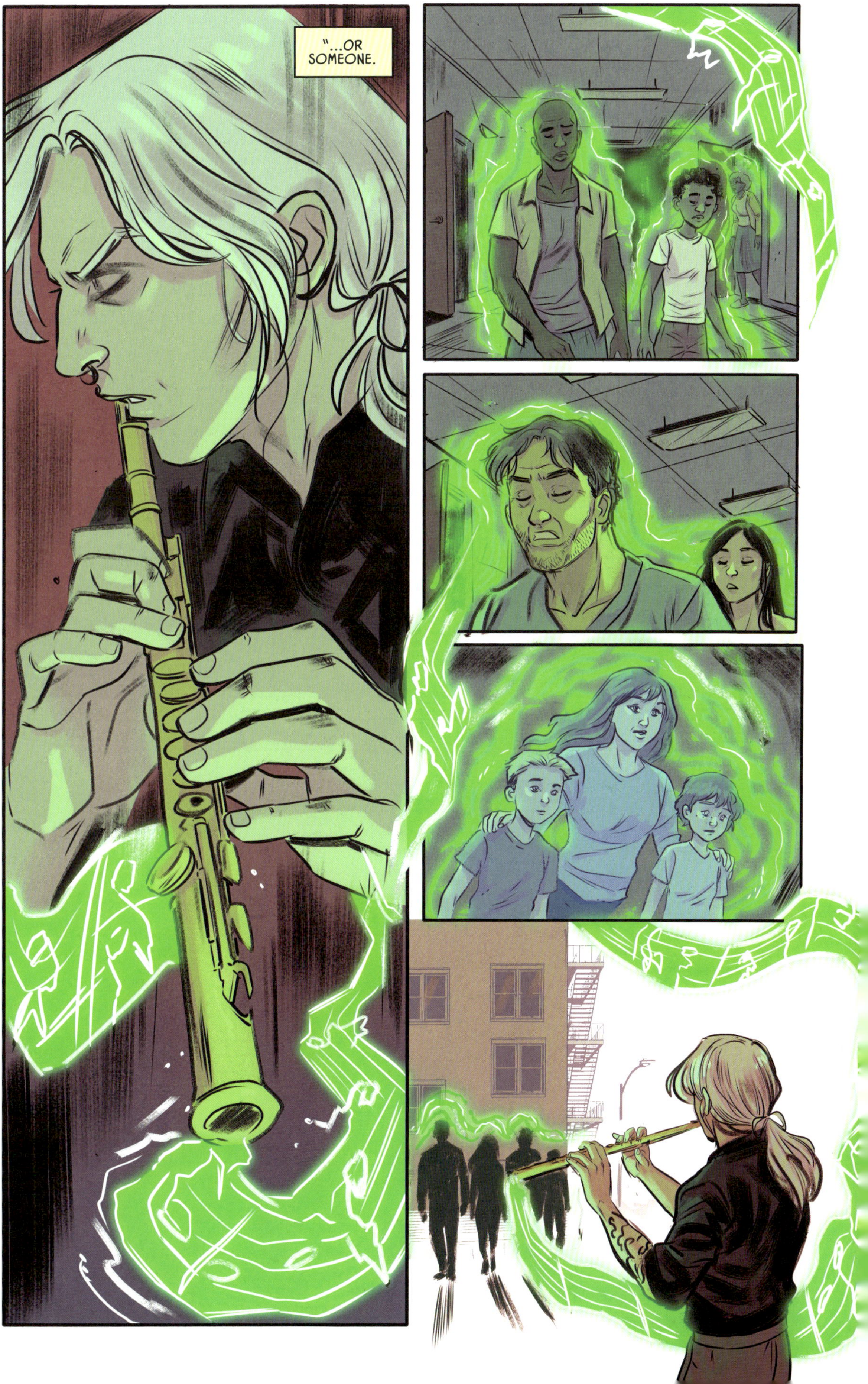
"...OR SOMEONE.

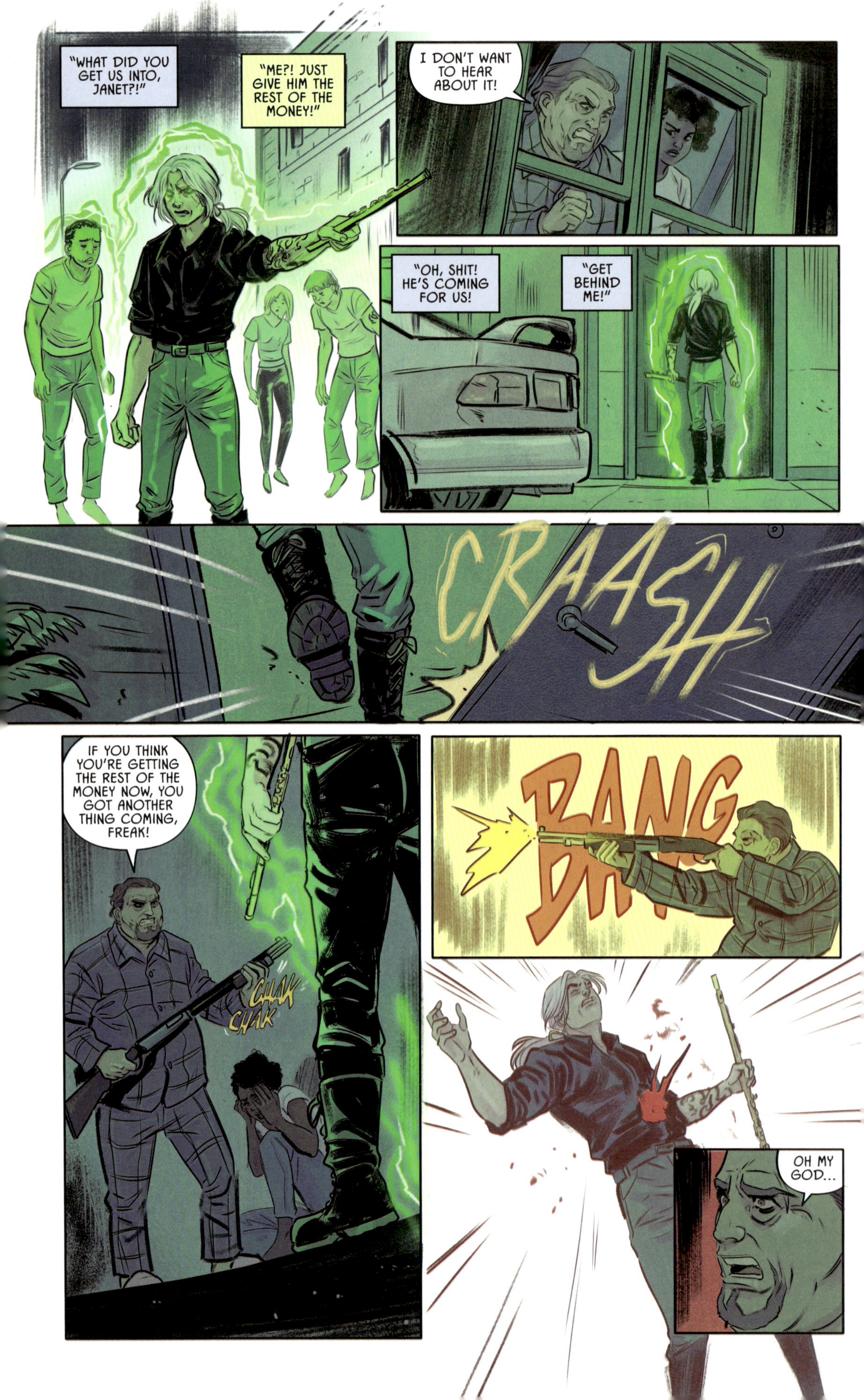
"WHAT DID YOU GET US INTO, JANET?!"
"ME?! JUST GIVE HIM THE REST OF THE MONEY!"
I DON'T WANT TO HEAR ABOUT IT!
"OH, SHIT! HE'S COMING FOR US!
"GET BEHIND ME!"
CRAASH
IF YOU THINK YOU'RE GETTING THE REST OF THE MONEY NOW, YOU GOT ANOTHER THING COMING, FREAK!
CHAK
CHAK
BANG
OH MY GOD...

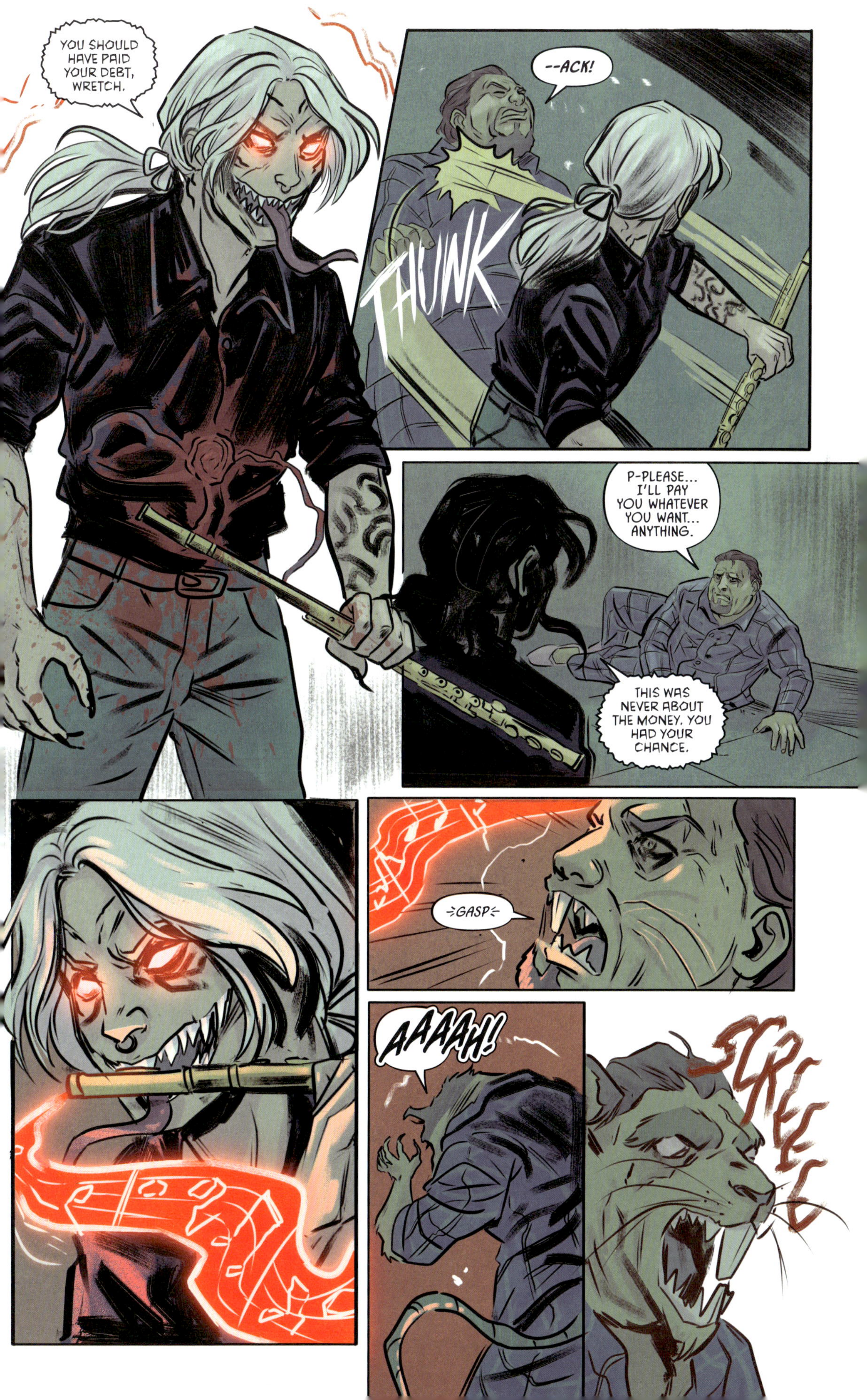
YOU SHOULD HAVE PAID YOUR DEBT, WRETCH.
--ACK!
THUNK
P-PLEASE... I'LL PAY YOU WHATEVER YOU WANT... ANYTHING.
THIS WAS NEVER ABOUT THE MONEY. YOU HAD YOUR CHANCE.
GASP
AAAAH!
SCREEE

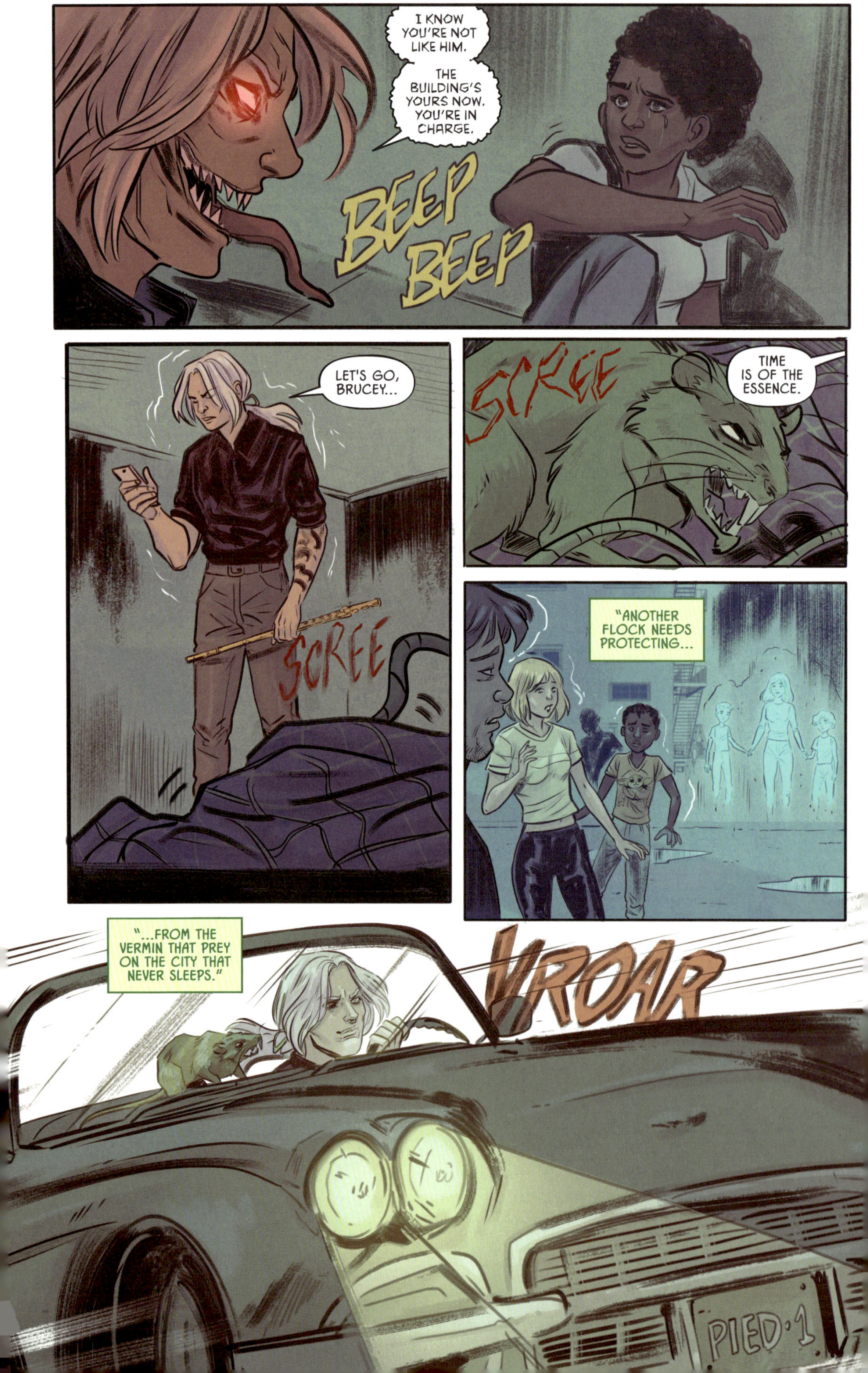
I KNOW YOU'RE NOT LIKE HIM.
THE BUILDING'S YOURS NOW. YOU'RE IN CHARGE.
BEEP BEEP
LET'S GO, BRUCEY...
SCREE
SCREE
TIME IS OF THE ESSENCE.
"ANOTHER FLOCK NEEDS PROTECTING...
"...FROM THE VERMIN THAT PREY ON THE CITY THAT NEVER SLEEPS."
VROAR
PIED·1

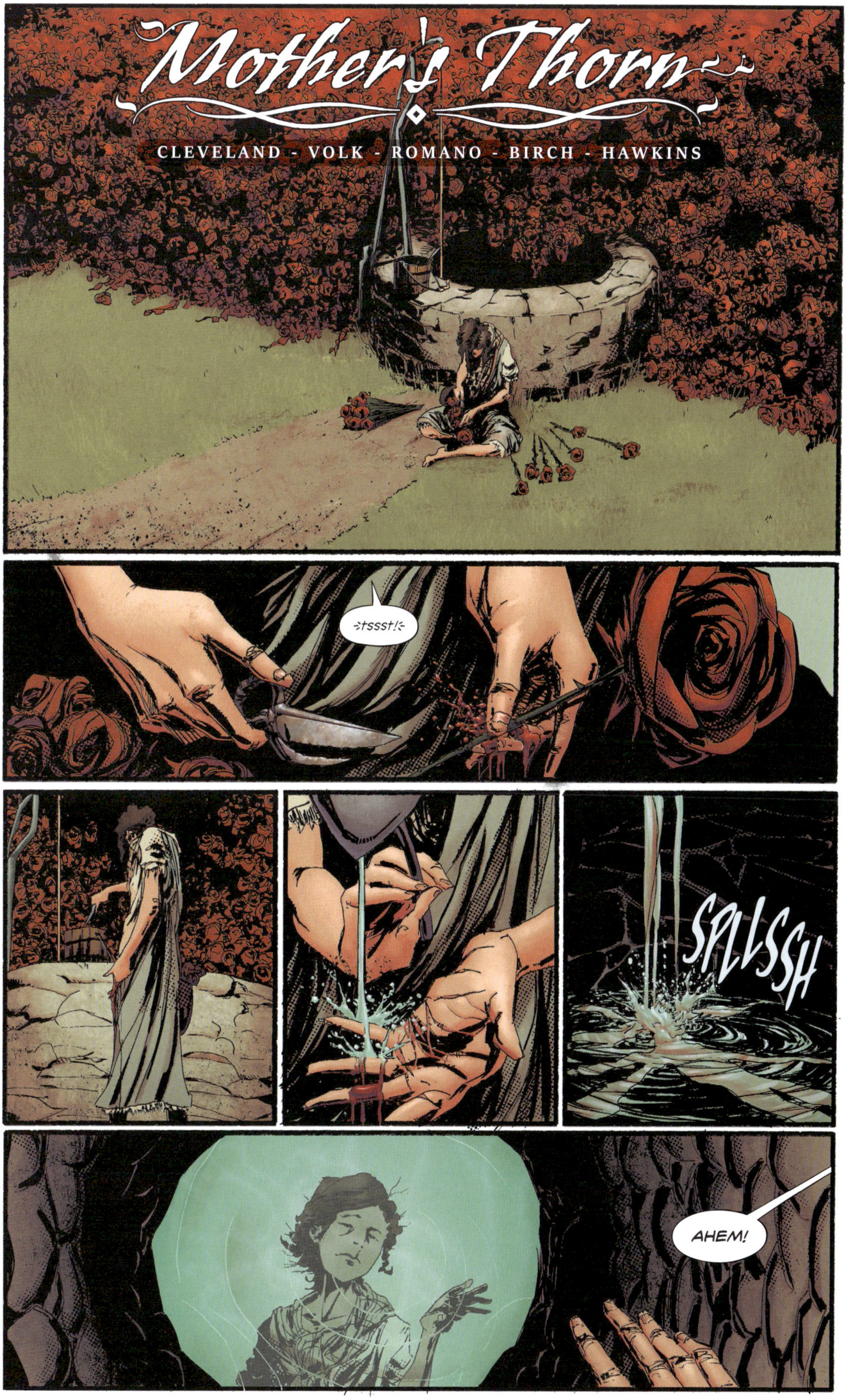
Mother's Thorn
CLEVELAND - VOLK - ROMANO - BIRCH - HAWKINS
⪢tssst!⪡
SPLISH
AHEM!

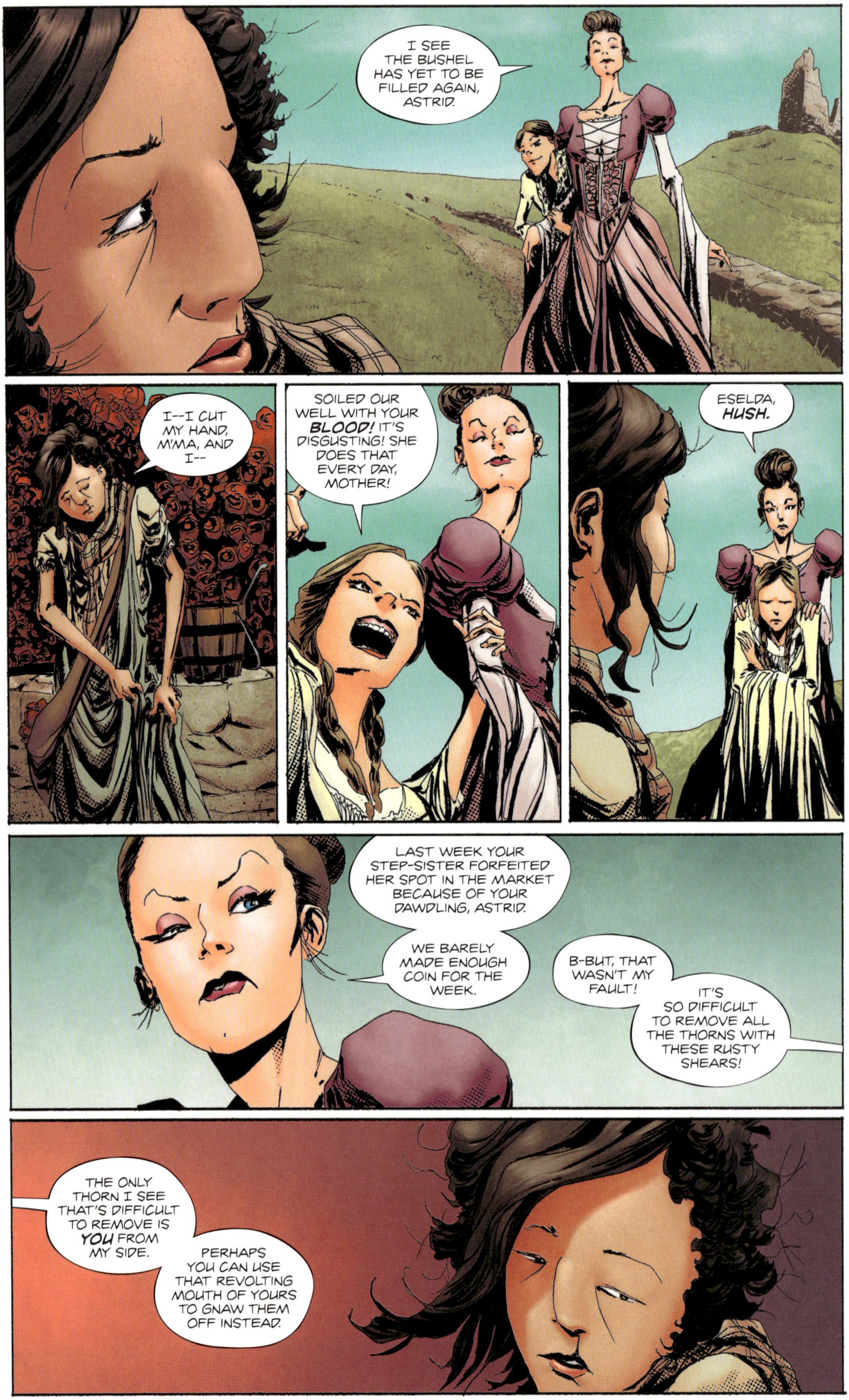
I SEE THE BUSHEL HAS YET TO BE FILLED AGAIN, ASTRID.
I--I CUT MY HAND, M'MA, AND I--
SOILED OUR WELL WITH YOUR **BLOOD!** IT'S DISGUSTING! SHE DOES THAT EVERY DAY, MOTHER!
ESELDA, **HUSH.**
LAST WEEK YOUR STEP-SISTER FORFEITED HER SPOT IN THE MARKET BECAUSE OF YOUR DAWDLING, ASTRID.
WE BARELY MADE ENOUGH COIN FOR THE WEEK.
B-BUT, THAT WASN'T MY FAULT!
IT'S SO DIFFICULT TO REMOVE ALL THE THORNS WITH THESE RUSTY SHEARS!
THE ONLY THORN I SEE THAT'S DIFFICULT TO REMOVE IS **YOU** FROM MY SIDE.
PERHAPS YOU CAN USE THAT REVOLTING MOUTH OF YOURS TO GNAW THEM OFF INSTEAD.

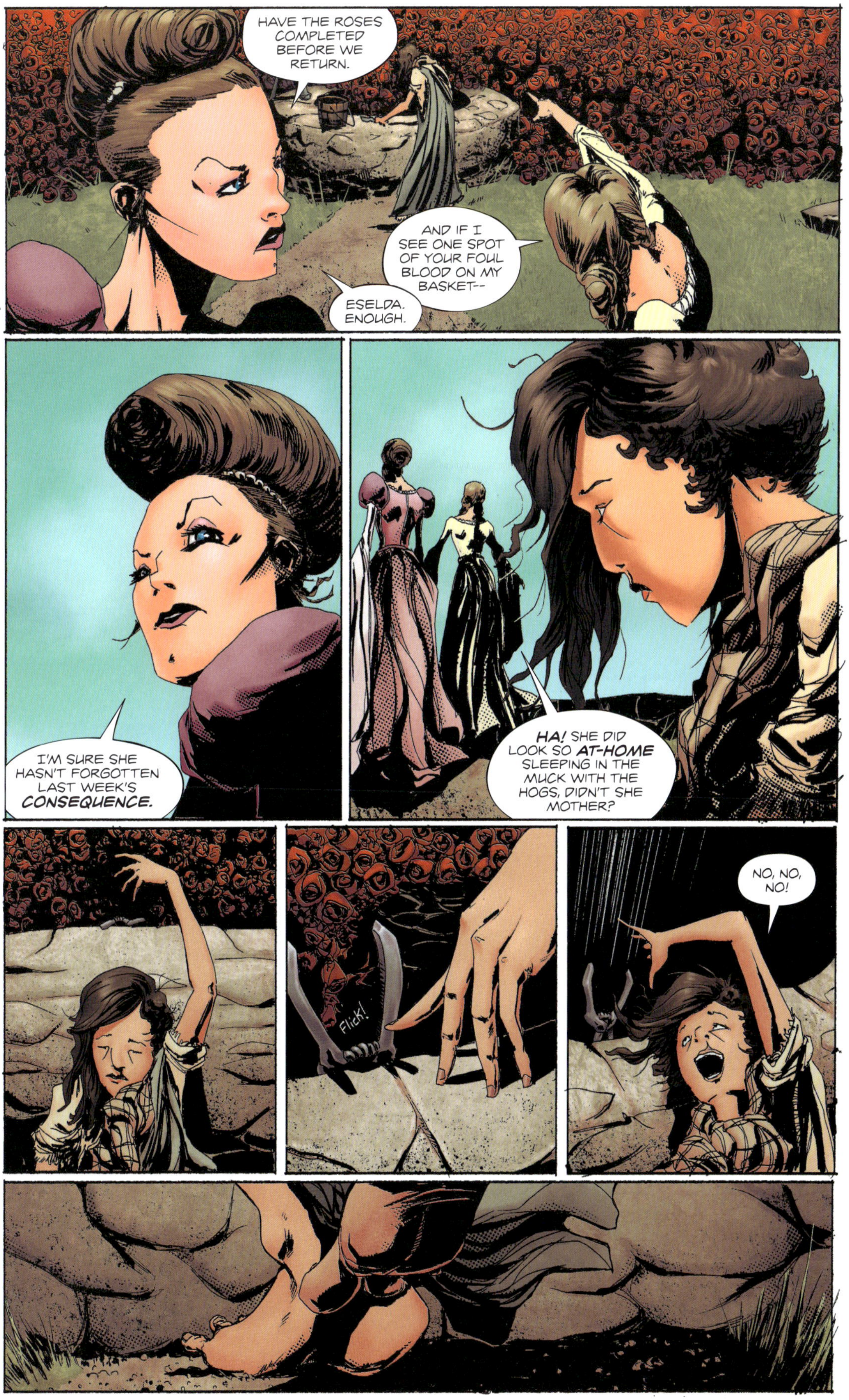
HAVE THE ROSES COMPLETED BEFORE WE RETURN.
AND IF I SEE ONE SPOT OF YOUR FOUL BLOOD ON MY BASKET--
ESELDA. ENOUGH.
I'M SURE SHE HASN'T FORGOTTEN LAST WEEK'S **CONSEQUENCE.**
HA! SHE DID LOOK SO **AT-HOME** SLEEPING IN THE MUCK WITH THE HOGS, DIDN'T SHE MOTHER?
Flick!
NO, NO, NO!

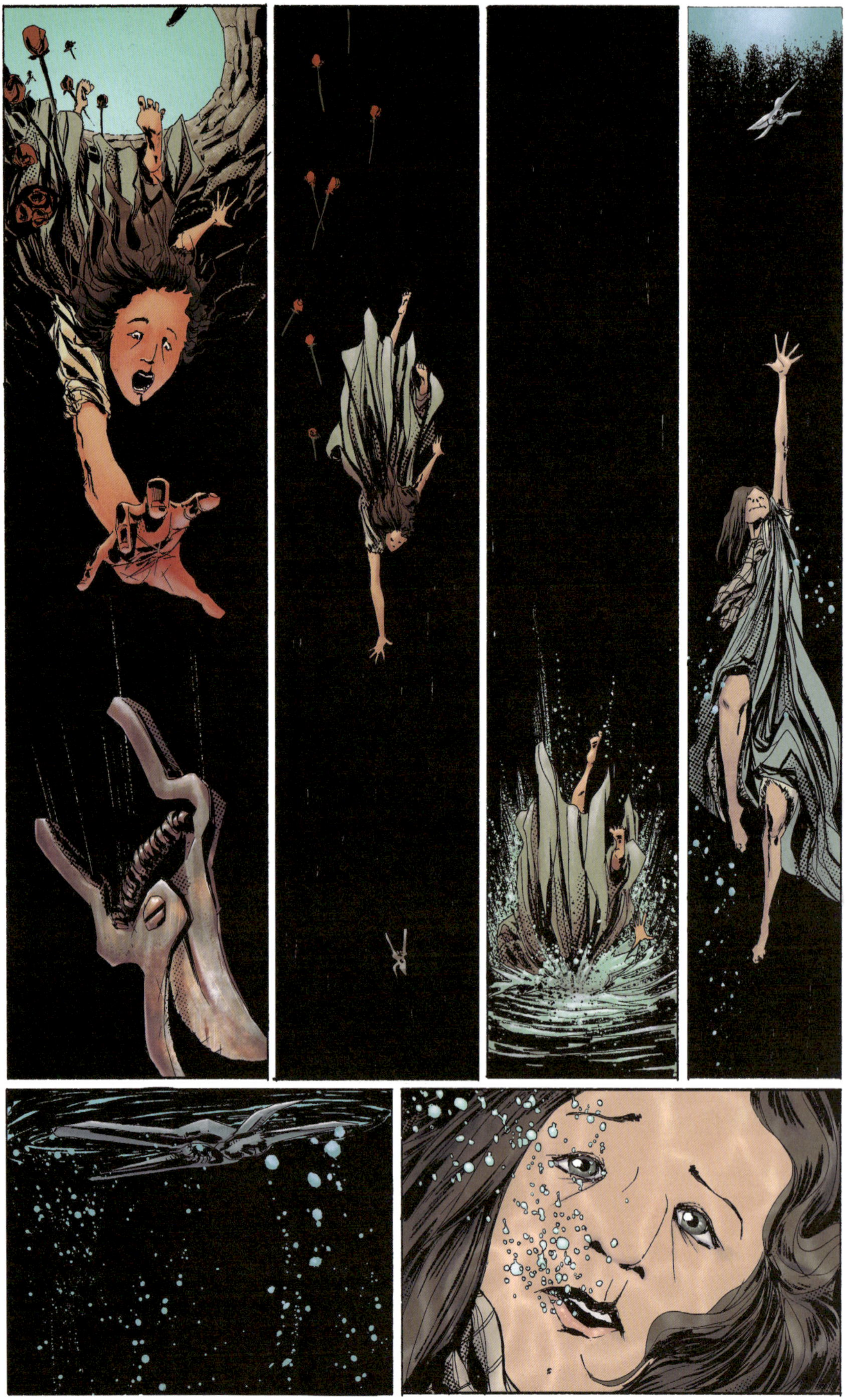

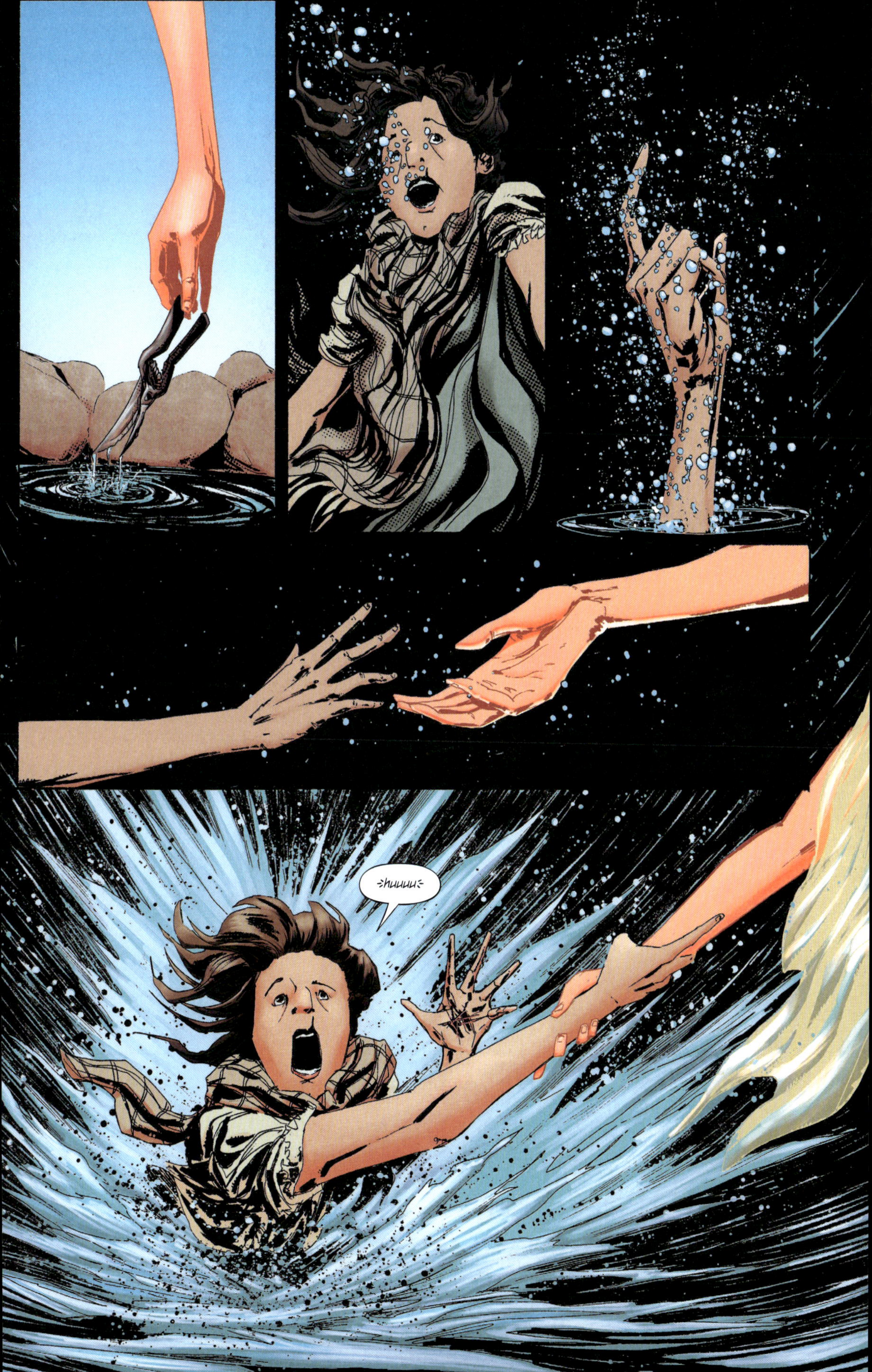
huuuu

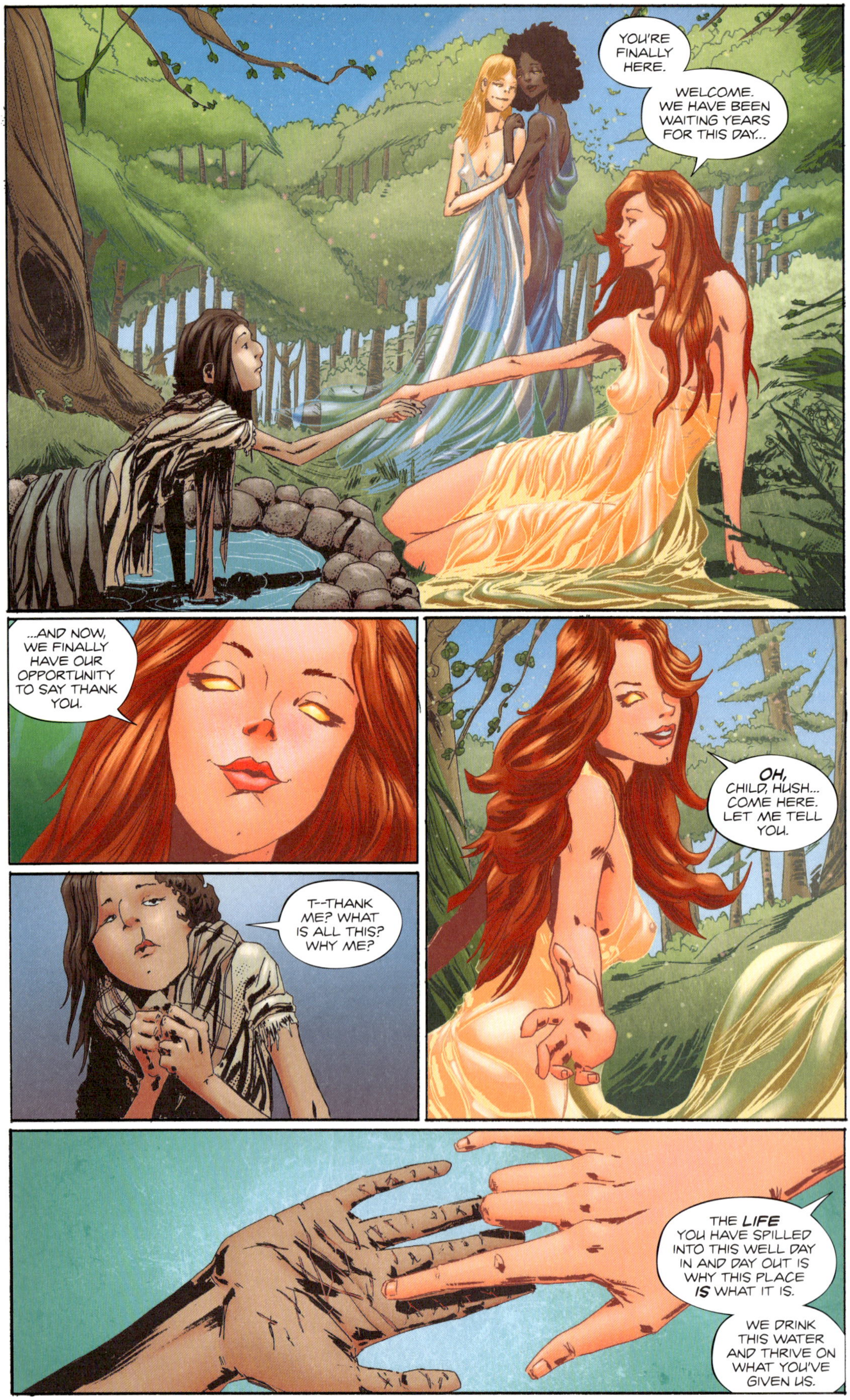
YOU'RE FINALLY HERE.
WELCOME. WE HAVE BEEN WAITING YEARS FOR THIS DAY...
...AND NOW, WE FINALLY HAVE OUR OPPORTUNITY TO SAY THANK YOU.
T--THANK ME? WHAT IS ALL THIS? WHY ME?
OH, CHILD, HUSH... COME HERE. LET ME TELL YOU.
THE LIFE YOU HAVE SPILLED INTO THIS WELL DAY IN AND DAY OUT IS WHY THIS PLACE IS WHAT IT IS.
WE DRINK THIS WATER AND THRIVE ON WHAT YOU'VE GIVEN US.

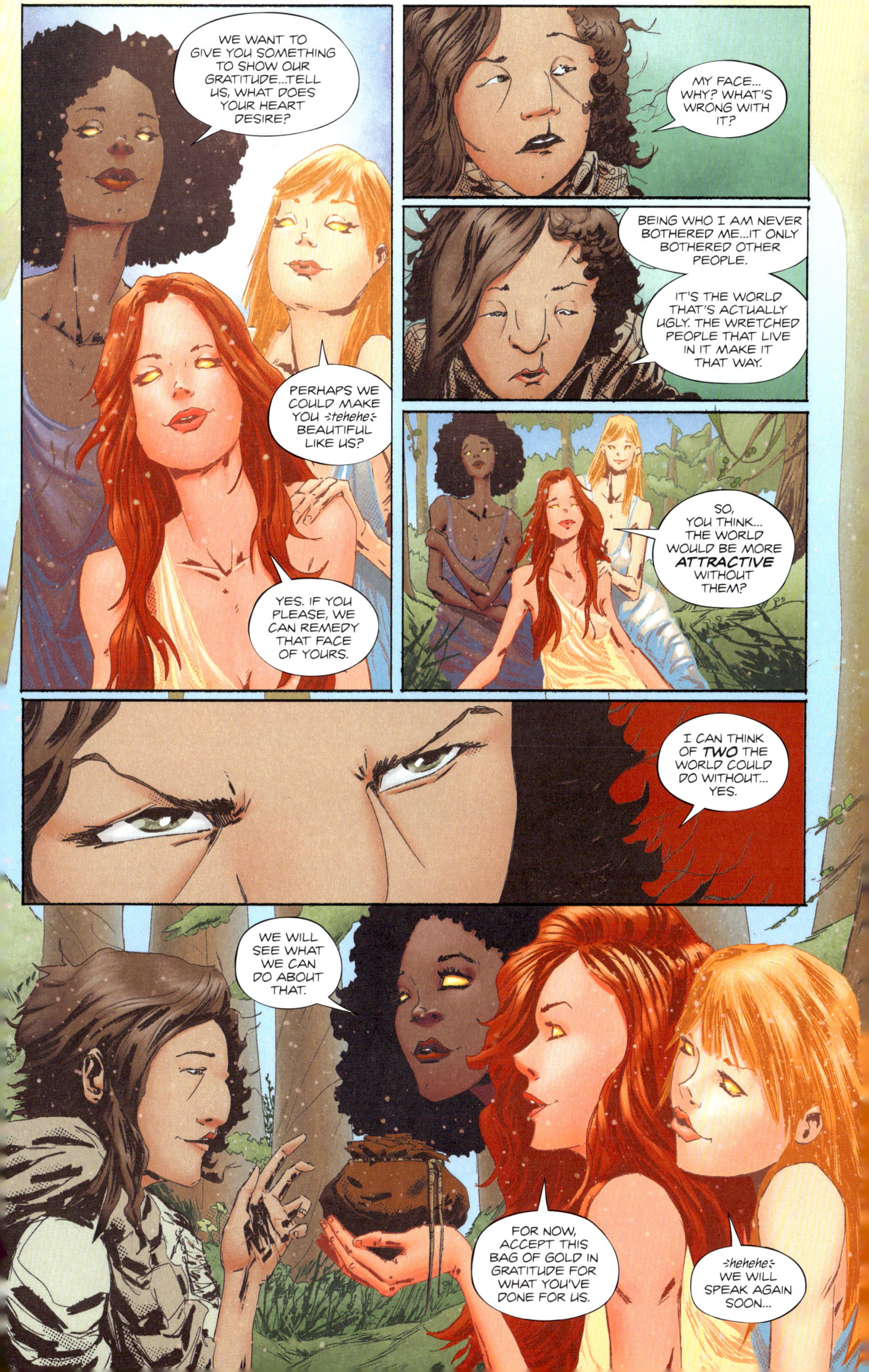

WE WANT TO GIVE YOU SOMETHING TO SHOW OUR GRATITUDE...TELL US, WHAT DOES YOUR HEART DESIRE?
PERHAPS WE COULD MAKE YOU ~tehehe~ BEAUTIFUL LIKE US?
YES. IF YOU PLEASE, WE CAN REMEDY THAT FACE OF YOURS.
MY FACE... WHY? WHAT'S WRONG WITH IT?
BEING WHO I AM NEVER BOTHERED ME...IT ONLY BOTHERED OTHER PEOPLE.
IT'S THE WORLD THAT'S ACTUALLY UGLY. THE WRETCHED PEOPLE THAT LIVE IN IT MAKE IT THAT WAY.
SO, YOU THINK... THE WORLD WOULD BE MORE ***ATTRACTIVE*** WITHOUT THEM?
I CAN THINK OF ***TWO*** THE WORLD COULD DO WITHOUT... YES.
WE WILL SEE WHAT WE CAN DO ABOUT THAT.
FOR NOW, ACCEPT THIS BAG OF GOLD IN GRATITUDE FOR WHAT YOU'VE DONE FOR US.
~hehehe~ WE WILL SPEAK AGAIN SOON...

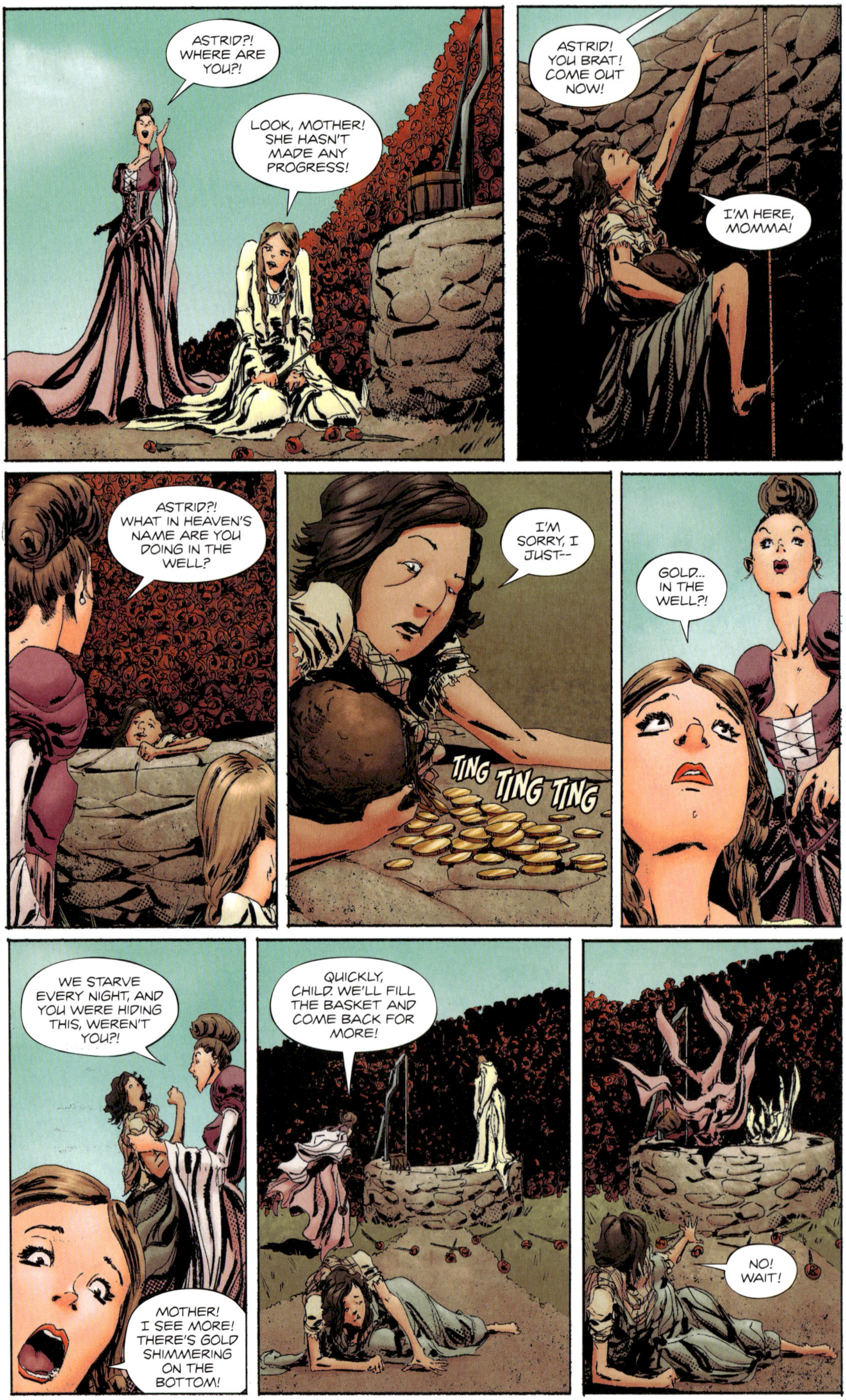
ASTRID?! WHERE ARE YOU?!
LOOK, MOTHER! SHE HASN'T MADE ANY PROGRESS!
ASTRID! YOU BRAT! COME OUT NOW!
I'M HERE, MOMMA!
ASTRID?! WHAT IN HEAVEN'S NAME ARE YOU DOING IN THE WELL?
I'M SORRY, I JUST--
TING TING TING
GOLD... IN THE WELL?!
WE STARVE EVERY NIGHT, AND YOU WERE HIDING THIS, WEREN'T YOU?!
MOTHER! I SEE MORE! THERE'S GOLD SHIMMERING ON THE BOTTOM!
QUICKLY, CHILD. WE'LL FILL THE BASKET AND COME BACK FOR MORE!
NO! WAIT!

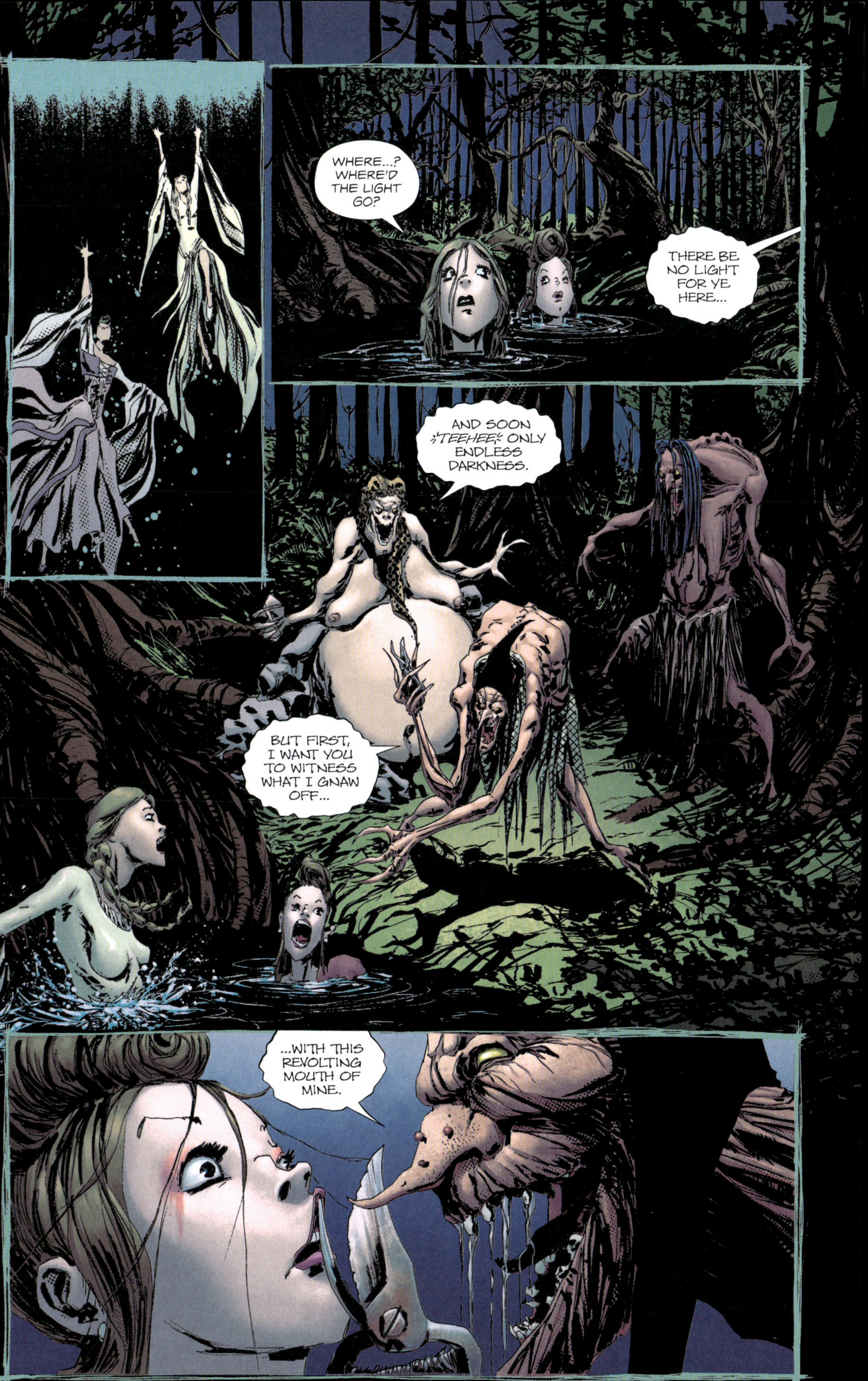
WHERE...? WHERE'D THE LIGHT GO?
THERE BE NO LIGHT FOR YE HERE...
AND SOON *TEEHEE* ONLY ENDLESS DARKNESS.
BUT FIRST, I WANT YOU TO WITNESS WHAT I GNAW OFF...
...WITH THIS REVOLTING MOUTH OF MINE.

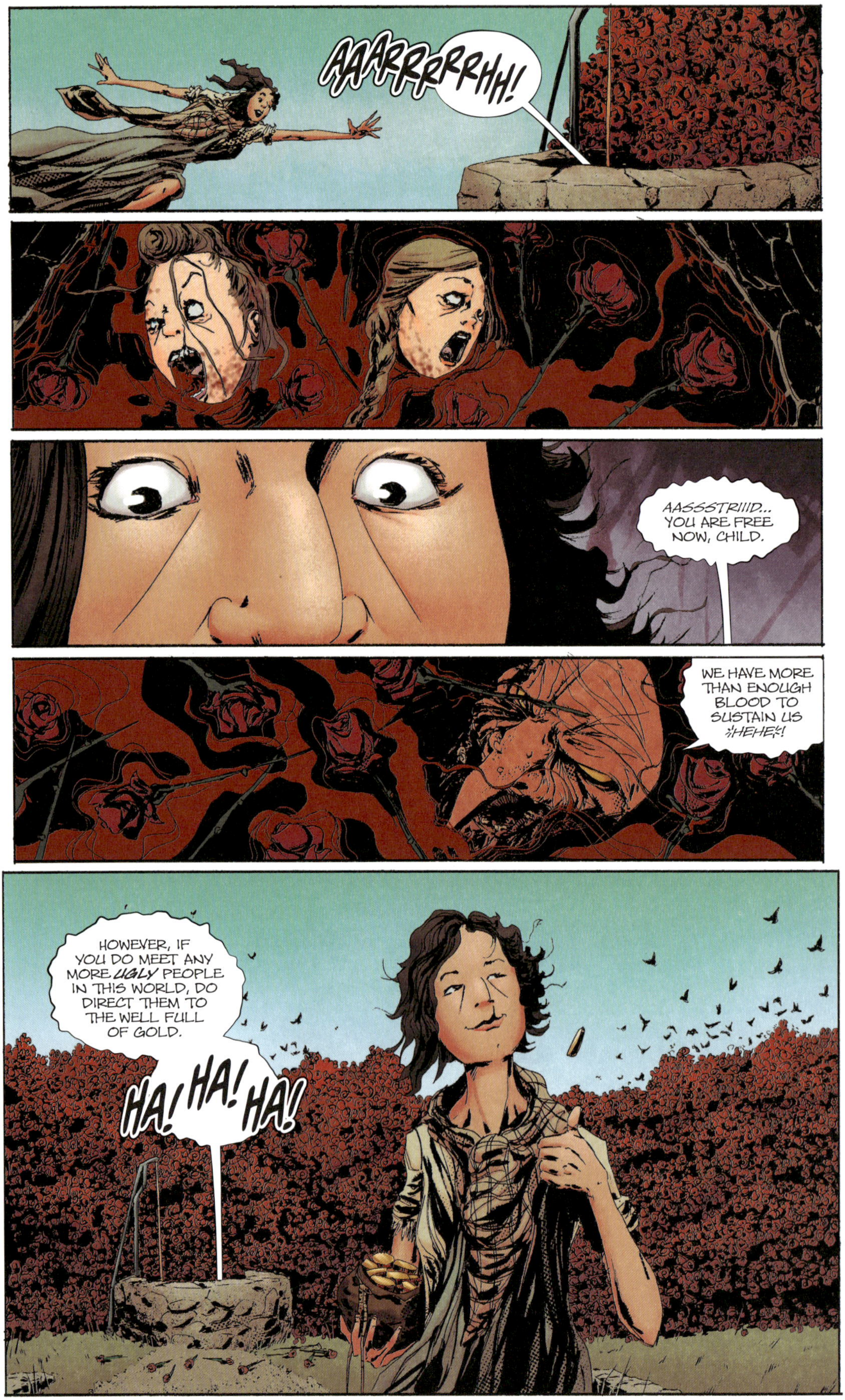
AAARRRRRHH!
AASSSTRIIID... YOU ARE FREE NOW, CHILD.
WE HAVE MORE THAN ENOUGH BLOOD TO SUSTAIN US *HEHE*!
HOWEVER, IF YOU DO MEET ANY MORE *UGLY* PEOPLE IN THIS WORLD, DO DIRECT THEM TO THE WELL FULL OF GOLD.
HA! HA! HA!

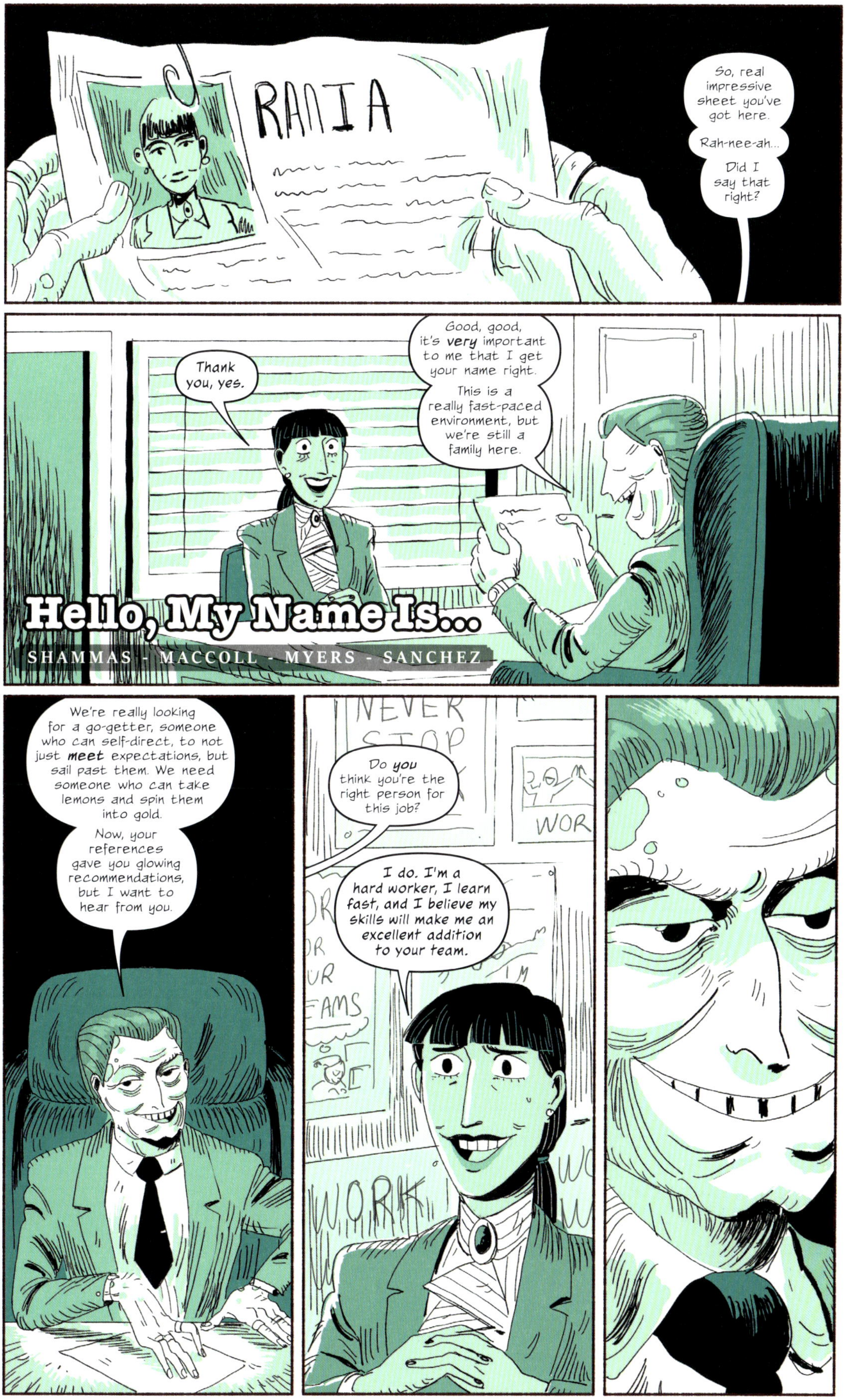
RANIA
So, real impressive sheet you've got here.
Rah-nee-ah...
Did I say that right?
Thank you, yes.
Good, good, it's **very** important to me that I get your name right.
This is a really fast-paced environment, but we're still a family here.
Hello, My Name Is...
SHAMMAS - MACCOLL - MYERS - SANCHEZ
We're really looking for a go-getter, someone who can self-direct, to not just **meet** expectations, but sail past them. We need someone who can take lemons and spin them into gold.
Now, your references gave you glowing recommendations, but I want to hear from you.
NEVER STOP
WOR
Do **you** think you're the right person for this job?
I do. I'm a hard worker, I learn fast, and I believe my skills will make me an excellent addition to your team.
WORK

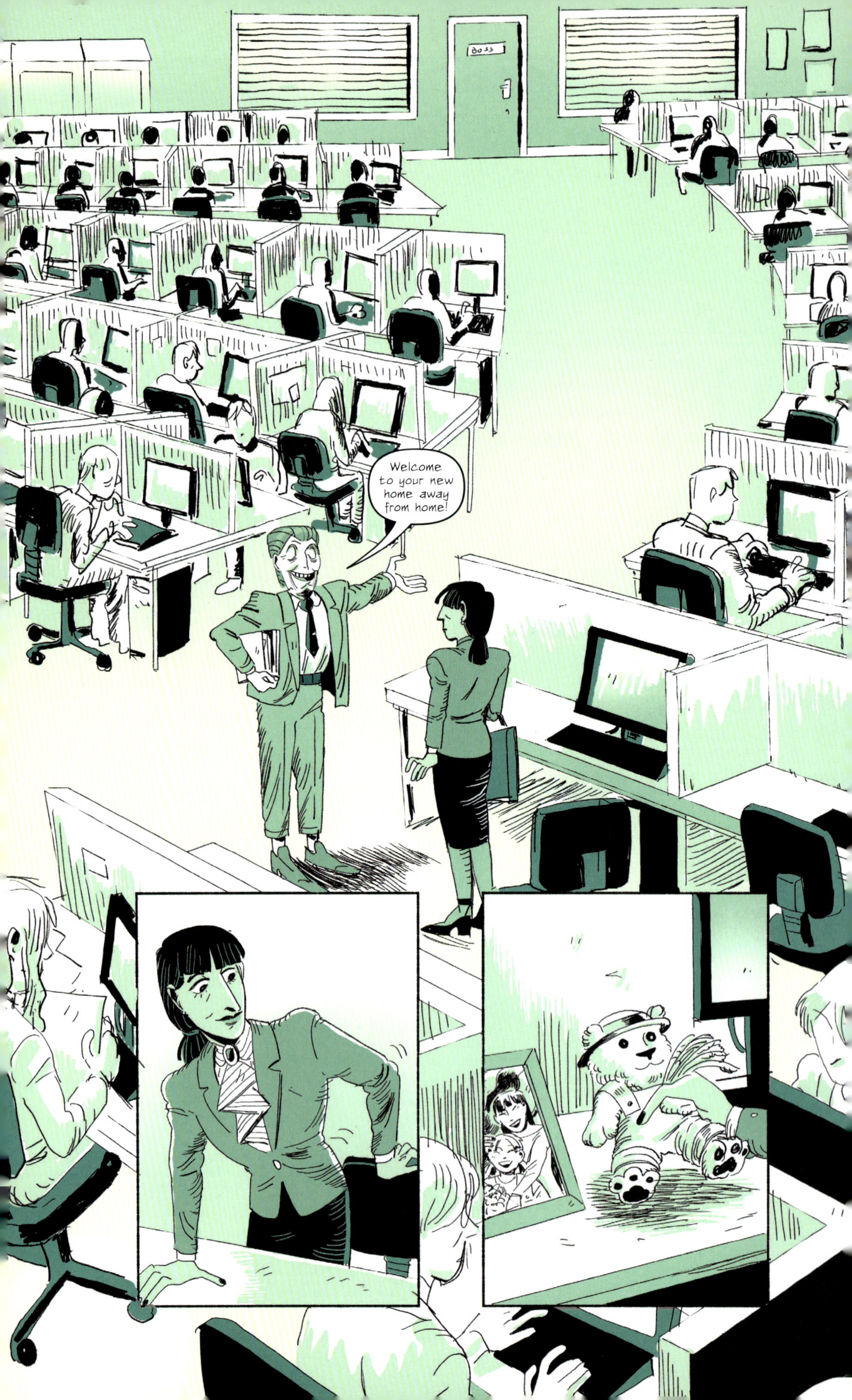
Welcome to your new home away from home!
BOSS

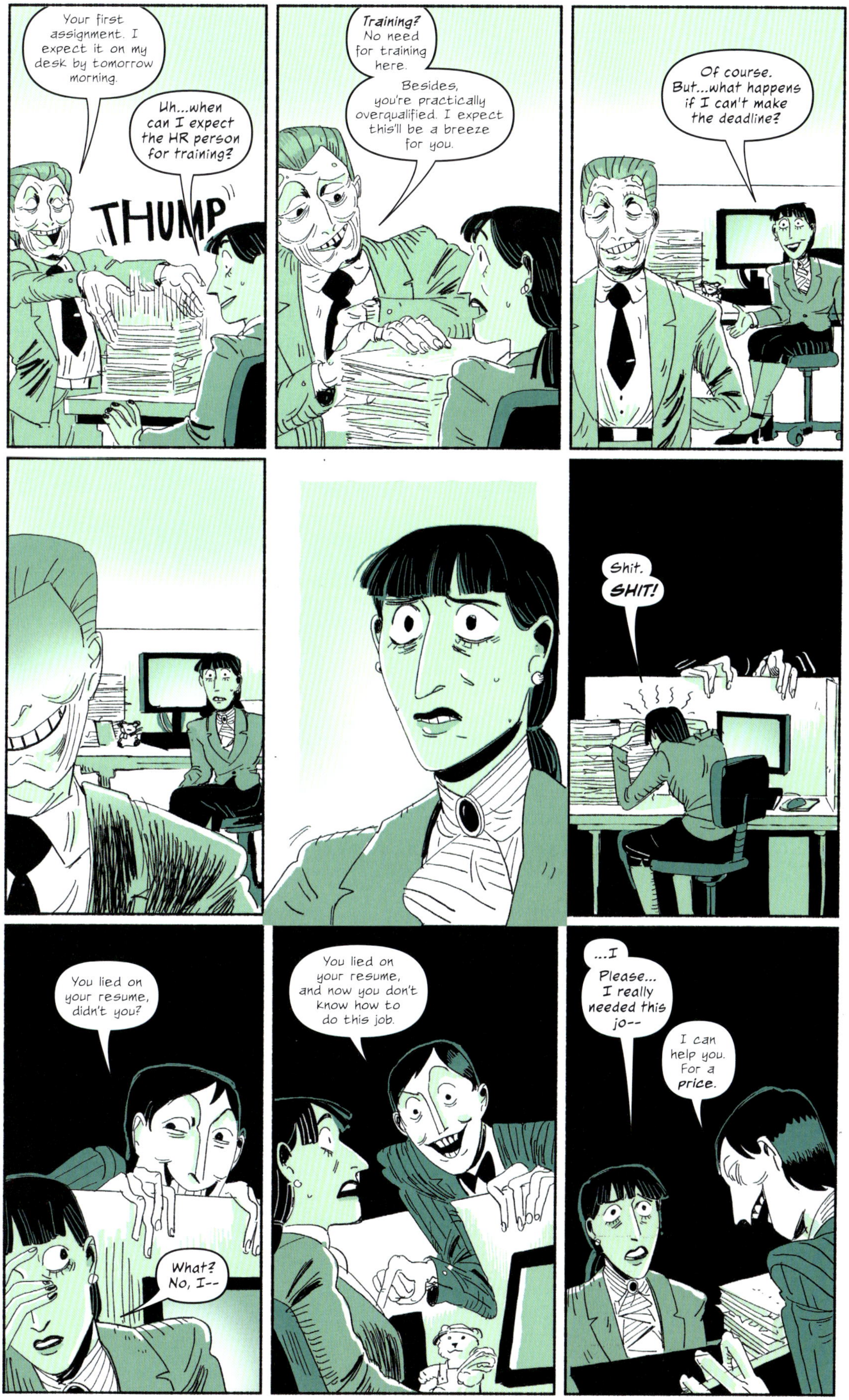
Your first assignment. I expect it on my desk by tomorrow morning.
Uh...when can I expect the HR person for training?
THUMP
Training? No need for training here.
Besides, you're practically overqualified. I expect this'll be a breeze for you.
Of course. But...what happens if I can't make the deadline?
Shit. SHIT!
You lied on your resume, didn't you?
What? No, I--
You lied on your resume, and now you don't know how to do this job.
...I
Please... I really needed this jo--
I can help you. For a price.

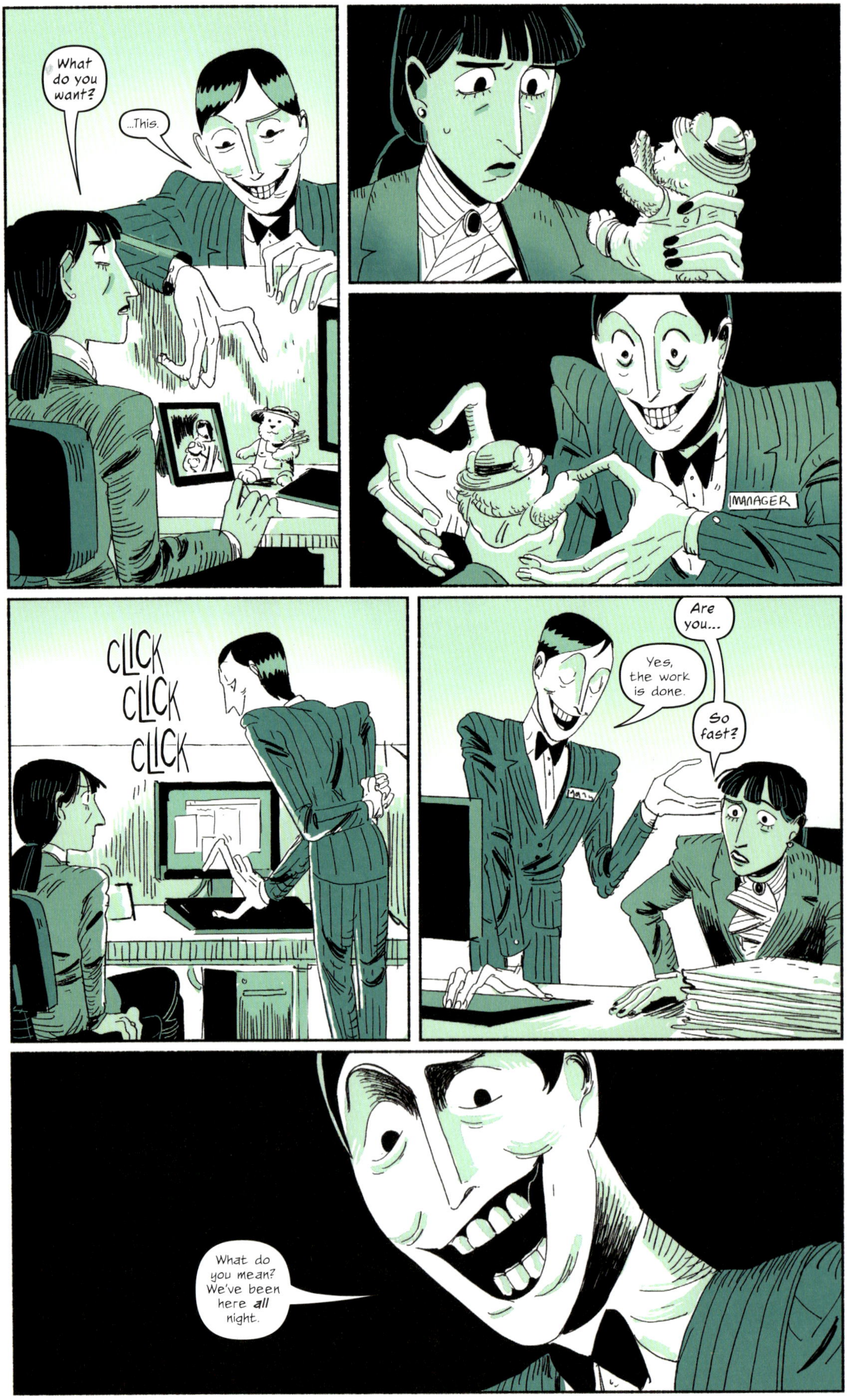
What do you want?
...This.
MANAGER
CLICK
CLICK
CLICK
Are you...
Yes, the work is done.
So fast?
What do you mean? We've been here ***all*** night.

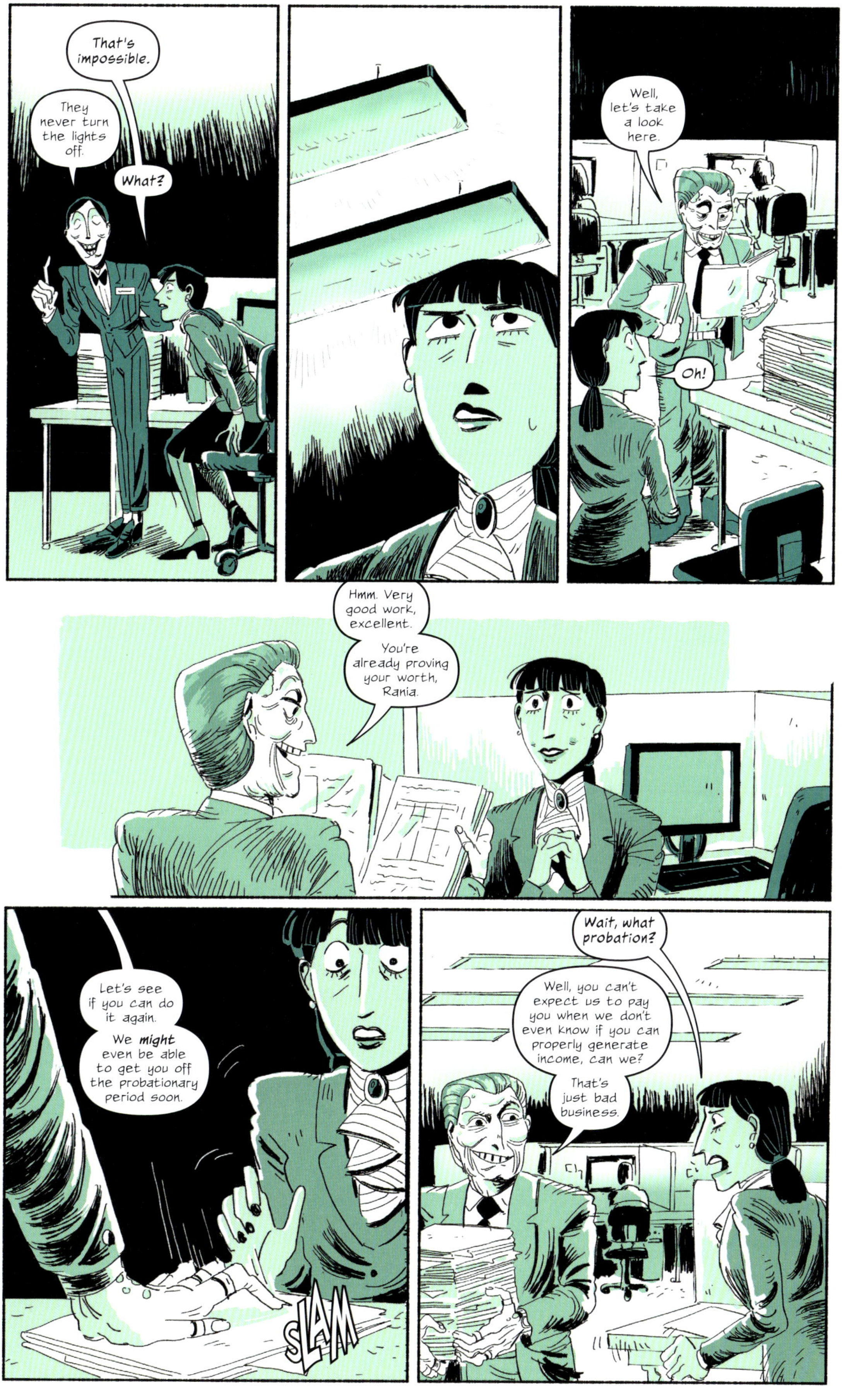

They never turn the lights off.
That's impossible.
What?
Well, let's take a look here.
Oh!
Hmm. Very good work, excellent.
You're already proving your worth, Rania.
Let's see if you can do it again.
We *might* even be able to get you off the probationary period soon.
SLAM
Wait, what probation?
Well, you can't expect us to pay you when we don't even know if you can properly generate income, can we?
That's just bad business.

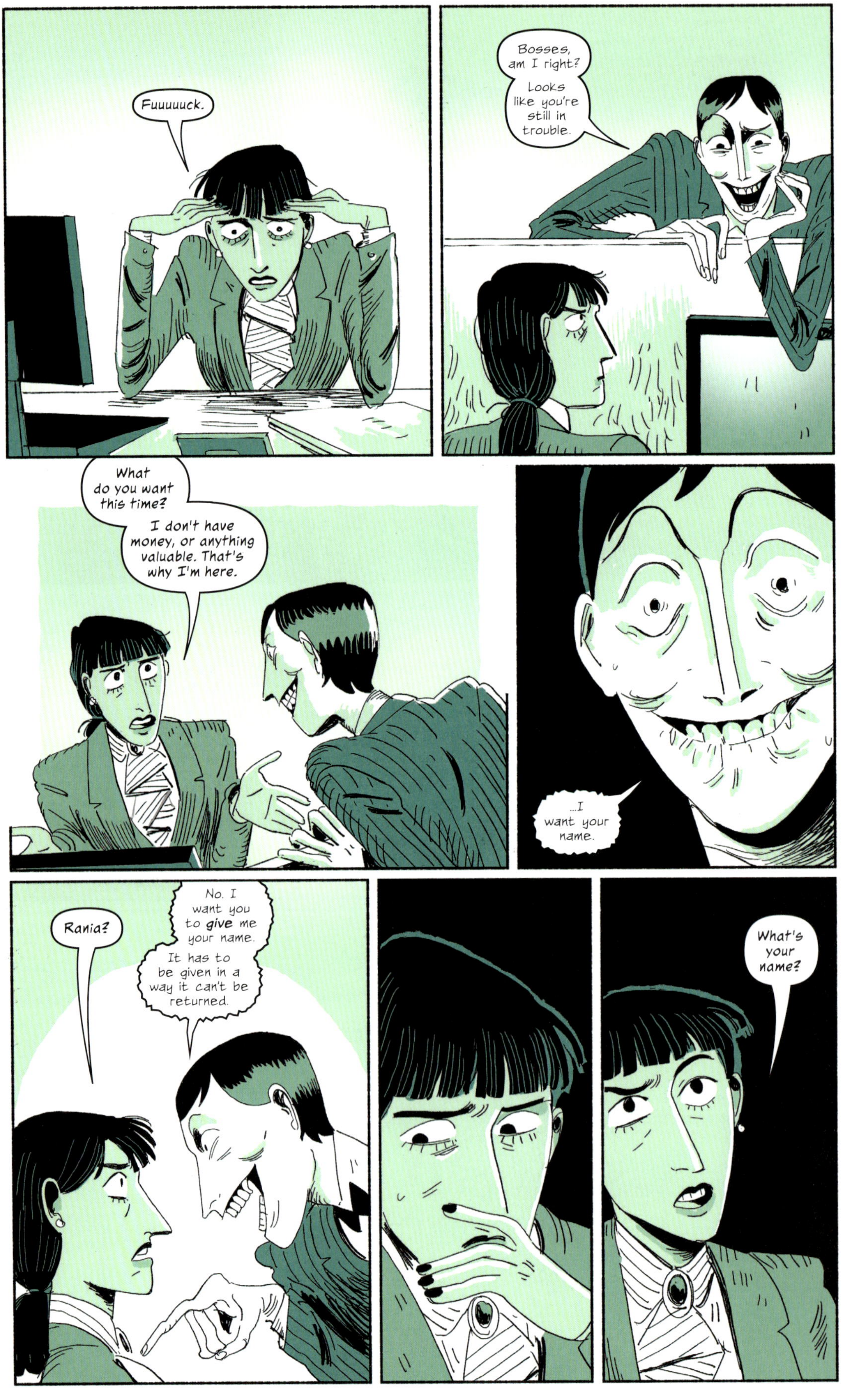
Fuuuuuck.
Bosses, am I right?
Looks like you're still in trouble.
What do you want this time?
I don't have money, or anything valuable. That's why I'm here.
...I want your name.
Rania?
No. I want you to give me your name.
It has to be given in a way it can't be returned.
What's your name?

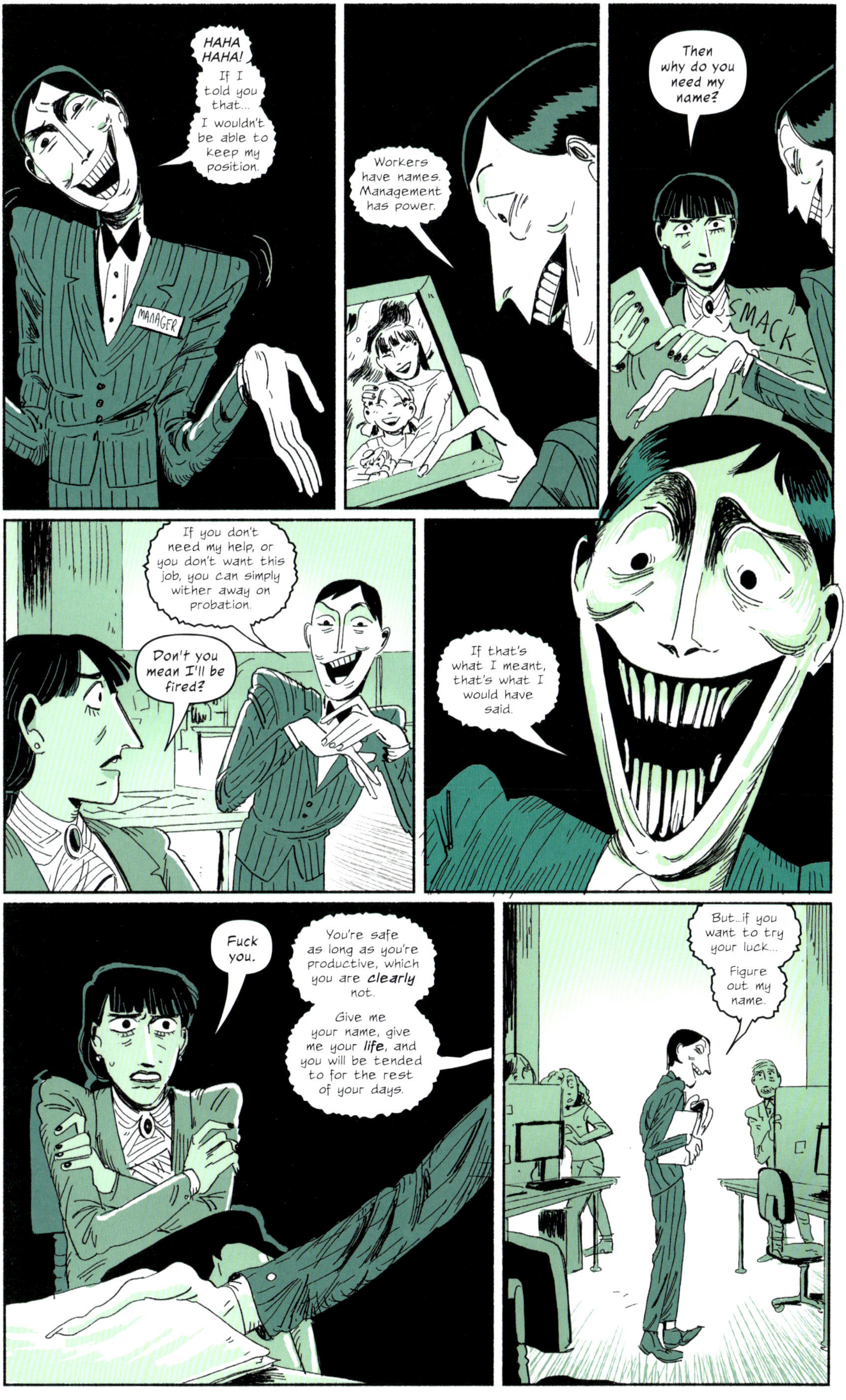
HAHA HAHA! If I told you that... I wouldn't be able to keep my position.
MANAGER
Workers have names. Management has power.
Then why do you need my name?
SMACK
If you don't need my help, or you don't want this job, you can simply wither away on probation.
Don't you mean I'll be fired?
If that's what I meant, that's what I would have said.
Fuck you.
You're safe as long as you're productive, which you are clearly not.
Give me your name, give me your life, and you will be tended to for the rest of your days.
But...if you want to try your luck...
Figure out my name.

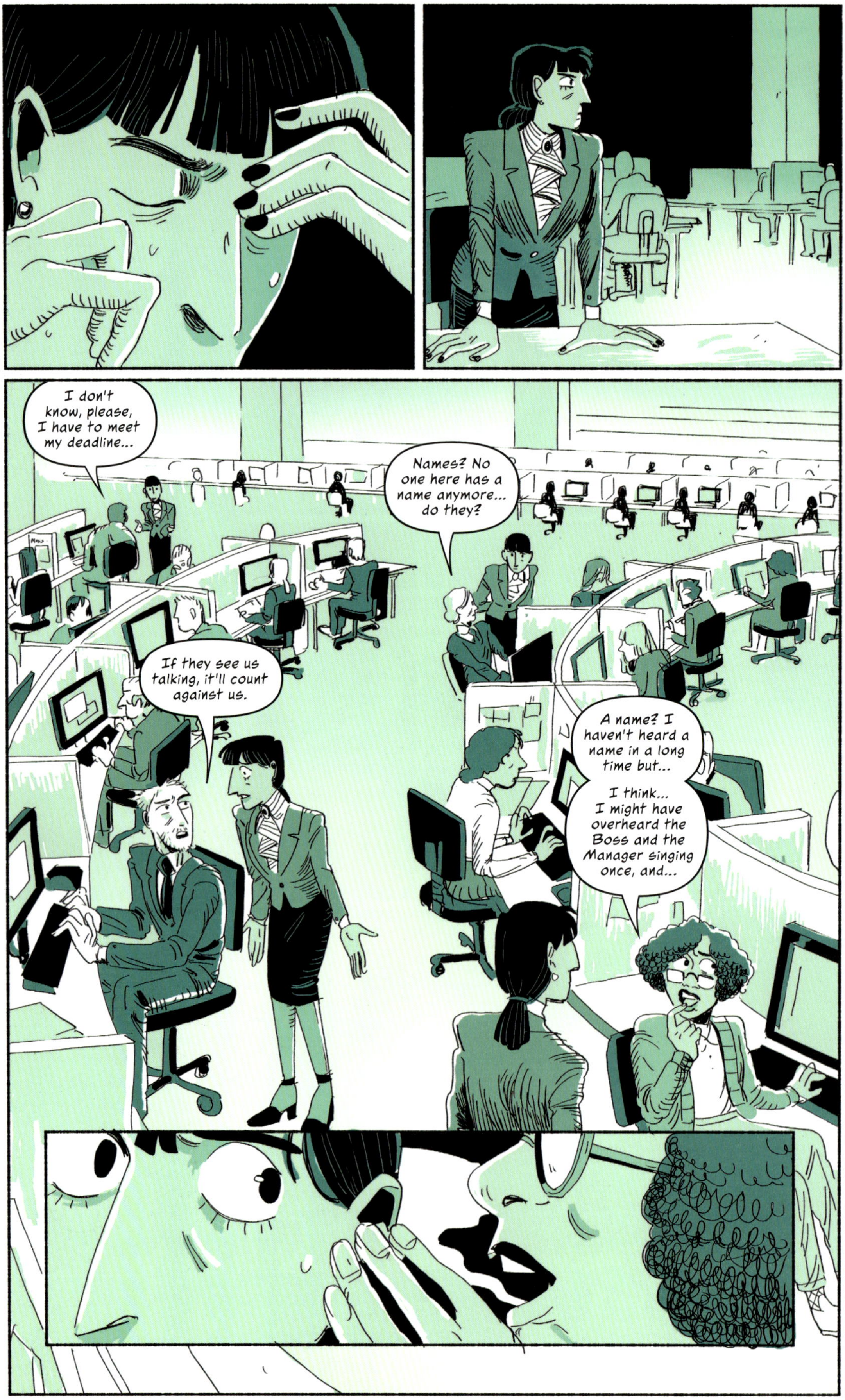
I don't know, please, I have to meet my deadline...
Names? No one here has a name anymore... do they?
If they see us talking, it'll count against us.
A name? I haven't heard a name in a long time but...
I think... I might have overheard the Boss and the Manager singing once, and...

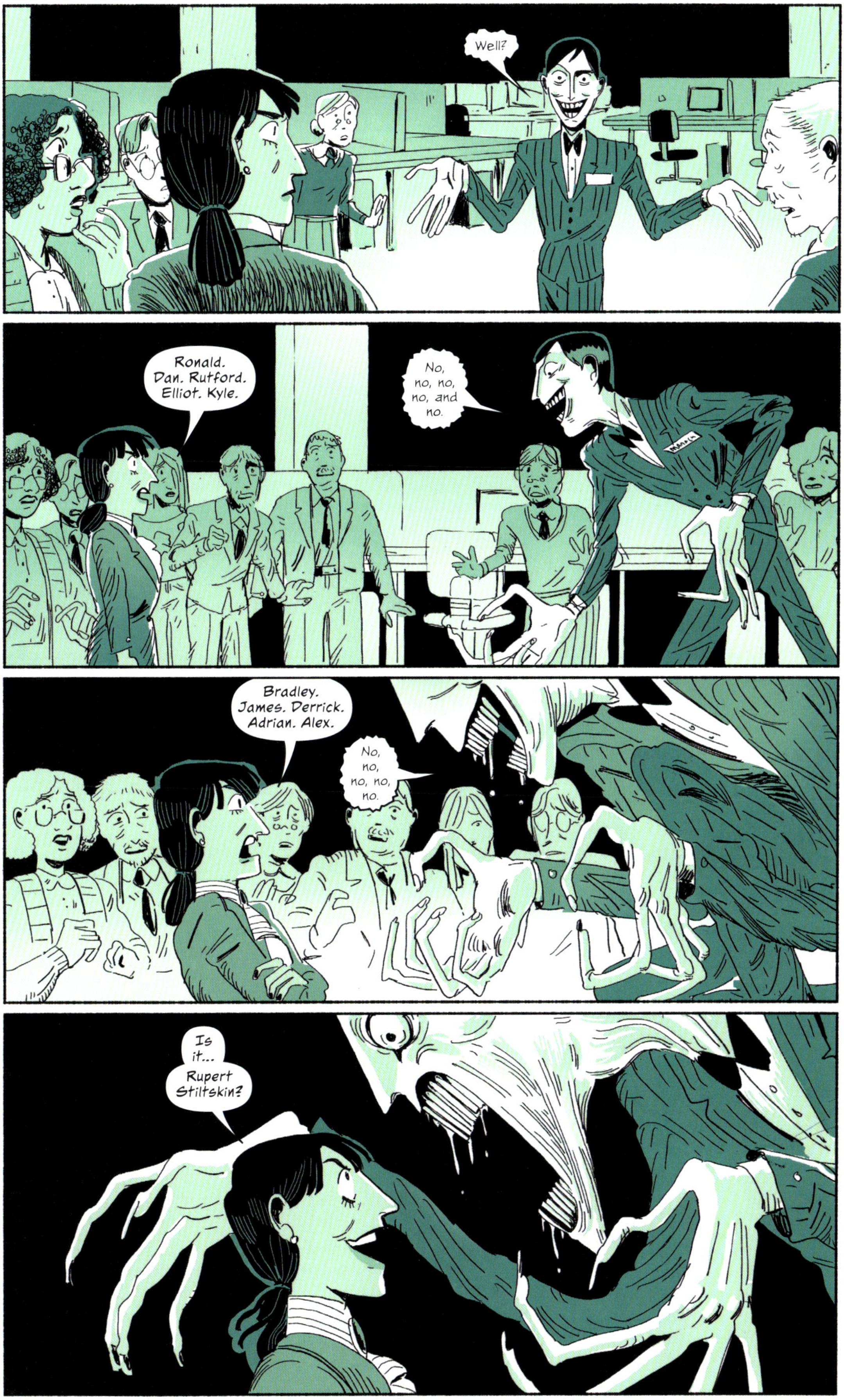
Well?
Ronald. Dan. Rutford. Elliot. Kyle.
No, no, no, no, and no.
Bradley. James. Derrick. Adrian. Alex.
No, no, no, no, no.
Is it... Rupert Stiltskin?

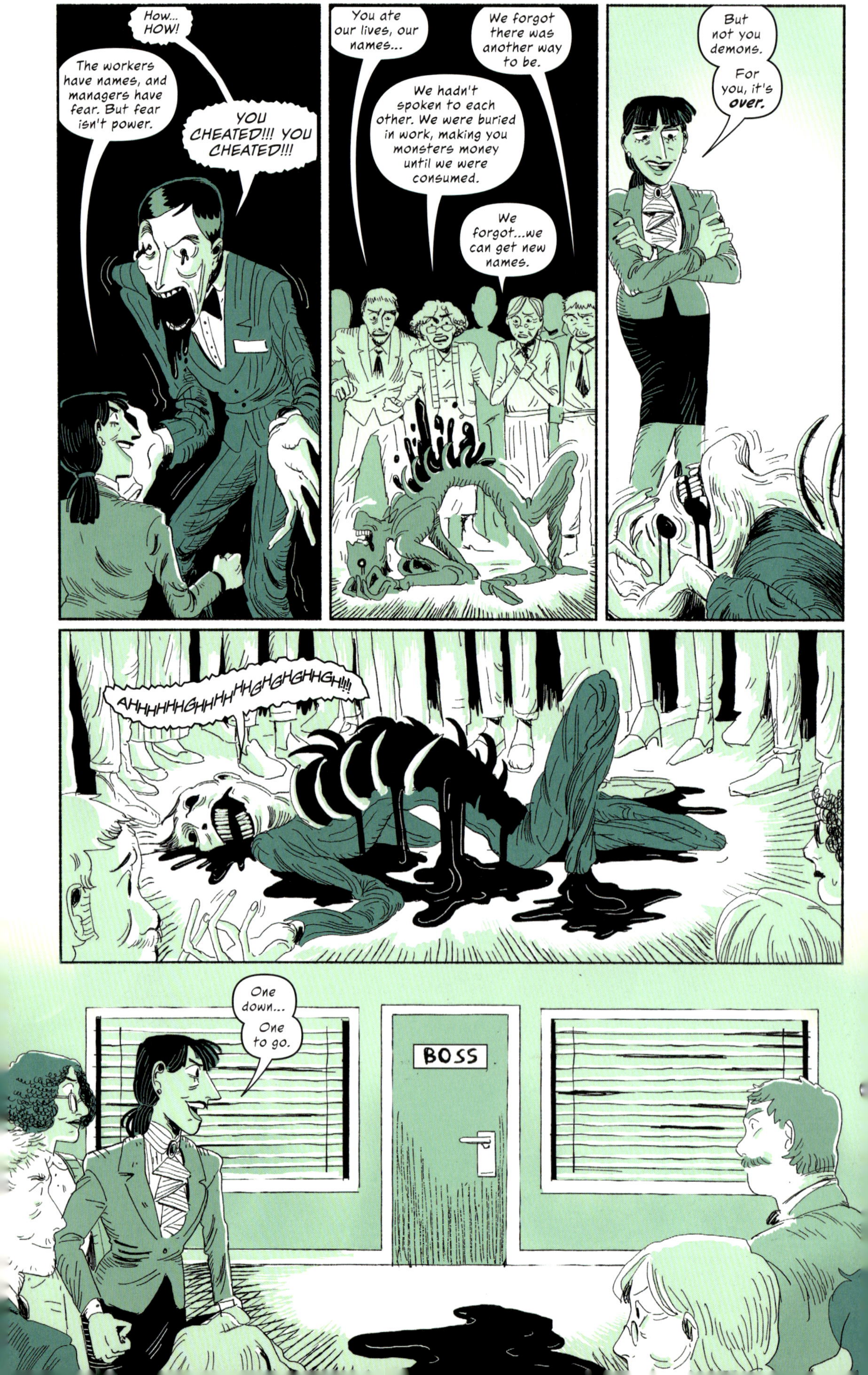
How... HOW!
The workers have names, and managers have fear. But fear isn't power.
YOU CHEATED!!! YOU CHEATED!!!
You ate our lives, our names...
We forgot there was another way to be.
We hadn't spoken to each other. We were buried in work, making you monsters money until we were consumed.
We forgot...we can get new names.
But not you demons.
For you, it's *over.*
AHHHHHHGHHHHHHGHGHGHHGH!!!
One down... One to go.
BOSS

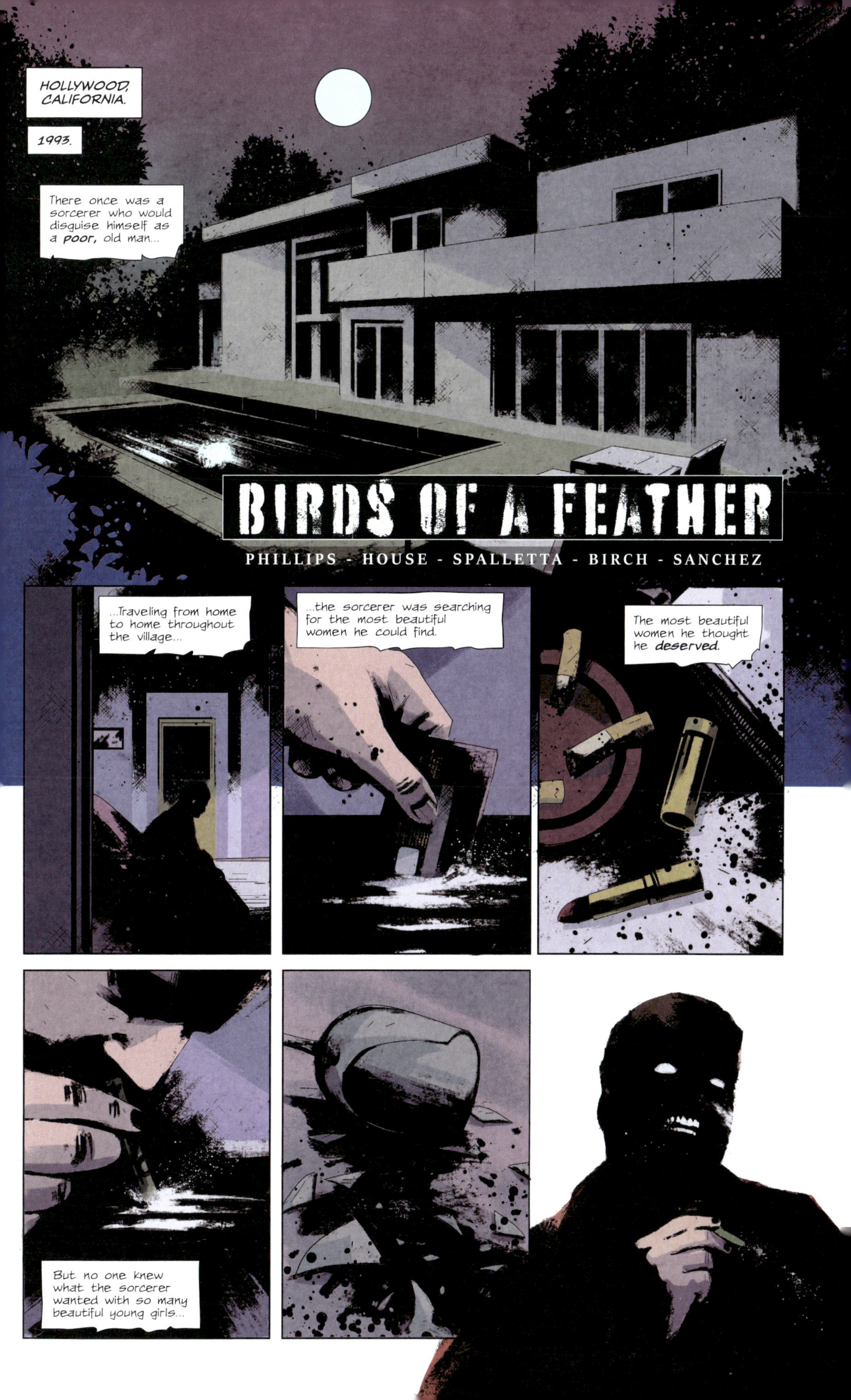
HOLLYWOOD, CALIFORNIA.
1993.
There once was a sorcerer who would disguise himself as a poor, old man...
BIRDS OF A FEATHER
PHILLIPS - HOUSE - SPALLETTA - BIRCH - SANCHEZ
...Traveling from home to home throughout the village...
...the sorcerer was searching for the most beautiful women he could find.
The most beautiful women he thought he deserved.
But no one knew what the sorcerer wanted with so many beautiful young girls...

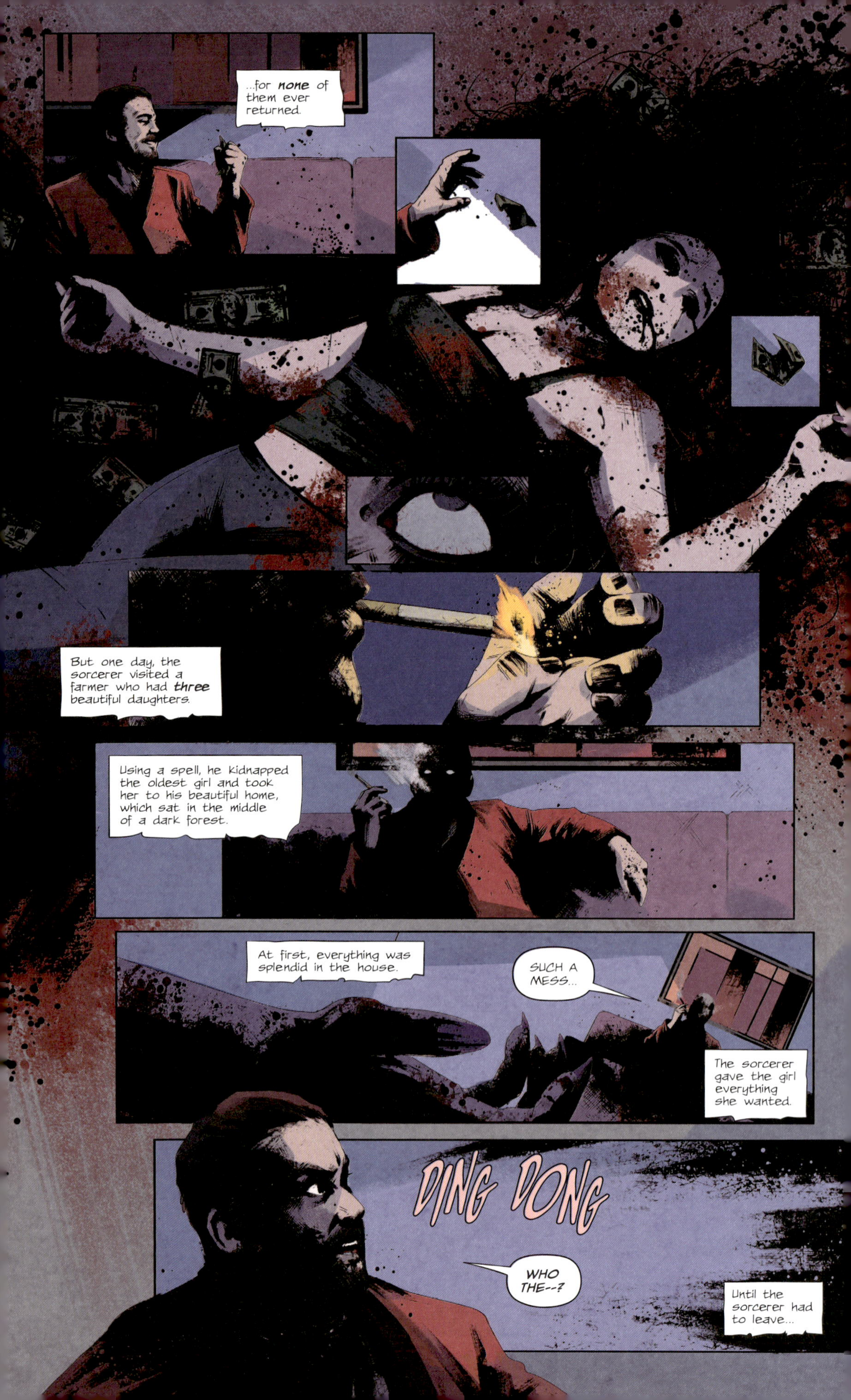

...for none of them ever returned.
But one day, the sorcerer visited a farmer who had three beautiful daughters.
Using a spell, he kidnapped the oldest girl and took her to his beautiful home, which sat in the middle of a dark forest.
At first, everything was splendid in the house.
SUCH A MESS...
The sorcerer gave the girl everything she wanted.
DING DONG
WHO THE--?
Until the sorcerer had to leave...

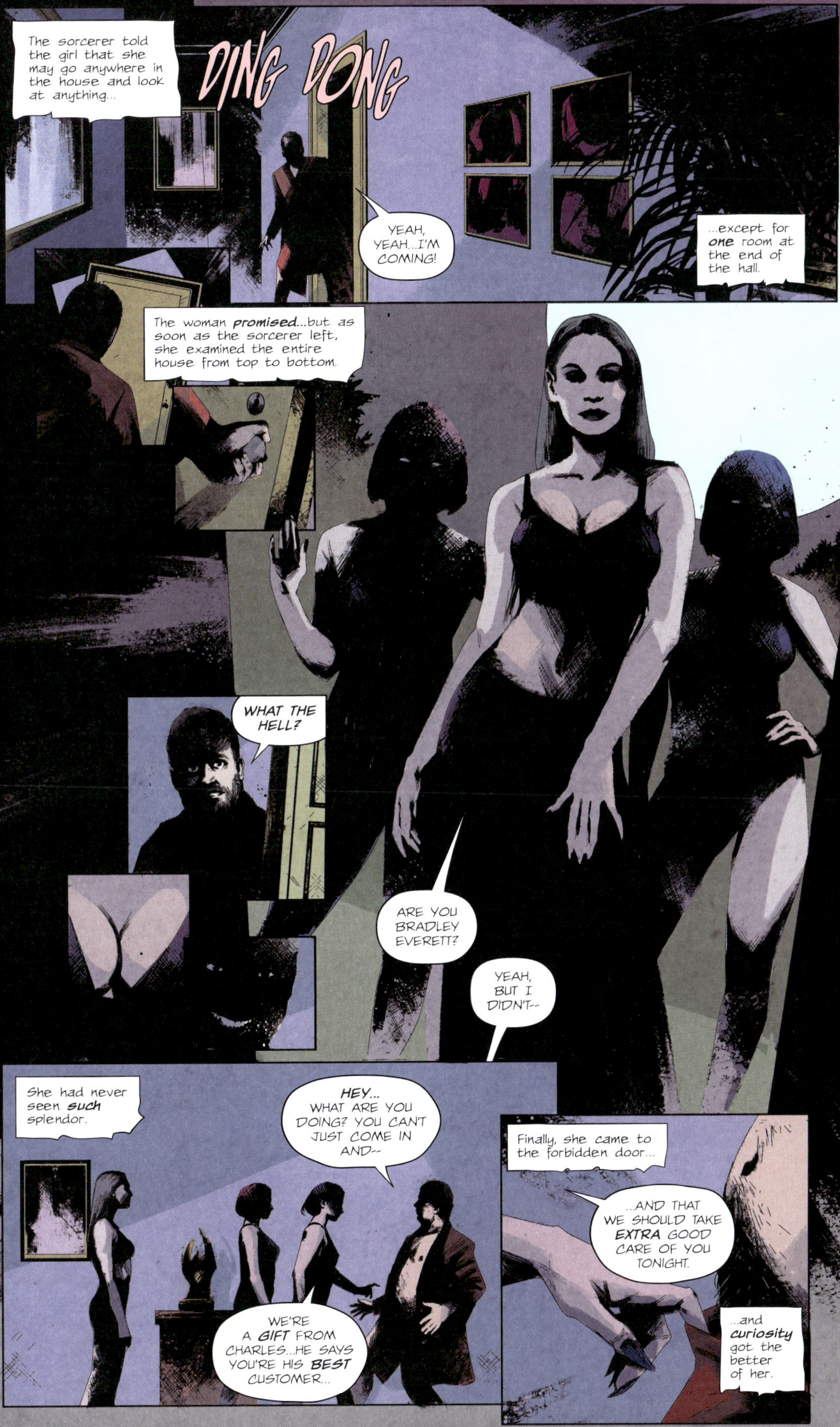
The sorcerer told the girl that she may go anywhere in the house and look at anything...
DING DONG
YEAH, YEAH...I'M COMING!
...except for one room at the end of the hall.
The woman promised...but as soon as the sorcerer left, she examined the entire house from top to bottom.
WHAT THE HELL?
ARE YOU BRADLEY EVERETT?
YEAH, BUT I DIDN'T--
She had never seen such splendor.
HEY... WHAT ARE YOU DOING? YOU CAN'T JUST COME IN AND--
WE'RE A GIFT FROM CHARLES...HE SAYS YOU'RE HIS BEST CUSTOMER...
Finally, she came to the forbidden door...
...AND THAT WE SHOULD TAKE EXTRA GOOD CARE OF YOU TONIGHT.
...and curiosity got the better of her.

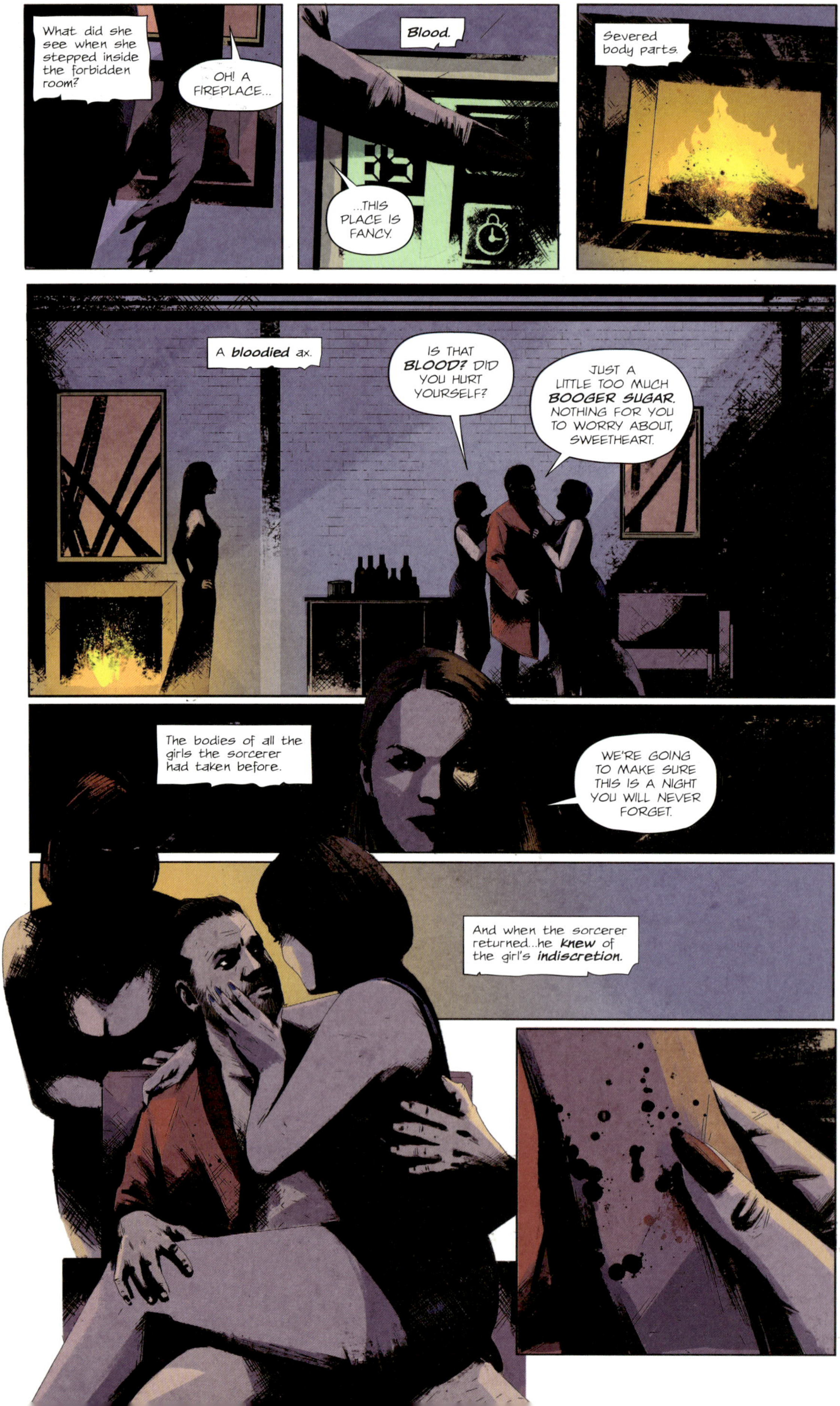
What did she see when she stepped inside the forbidden room?
OH! A FIREPLACE...
Blood.
...THIS PLACE IS FANCY.
Severed body parts.
A bloodied ax.
IS THAT BLOOD? DID YOU HURT YOURSELF?
JUST A LITTLE TOO MUCH BOOGER SUGAR. NOTHING FOR YOU TO WORRY ABOUT, SWEETHEART.
The bodies of all the girls the sorcerer had taken before.
WE'RE GOING TO MAKE SURE THIS IS A NIGHT YOU WILL NEVER FORGET.
And when the sorcerer returned...he knew of the girl's indiscretion.

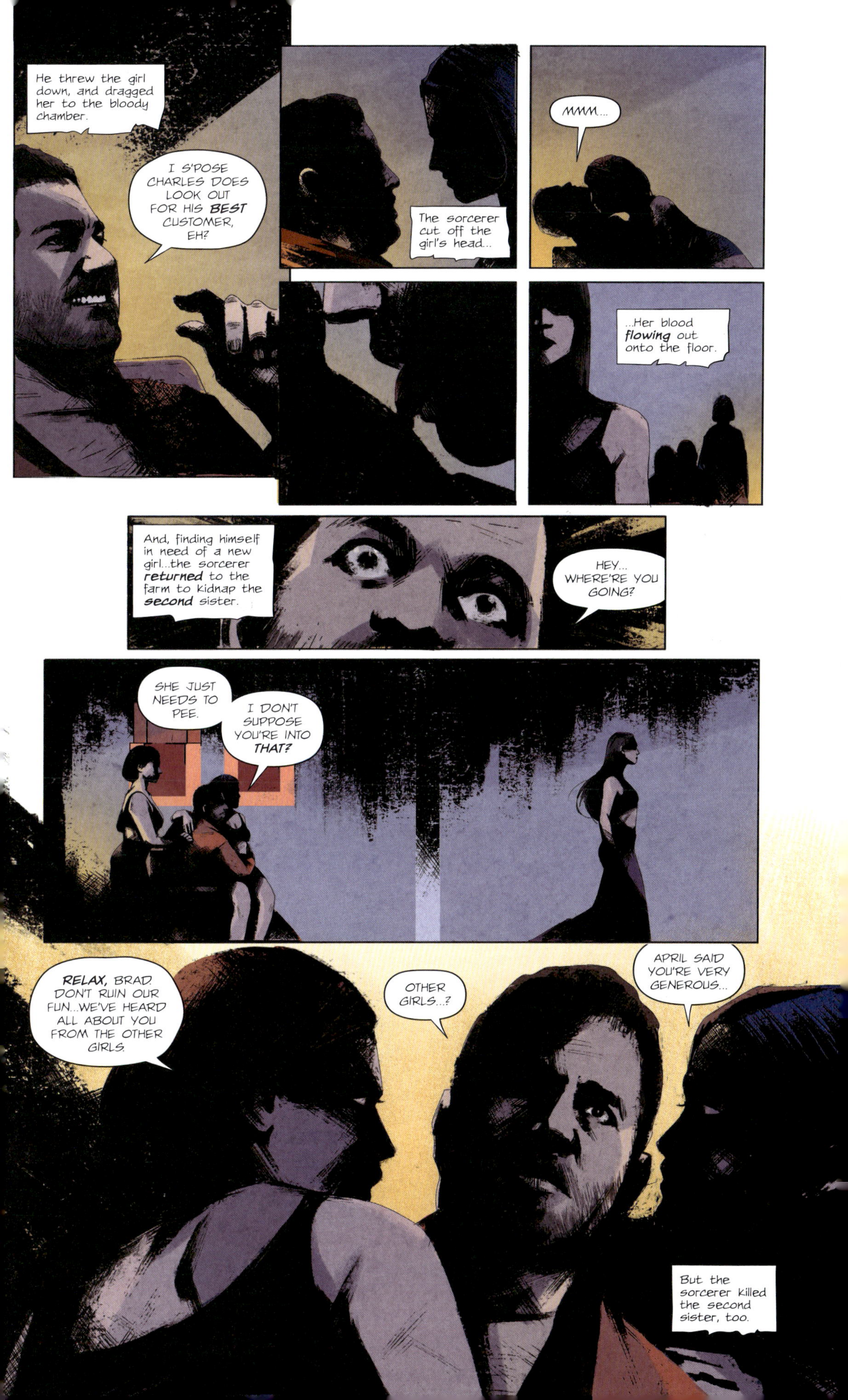
He threw the girl down, and dragged her to the bloody chamber.
I S'POSE CHARLES DOES LOOK OUT FOR HIS **BEST** CUSTOMER, EH?
The sorcerer cut off the girl's head...
MMM...
...Her blood **flowing** out onto the floor.
And, finding himself in need of a new girl...the sorcerer **returned** to the farm to kidnap the **second** sister.
HEY... WHERE'RE YOU GOING?
SHE JUST NEEDS TO PEE.
I DON'T SUPPOSE YOU'RE INTO **THAT?**
RELAX, BRAD. DON'T RUIN OUR FUN...WE'VE HEARD ALL ABOUT YOU FROM THE OTHER GIRLS.
OTHER GIRLS...?
APRIL SAID YOU'RE VERY GENEROUS...
But the sorcerer killed the second sister, too.

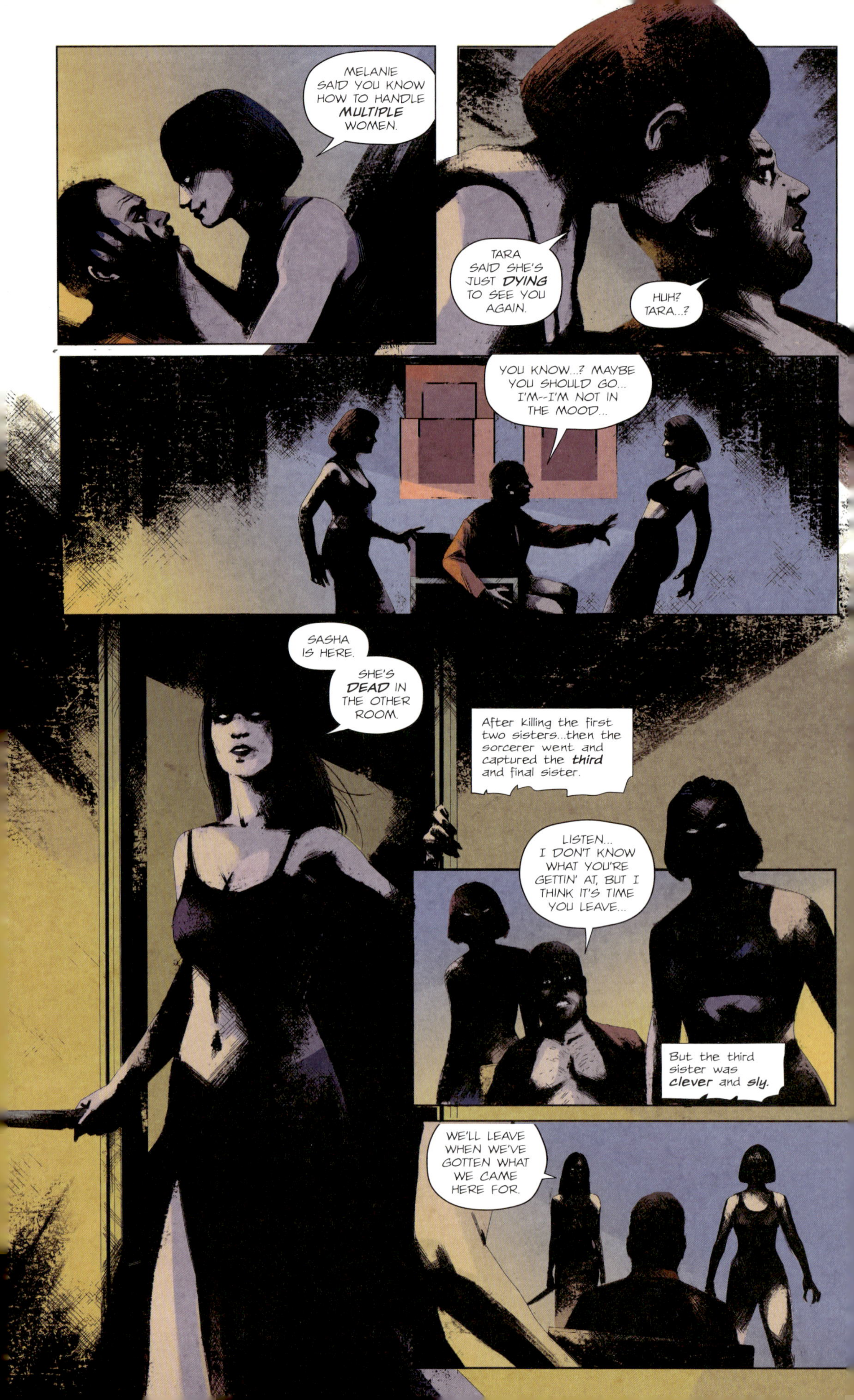

MELANIE SAID YOU KNOW HOW TO HANDLE **MULTIPLE** WOMEN.
TARA SAID SHE'S JUST **DYING** TO SEE YOU AGAIN.
HUH? TARA...?
YOU KNOW...? MAYBE YOU SHOULD GO... I'M--I'M NOT IN THE MOOD...
SASHA IS HERE.
SHE'S **DEAD** IN THE OTHER ROOM.
After killing the first two sisters...then the sorcerer went and captured the ***third*** and final sister.
LISTEN... I DON'T KNOW WHAT YOU'RE GETTIN' AT, BUT I THINK IT'S TIME YOU LEAVE...
But the third sister was ***clever*** and ***sly.***
WE'LL LEAVE WHEN WE'VE GOTTEN WHAT WE CAME HERE FOR.

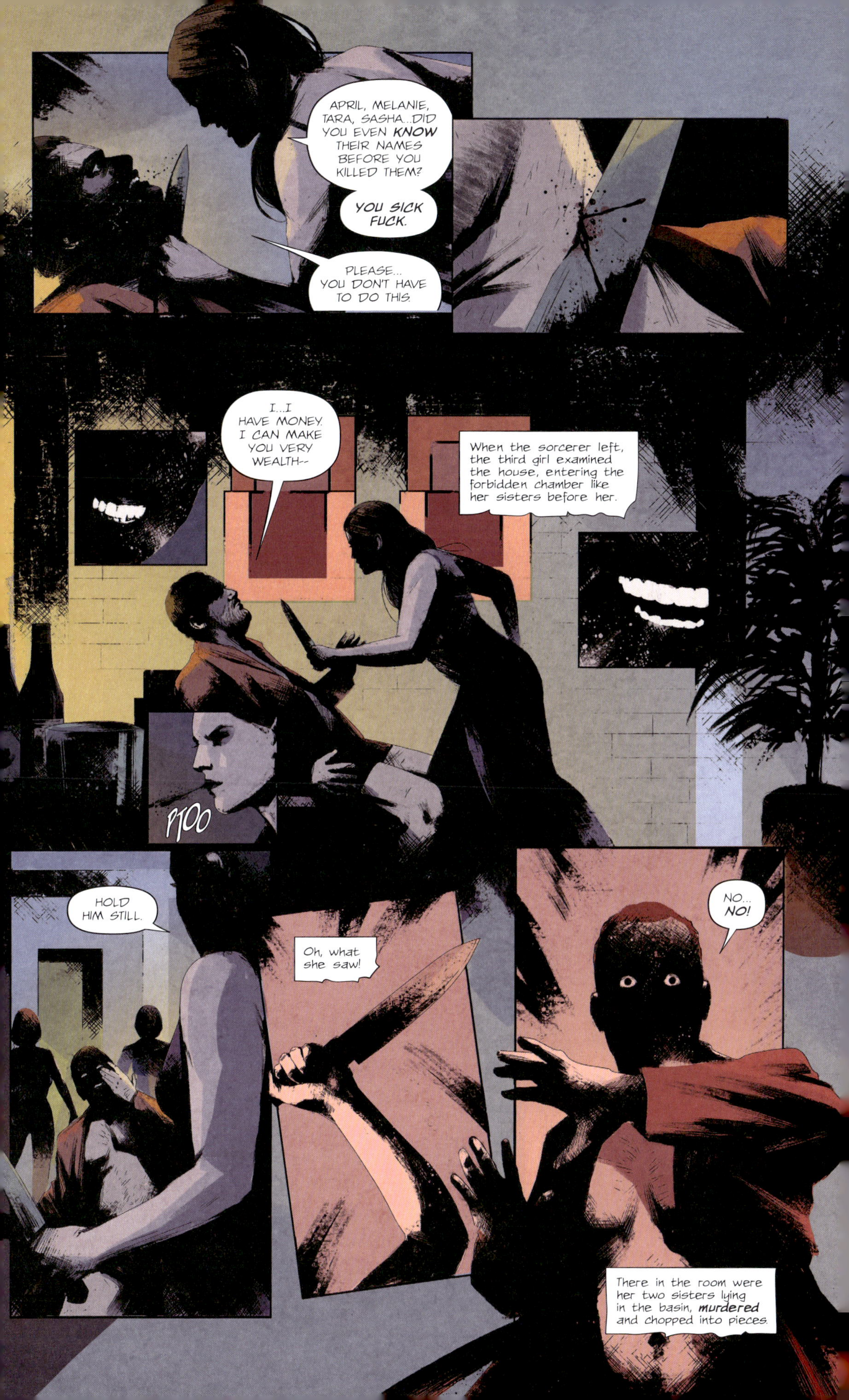
APRIL, MELANIE, TARA, SASHA...DID YOU EVEN KNOW THEIR NAMES BEFORE YOU KILLED THEM?
YOU SICK FUCK.
PLEASE... YOU DON'T HAVE TO DO THIS.
I...I HAVE MONEY. I CAN MAKE YOU VERY WEALTH--
When the sorcerer left, the third girl examined the house, entering the forbidden chamber like her sisters before her.
PTOO
HOLD HIM STILL.
Oh, what she saw!
NO... NO!
There in the room were her two sisters lying in the basin, murdered and chopped into pieces.

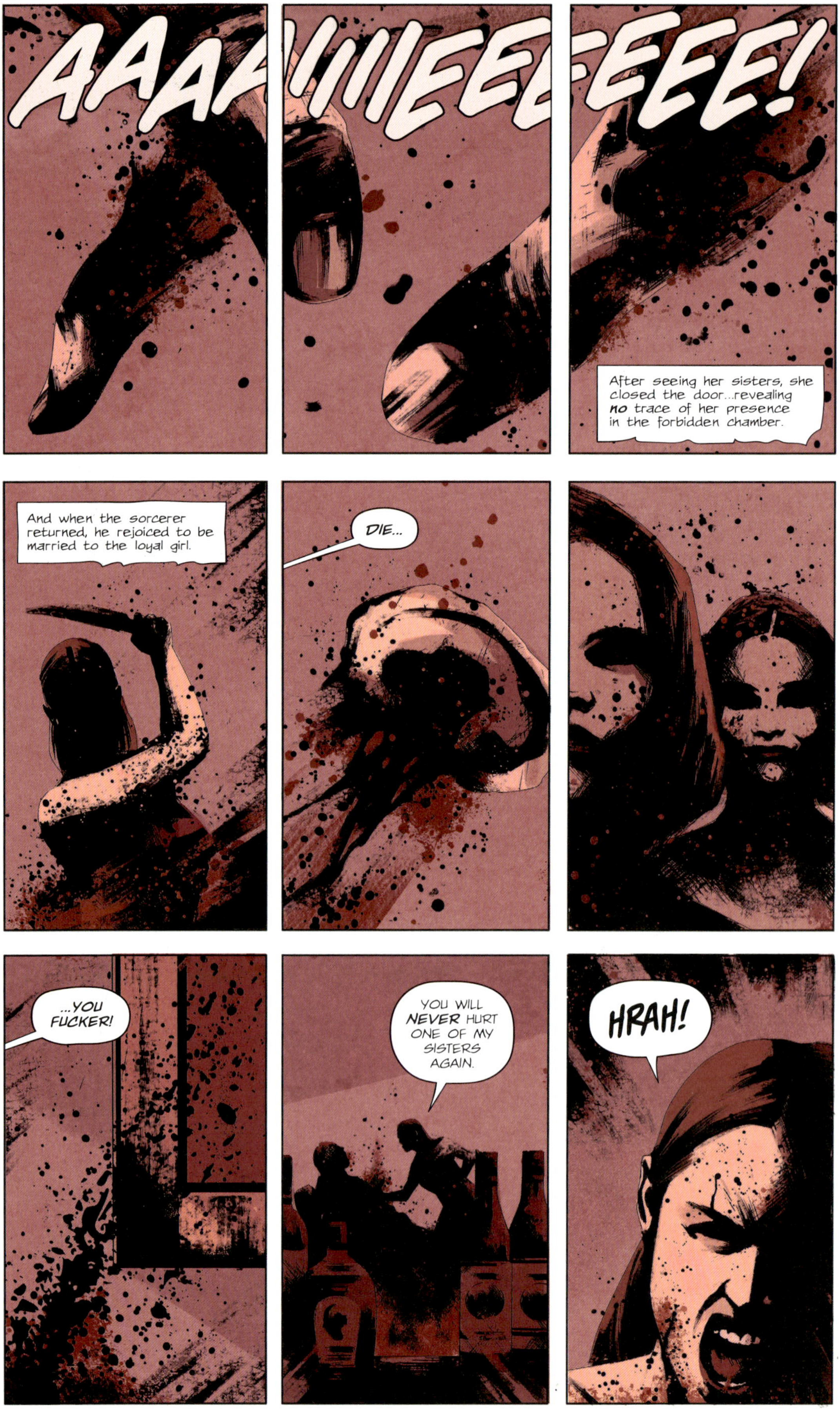
AAAIIIIEEEEEEE!
After seeing her sisters, she closed the door...revealing **no** trace of her presence in the forbidden chamber.
And when the sorcerer returned, he rejoiced to be married to the loyal girl.
DIE...
...YOU FUCKER!
YOU WILL **NEVER** HURT ONE OF MY SISTERS AGAIN.
HRAH!

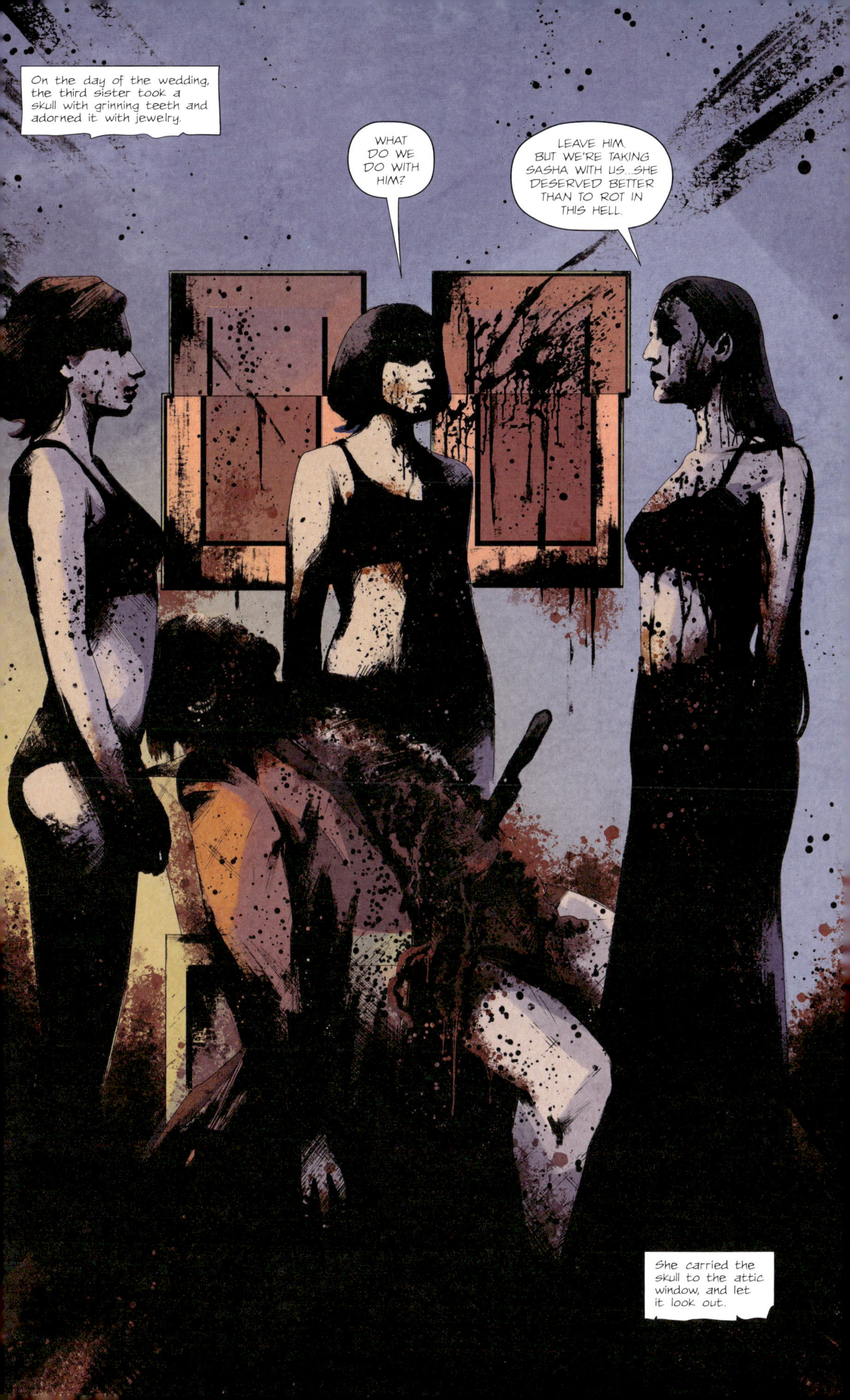

On the day of the wedding, the third sister took a skull with grinning teeth and adorned it with jewelry.
WHAT DO WE DO WITH HIM?
LEAVE HIM. BUT WE'RE TAKING SASHA WITH US...SHE DESERVED BETTER THAN TO ROT IN THIS HELL.
She carried the skull to the attic window, and let it look out.

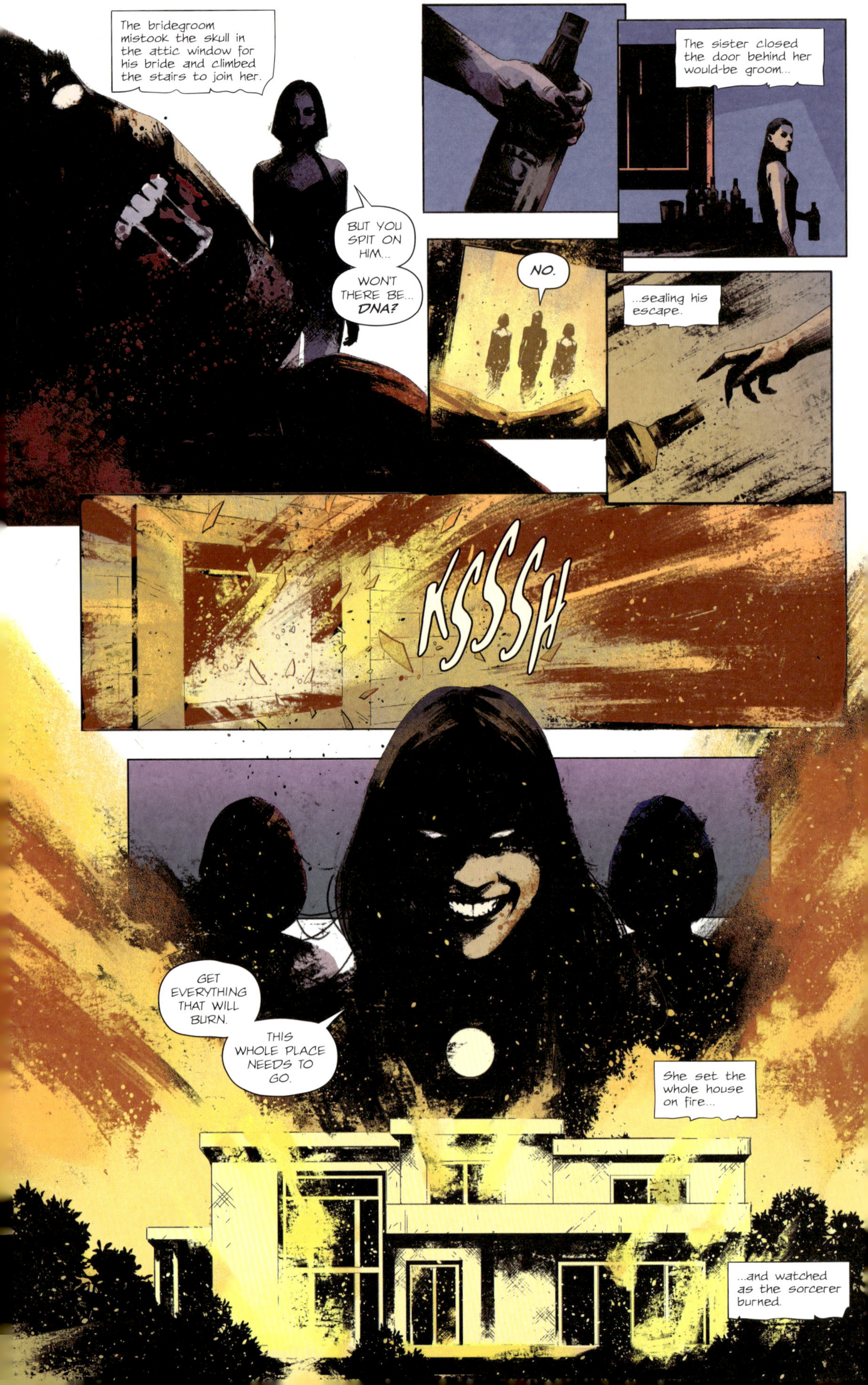

The bridegroom mistook the skull in the attic window for his bride and climbed the stairs to join her.
BUT YOU SPIT ON HIM...
WON'T THERE BE... DNA?
NO.
The sister closed the door behind her would-be groom...
...sealing his escape.
KSSSH
GET EVERYTHING THAT WILL BURN.
THIS WHOLE PLACE NEEDS TO GO.
She set the whole house on fire...
...and watched as the sorcerer burned.

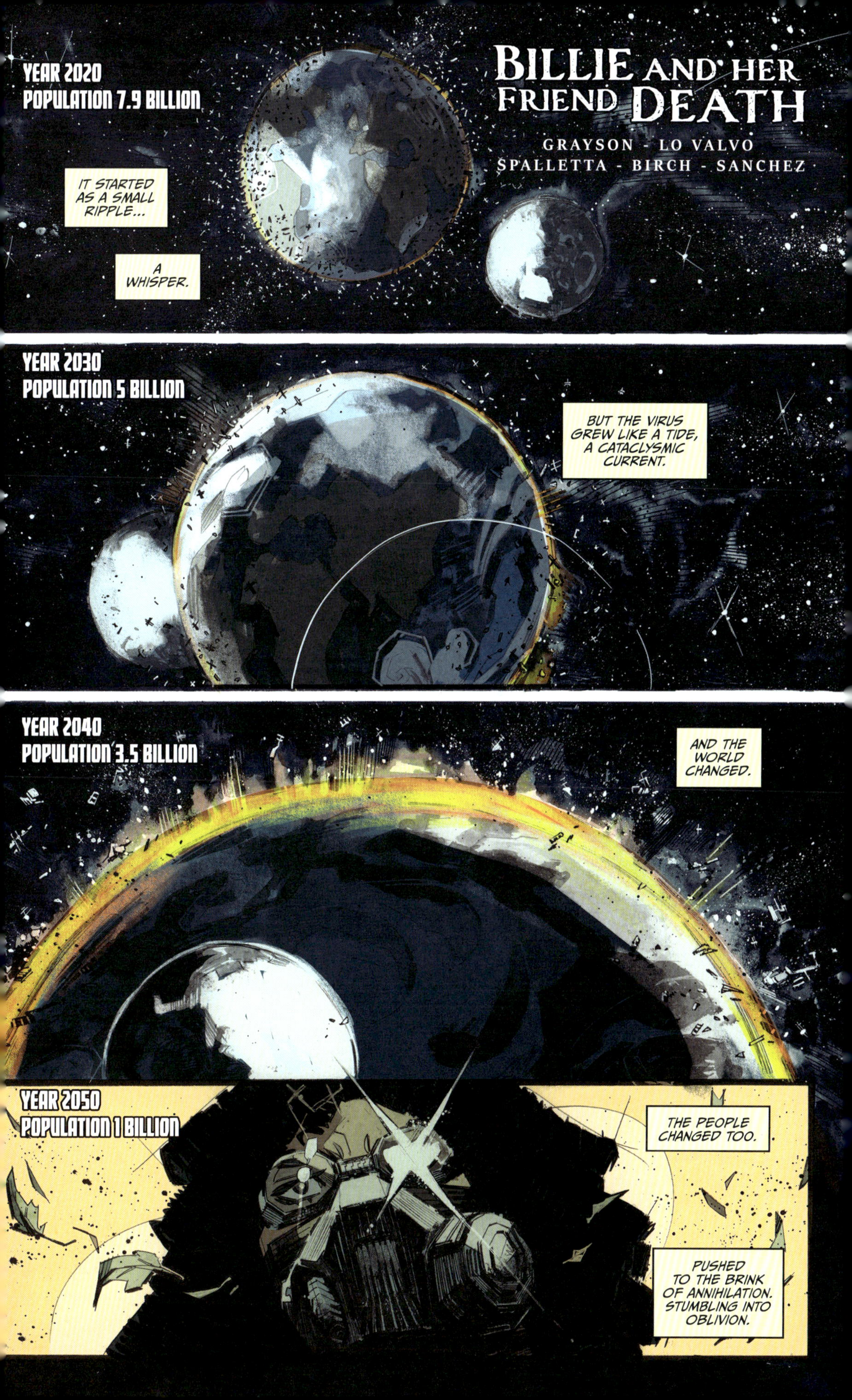

BILLIE AND HER FRIEND DEATH
GRAYSON - LO VALVO
SPALLETTA - BIRCH - SANCHEZ
YEAR 2020
POPULATION 7.9 BILLION
IT STARTED AS A SMALL RIPPLE...
A WHISPER.
YEAR 2030
POPULATION 5 BILLION
BUT THE VIRUS GREW LIKE A TIDE, A CATACLYSMIC CURRENT.
YEAR 2040
POPULATION 3.5 BILLION
AND THE WORLD CHANGED.
YEAR 2050
POPULATION 1 BILLION
THE PEOPLE CHANGED TOO.
PUSHED TO THE BRINK OF ANNIHILATION. STUMBLING INTO OBLIVION.

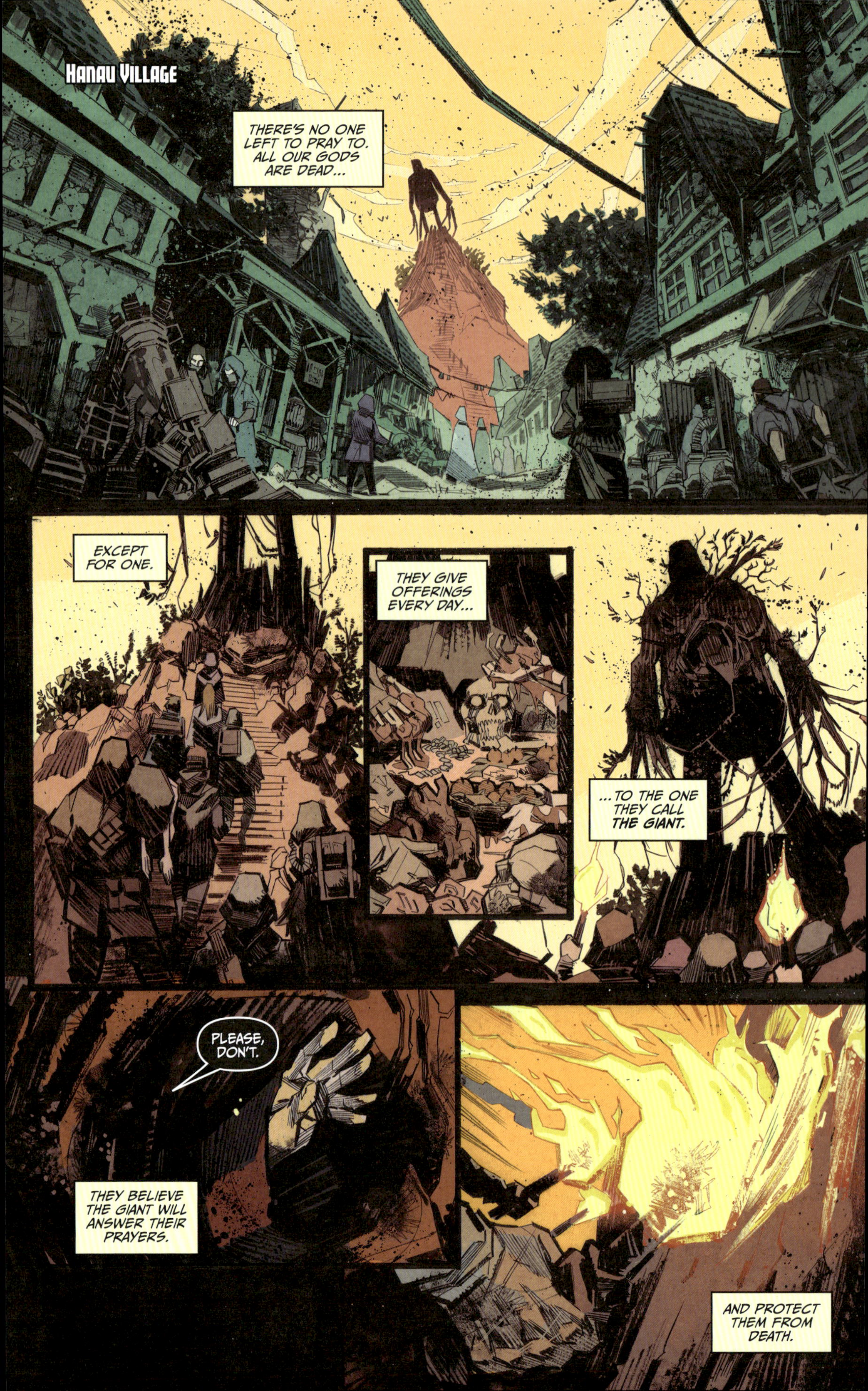
HANAU VILLAGE
THERE'S NO ONE LEFT TO PRAY TO. ALL OUR GODS ARE DEAD...
EXCEPT FOR ONE.
THEY GIVE OFFERINGS EVERY DAY...
...TO THE ONE THEY CALL THE GIANT.
PLEASE, DON'T.
THEY BELIEVE THE GIANT WILL ANSWER THEIR PRAYERS.
AND PROTECT THEM FROM DEATH.

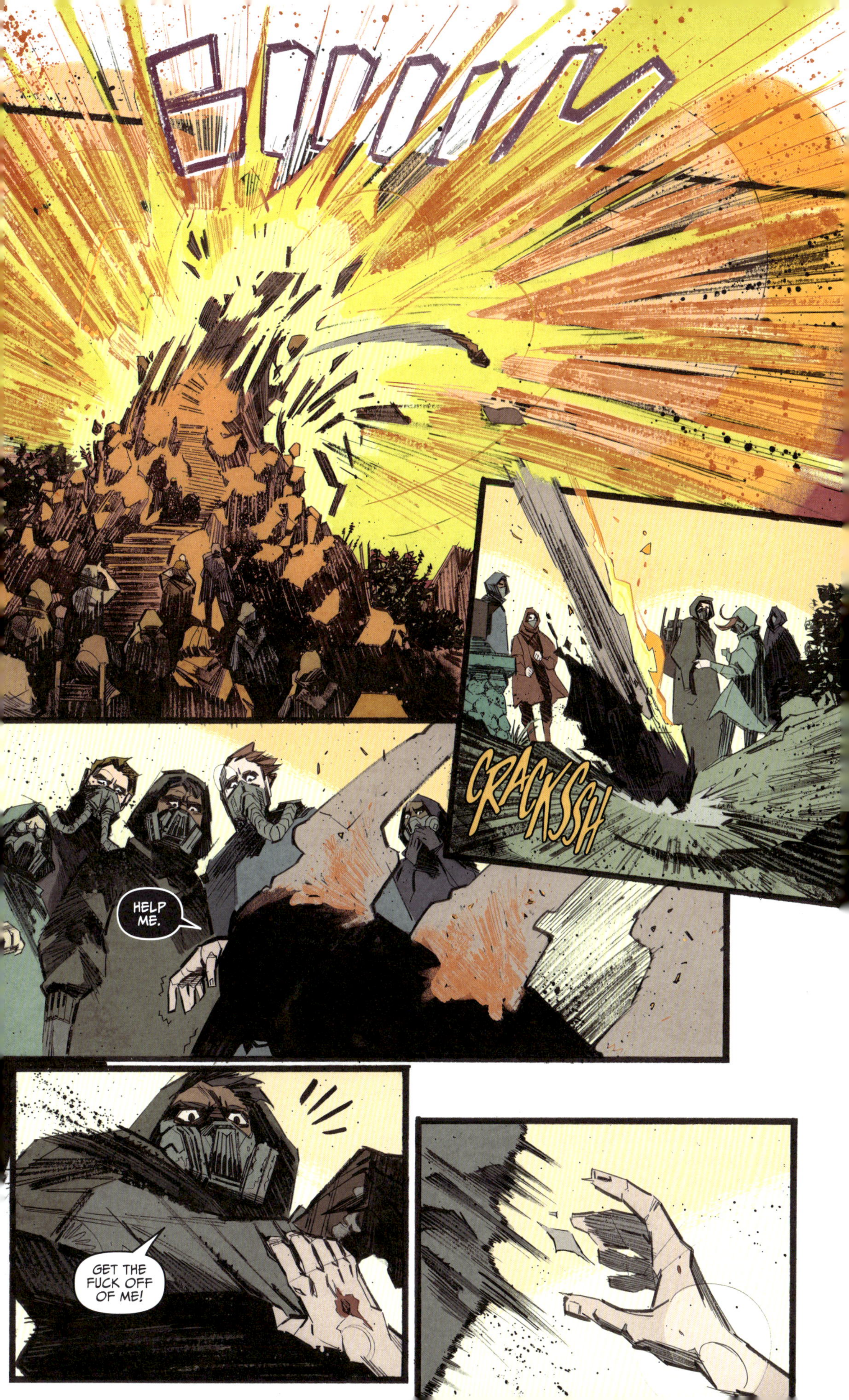
BOOOOM
CRACKSSH
HELP ME.
GET THE FUCK OFF OF ME!

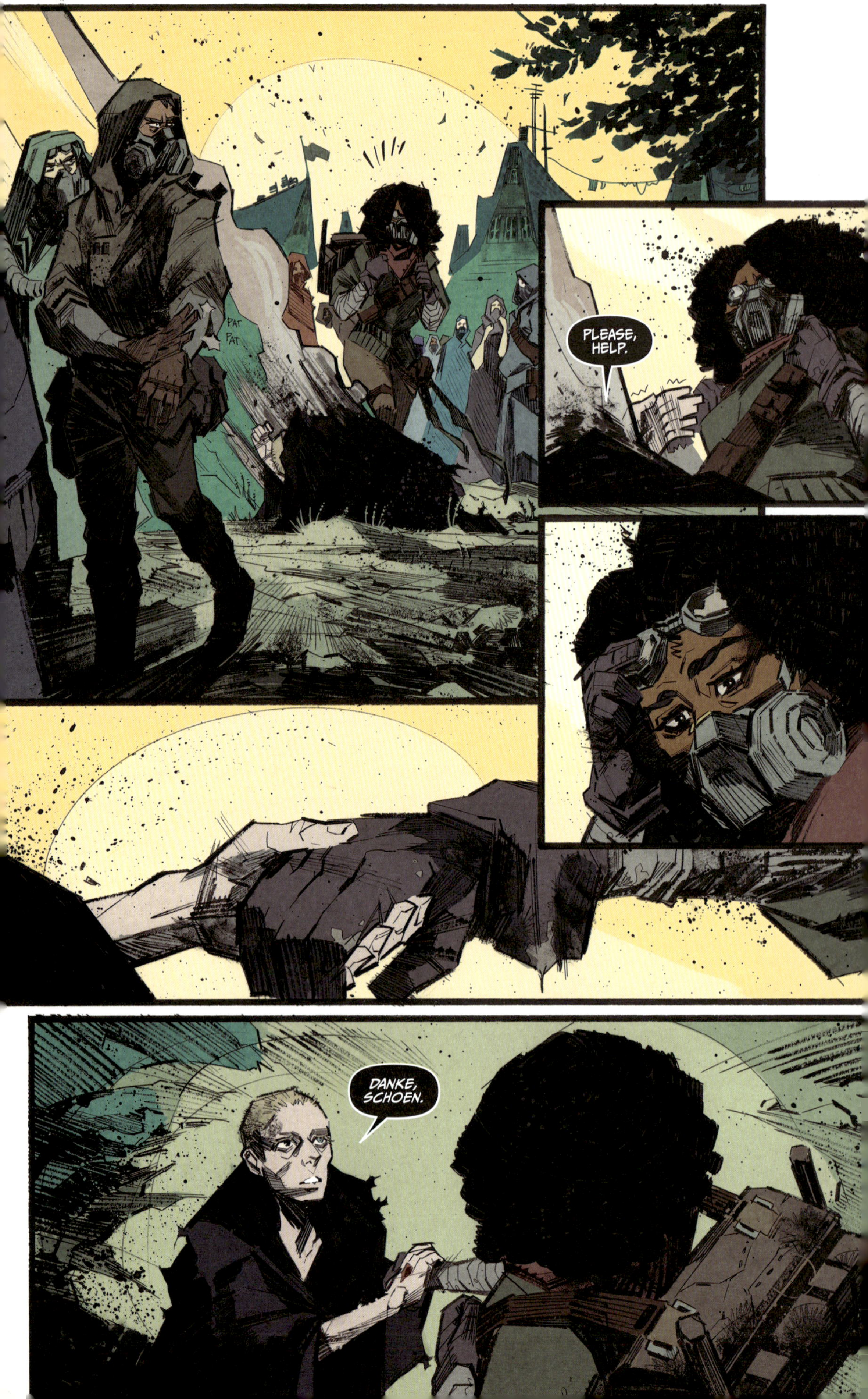
PAT PAT
PLEASE, HELP.
DANKE, SCHOEN.

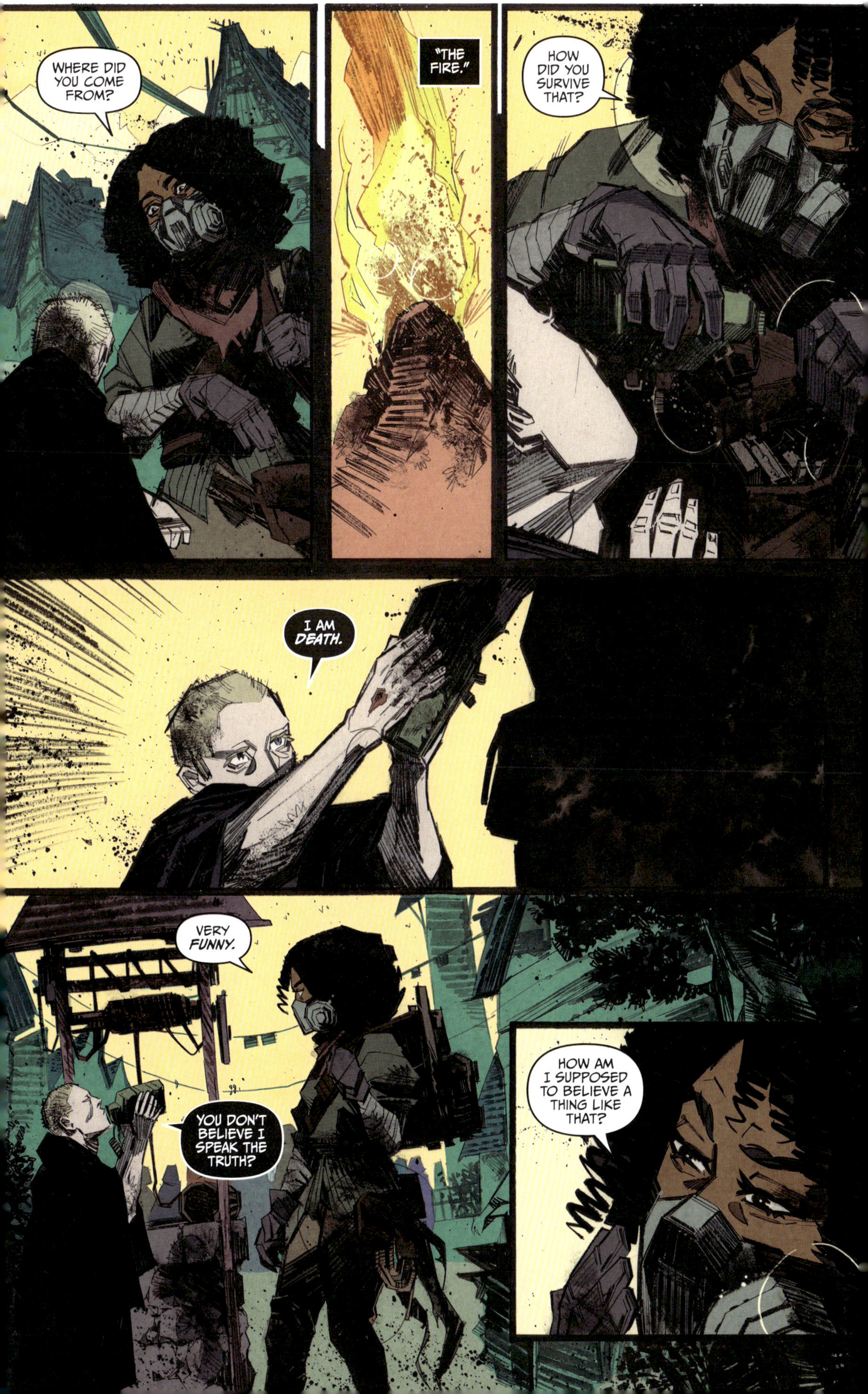
WHERE DID YOU COME FROM?
"THE FIRE."
HOW DID YOU SURVIVE THAT?
I AM *DEATH.*
VERY *FUNNY.*
YOU DON'T BELIEVE I SPEAK THE TRUTH?
HOW AM I SUPPOSED TO BELIEVE A THING LIKE THAT?

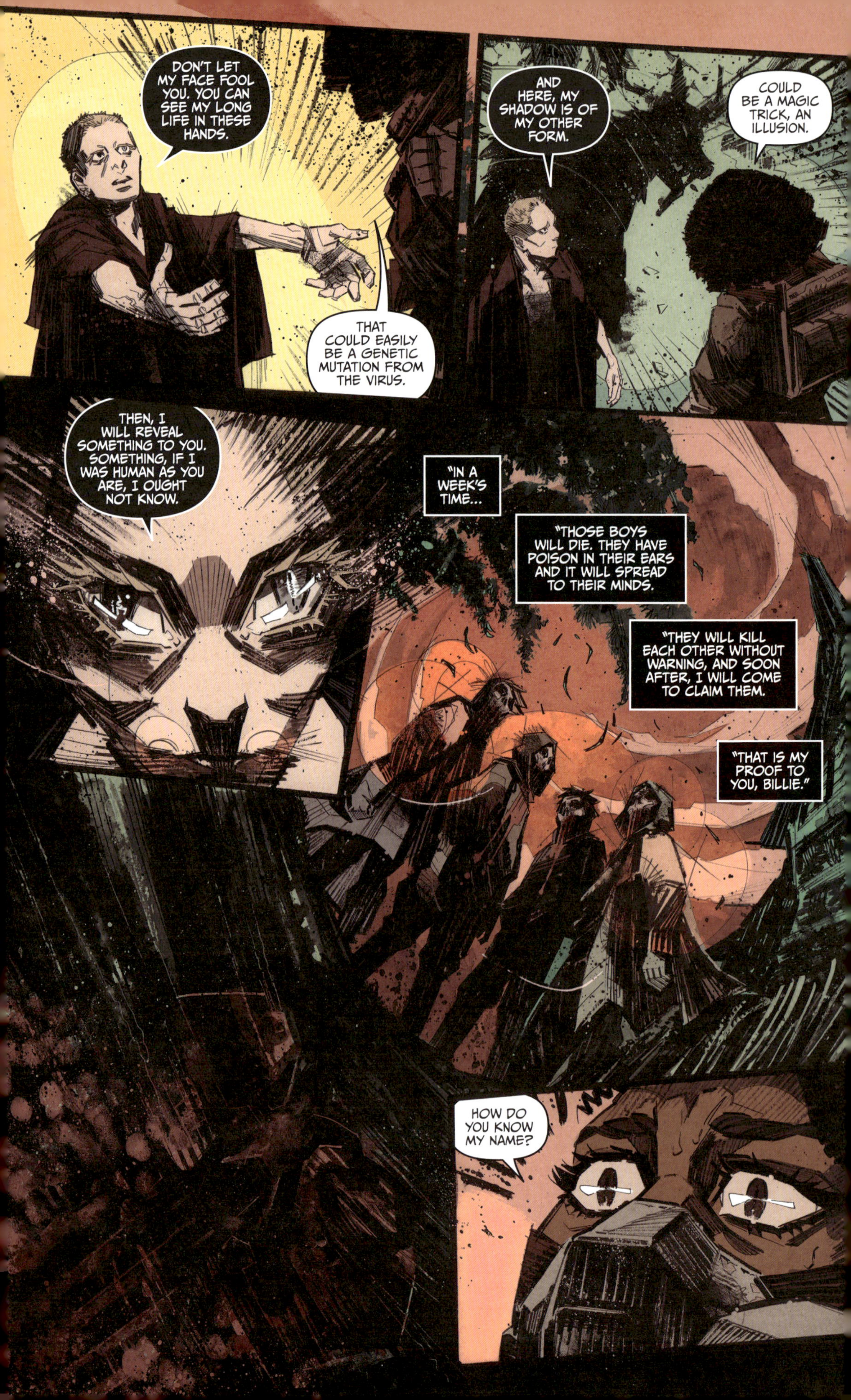
DON'T LET MY FACE FOOL YOU. YOU CAN SEE MY LONG LIFE IN THESE HANDS.
THAT COULD EASILY BE A GENETIC MUTATION FROM THE VIRUS.
AND HERE, MY SHADOW IS OF MY OTHER FORM.
COULD BE A MAGIC TRICK, AN ILLUSION.
THEN, I WILL REVEAL SOMETHING TO YOU. SOMETHING, IF I WAS HUMAN AS YOU ARE, I OUGHT NOT KNOW.
"IN A WEEK'S TIME...
"THOSE BOYS WILL DIE. THEY HAVE POISON IN THEIR EARS AND IT WILL SPREAD TO THEIR MINDS.
"THEY WILL KILL EACH OTHER WITHOUT WARNING, AND SOON AFTER, I WILL COME TO CLAIM THEM.
"THAT IS MY PROOF TO YOU, BILLIE."
HOW DO YOU KNOW MY NAME?

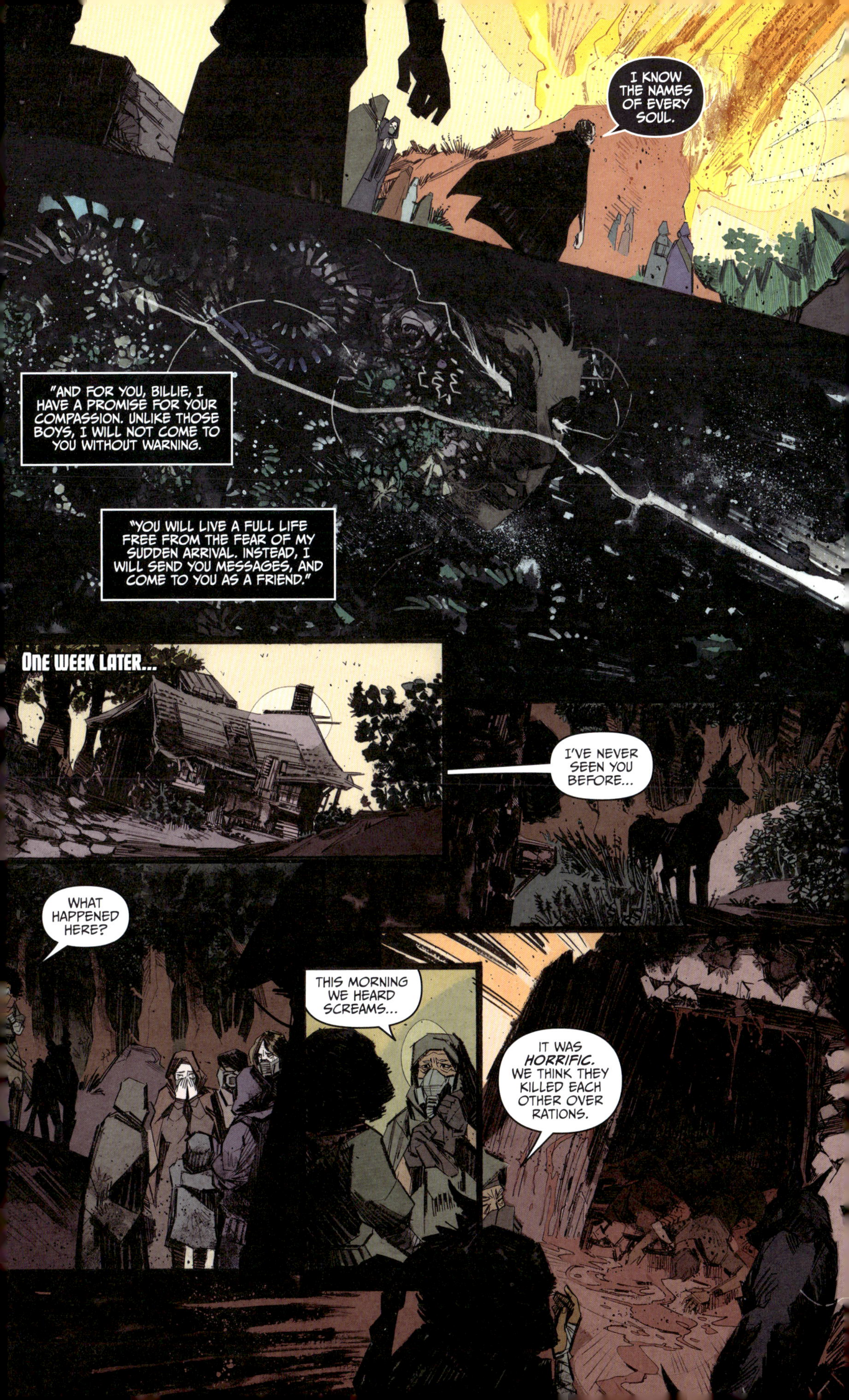
I KNOW THE NAMES OF EVERY SOUL.
"AND FOR YOU, BILLIE, I HAVE A PROMISE FOR YOUR COMPASSION. UNLIKE THOSE BOYS, I WILL NOT COME TO YOU WITHOUT WARNING.
"YOU WILL LIVE A FULL LIFE FREE FROM THE FEAR OF MY SUDDEN ARRIVAL. INSTEAD, I WILL SEND YOU MESSAGES, AND COME TO YOU AS A FRIEND."
ONE WEEK LATER...
I'VE NEVER SEEN YOU BEFORE...
WHAT HAPPENED HERE?
THIS MORNING WE HEARD SCREAMS...
IT WAS HORRIFIC. WE THINK THEY KILLED EACH OTHER OVER RATIONS.

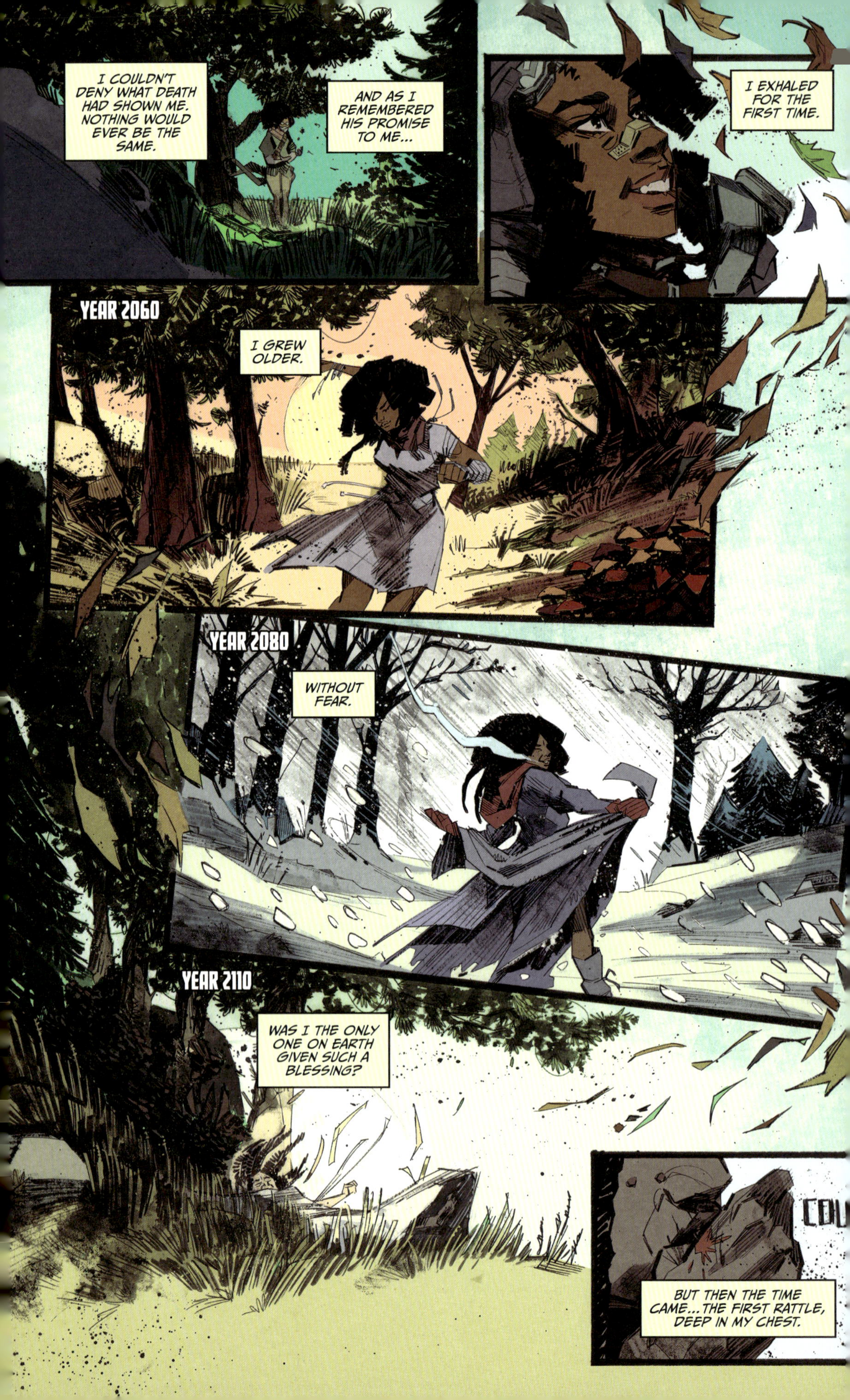
I COULDN'T DENY WHAT DEATH HAD SHOWN ME. NOTHING WOULD EVER BE THE SAME.
AND AS I REMEMBERED HIS PROMISE TO ME...
I EXHALED FOR THE FIRST TIME.
YEAR 2060
I GREW OLDER.
YEAR 2080
WITHOUT FEAR.
YEAR 2110
WAS I THE ONLY ONE ON EARTH GIVEN SUCH A BLESSING?
BUT THEN THE TIME CAME... THE FIRST RATTLE, DEEP IN MY CHEST.

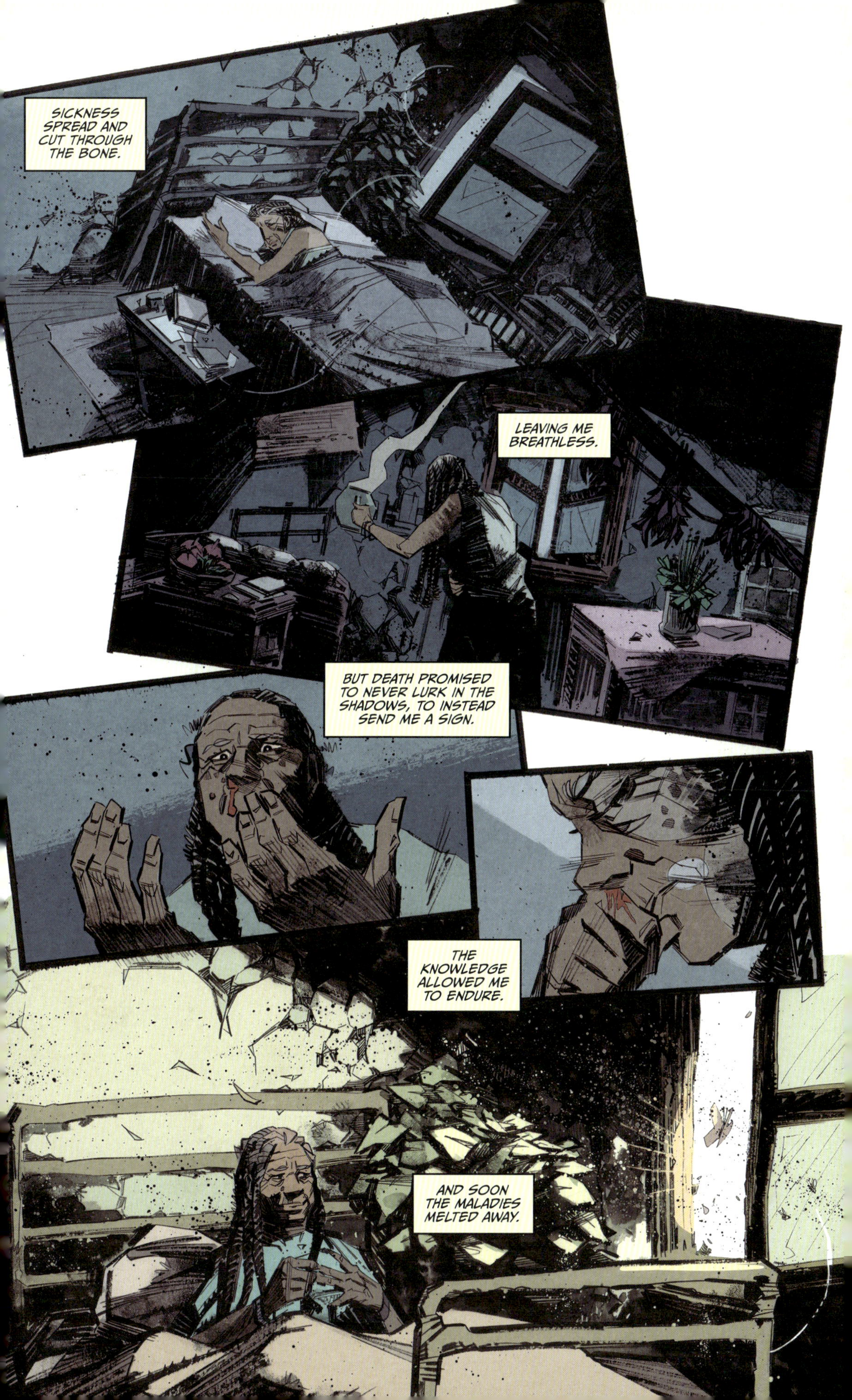
SICKNESS SPREAD AND CUT THROUGH THE BONE.
LEAVING ME BREATHLESS.
BUT DEATH PROMISED TO NEVER LURK IN THE SHADOWS, TO INSTEAD SEND ME A SIGN.
THE KNOWLEDGE ALLOWED ME TO ENDURE.
AND SOON THE MALADIES MELTED AWAY.

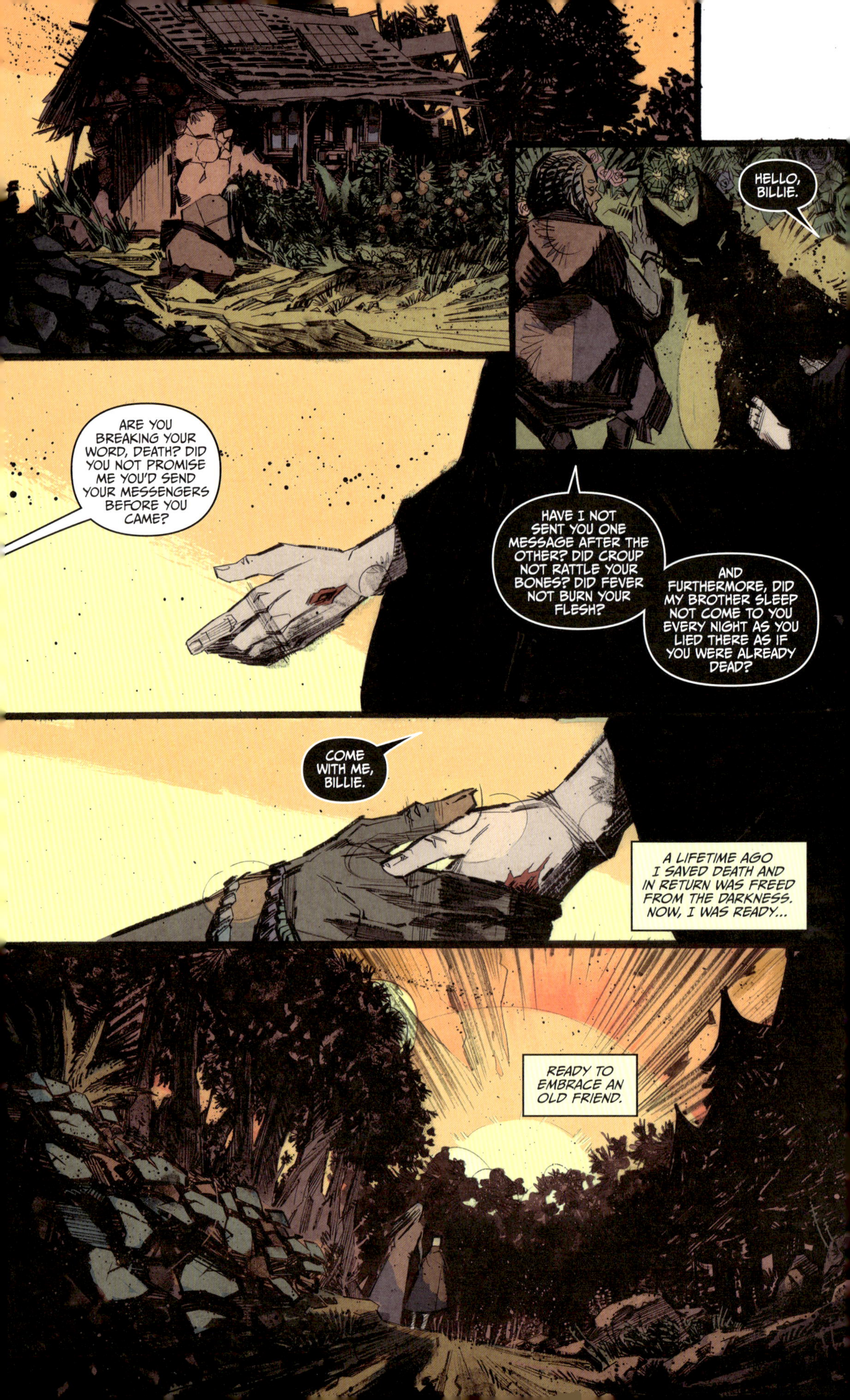
HELLO, BILLIE.
ARE YOU BREAKING YOUR WORD, DEATH? DID YOU NOT PROMISE ME YOU'D SEND YOUR MESSENGERS BEFORE YOU CAME?
HAVE I NOT SENT YOU ONE MESSAGE AFTER THE OTHER? DID CROUP NOT RATTLE YOUR BONES? DID FEVER NOT BURN YOUR FLESH?
AND FURTHERMORE, DID MY BROTHER SLEEP NOT COME TO YOU EVERY NIGHT AS YOU LIED THERE AS IF YOU WERE ALREADY DEAD?
COME WITH ME, BILLIE.
A LIFETIME AGO I SAVED DEATH AND IN RETURN WAS FREED FROM THE DARKNESS. NOW, I WAS READY...
READY TO EMBRACE AN OLD FRIEND.

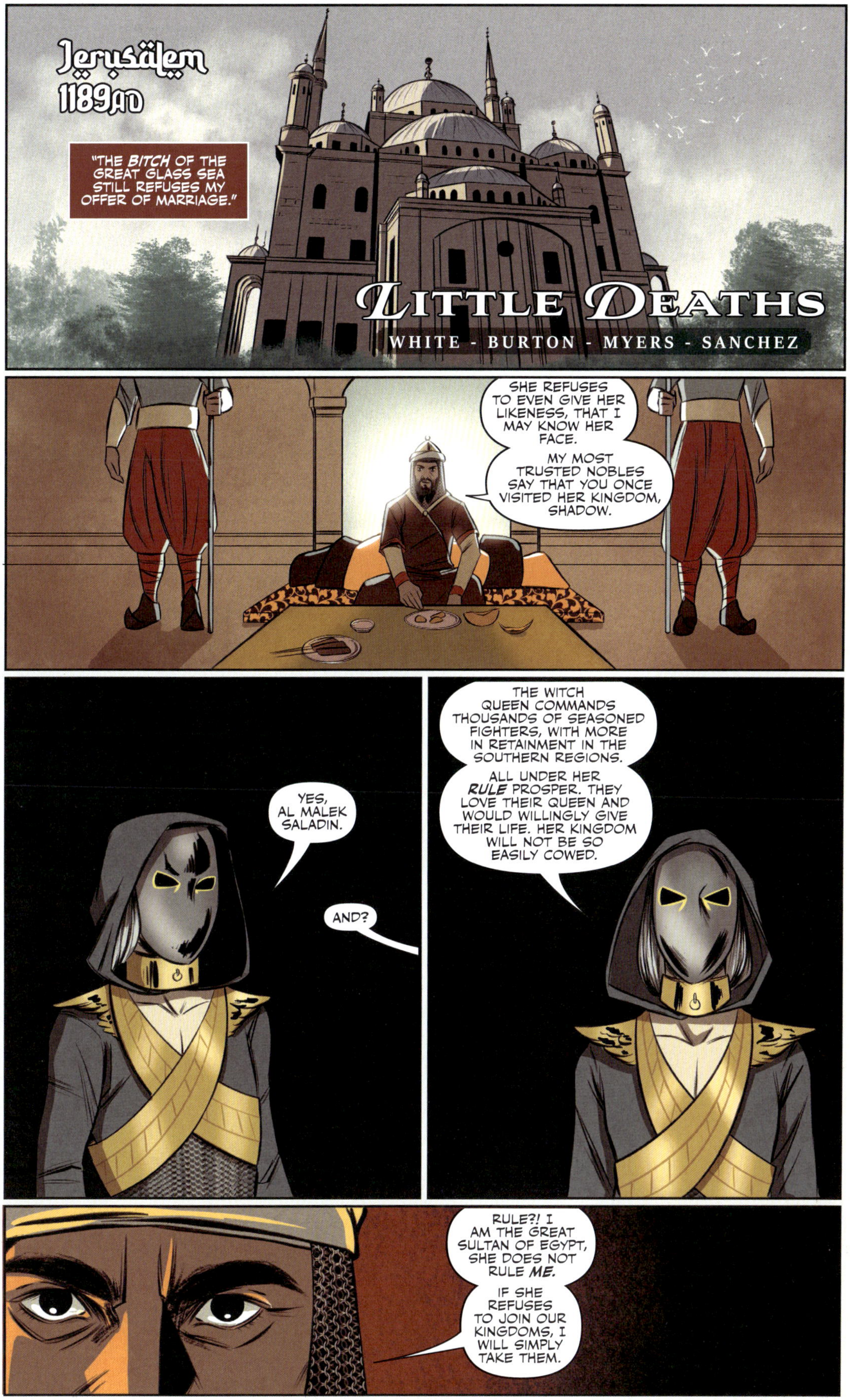
Jerusalem
1189AD
"THE BITCH OF THE GREAT GLASS SEA STILL REFUSES MY OFFER OF MARRIAGE."
LITTLE DEATHS
WHITE - BURTON - MYERS - SANCHEZ
SHE REFUSES TO EVEN GIVE HER LIKENESS, THAT I MAY KNOW HER FACE.
MY MOST TRUSTED NOBLES SAY THAT YOU ONCE VISITED HER KINGDOM, SHADOW.
YES, AL MALEK SALADIN.
AND?
THE WITCH QUEEN COMMANDS THOUSANDS OF SEASONED FIGHTERS, WITH MORE IN RETAINMENT IN THE SOUTHERN REGIONS.
ALL UNDER HER RULE PROSPER. THEY LOVE THEIR QUEEN AND WOULD WILLINGLY GIVE THEIR LIFE. HER KINGDOM WILL NOT BE SO EASILY COWED.
RULE?! I AM THE GREAT SULTAN OF EGYPT, SHE DOES NOT RULE ME.
IF SHE REFUSES TO JOIN OUR KINGDOMS, I WILL SIMPLY TAKE THEM.

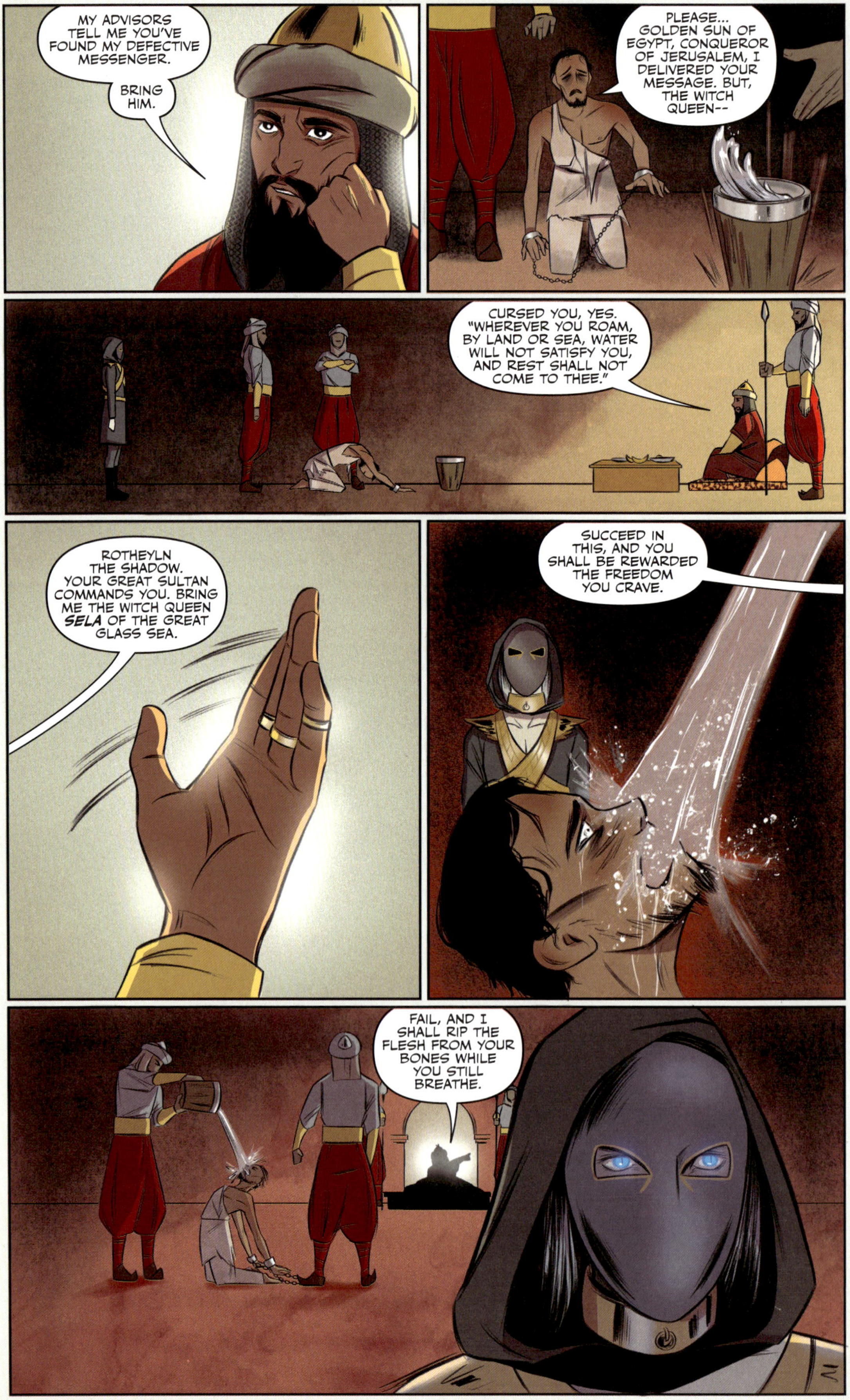
MY ADVISORS TELL ME YOU'VE FOUND MY DEFECTIVE MESSENGER.
BRING HIM.
PLEASE... GOLDEN SUN OF EGYPT, CONQUEROR OF JERUSALEM, I DELIVERED YOUR MESSAGE. BUT, THE WITCH QUEEN--
CURSED YOU, YES. "WHEREVER YOU ROAM, BY LAND OR SEA, WATER WILL NOT SATISFY YOU, AND REST SHALL NOT COME TO THEE."
ROTHEYLN THE SHADOW. YOUR GREAT SULTAN COMMANDS YOU. BRING ME THE WITCH QUEEN *SELA* OF THE GREAT GLASS SEA.
SUCCEED IN THIS, AND YOU SHALL BE REWARDED THE FREEDOM YOU CRAVE.
FAIL, AND I SHALL RIP THE FLESH FROM YOUR BONES WHILE YOU STILL BREATHE.

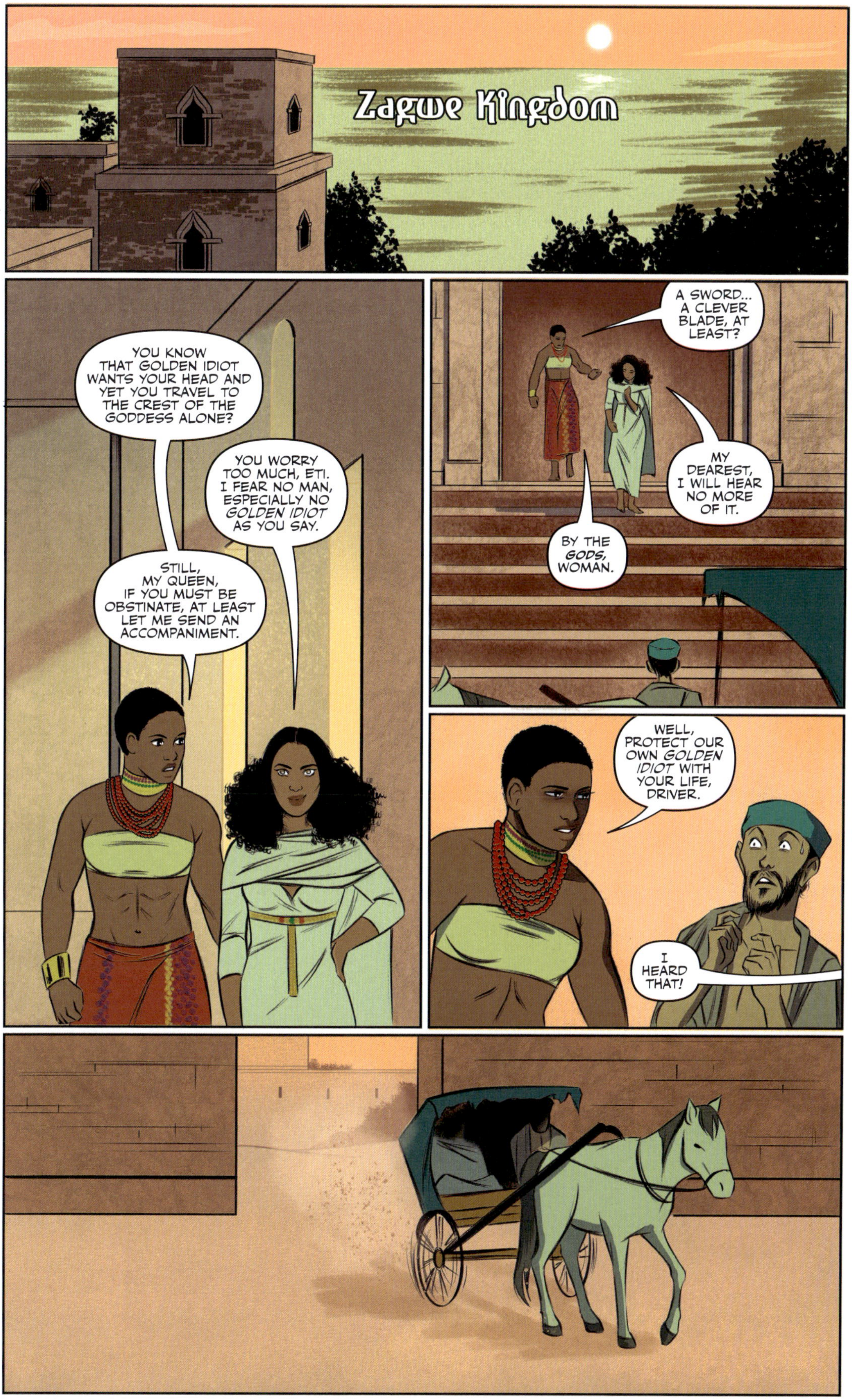
Zagwe Kingdom
YOU KNOW THAT GOLDEN IDIOT WANTS YOUR HEAD AND YET YOU TRAVEL TO THE CREST OF THE GODDESS ALONE?
YOU WORRY TOO MUCH, ETI. I FEAR NO MAN, ESPECIALLY NO GOLDEN IDIOT AS YOU SAY.
STILL, MY QUEEN, IF YOU MUST BE OBSTINATE, AT LEAST LET ME SEND AN ACCOMPANIMENT.
A SWORD... A CLEVER BLADE, AT LEAST?
MY DEAREST, I WILL HEAR NO MORE OF IT.
BY THE GODS, WOMAN.
WELL, PROTECT OUR OWN GOLDEN IDIOT WITH YOUR LIFE, DRIVER.
I HEARD THAT!

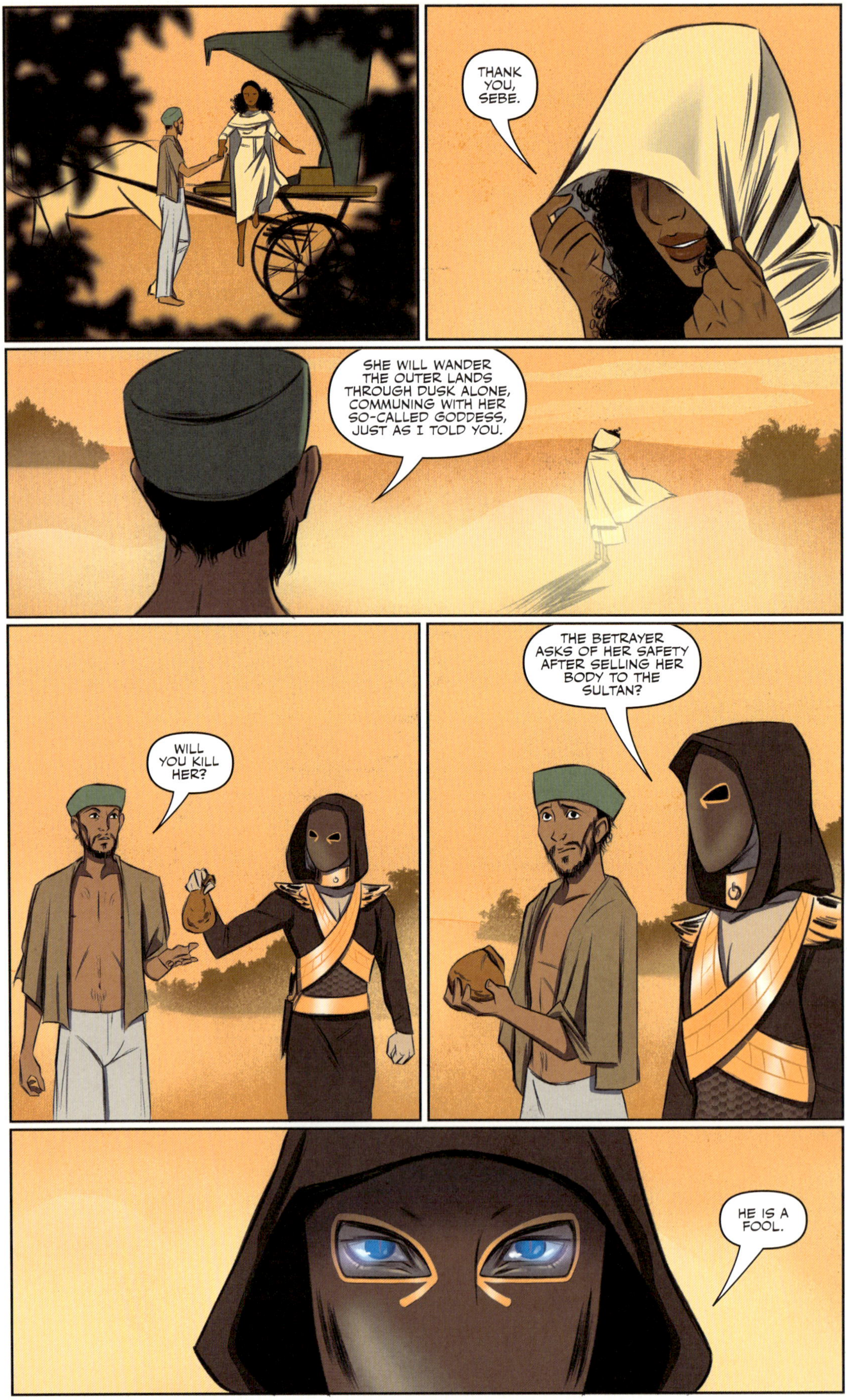
THANK YOU, SEBE.
SHE WILL WANDER THE OUTER LANDS THROUGH DUSK ALONE, COMMUNING WITH HER SO-CALLED GODDESS, JUST AS I TOLD YOU.
WILL YOU KILL HER?
THE BETRAYER ASKS OF HER SAFETY AFTER SELLING HER BODY TO THE SULTAN?
HE IS A FOOL.

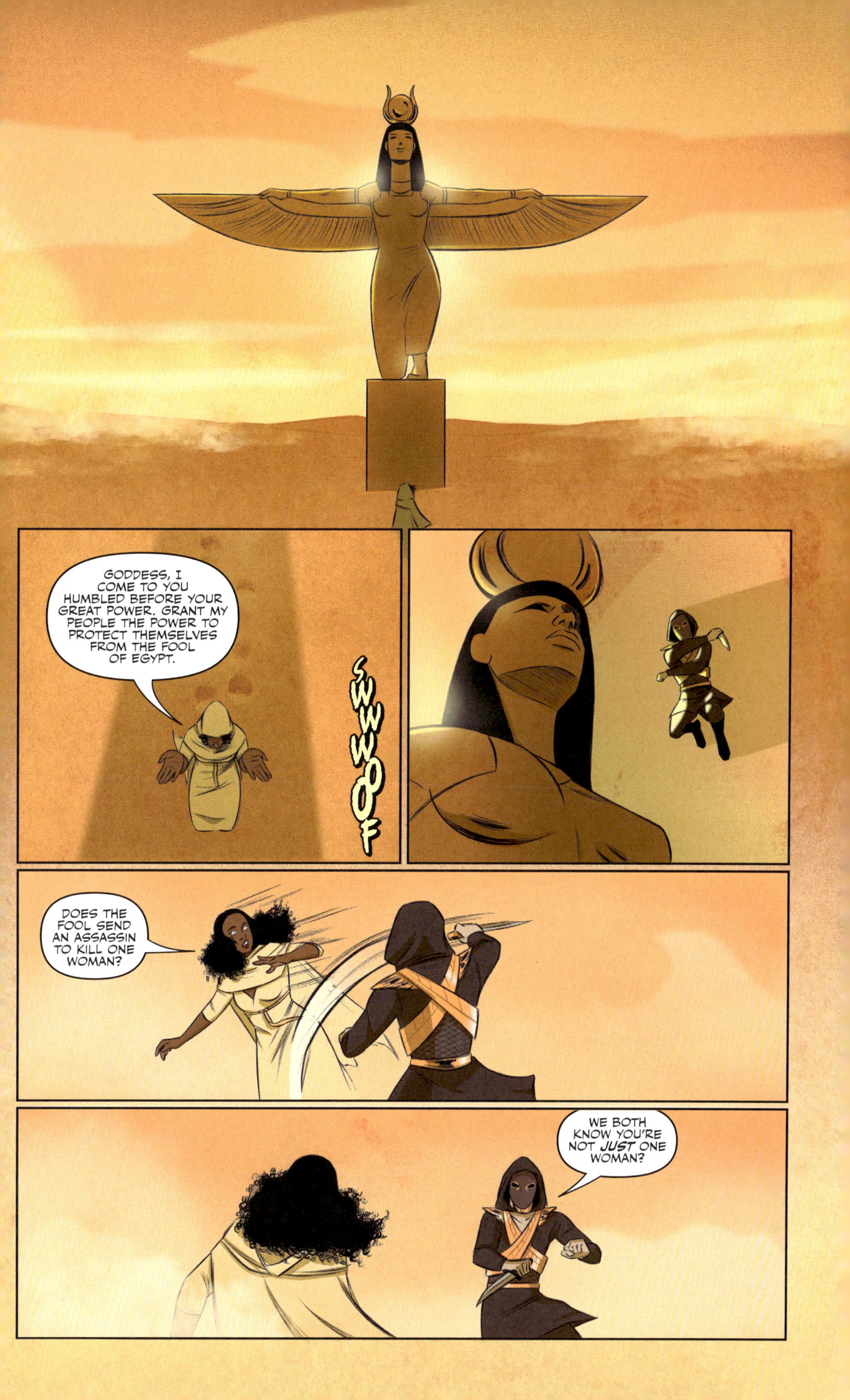
GODDESS, I COME TO YOU HUMBLED BEFORE YOUR GREAT POWER. GRANT MY PEOPLE THE POWER TO PROTECT THEMSELVES FROM THE FOOL OF EGYPT.
SWWWOOF
DOES THE FOOL SEND AN ASSASSIN TO KILL ONE WOMAN?
WE BOTH KNOW YOU'RE NOT *JUST* ONE WOMAN?

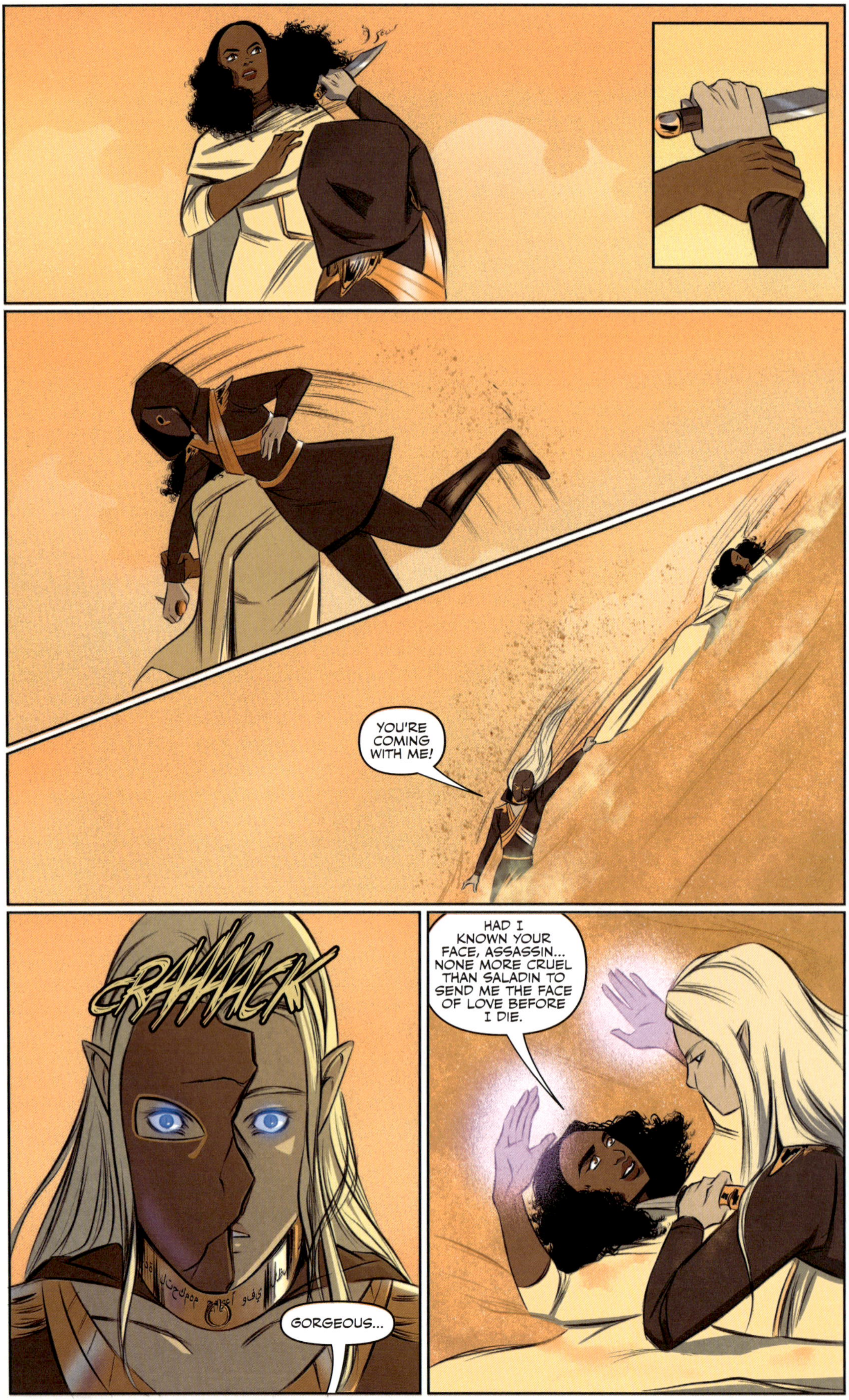
YOU'RE COMING WITH ME!
CRAAAACK
GORGEOUS...
HAD I KNOWN YOUR FACE, ASSASSIN... NONE MORE CRUEL THAN SALADIN TO SEND ME THE FACE OF LOVE BEFORE I DIE.

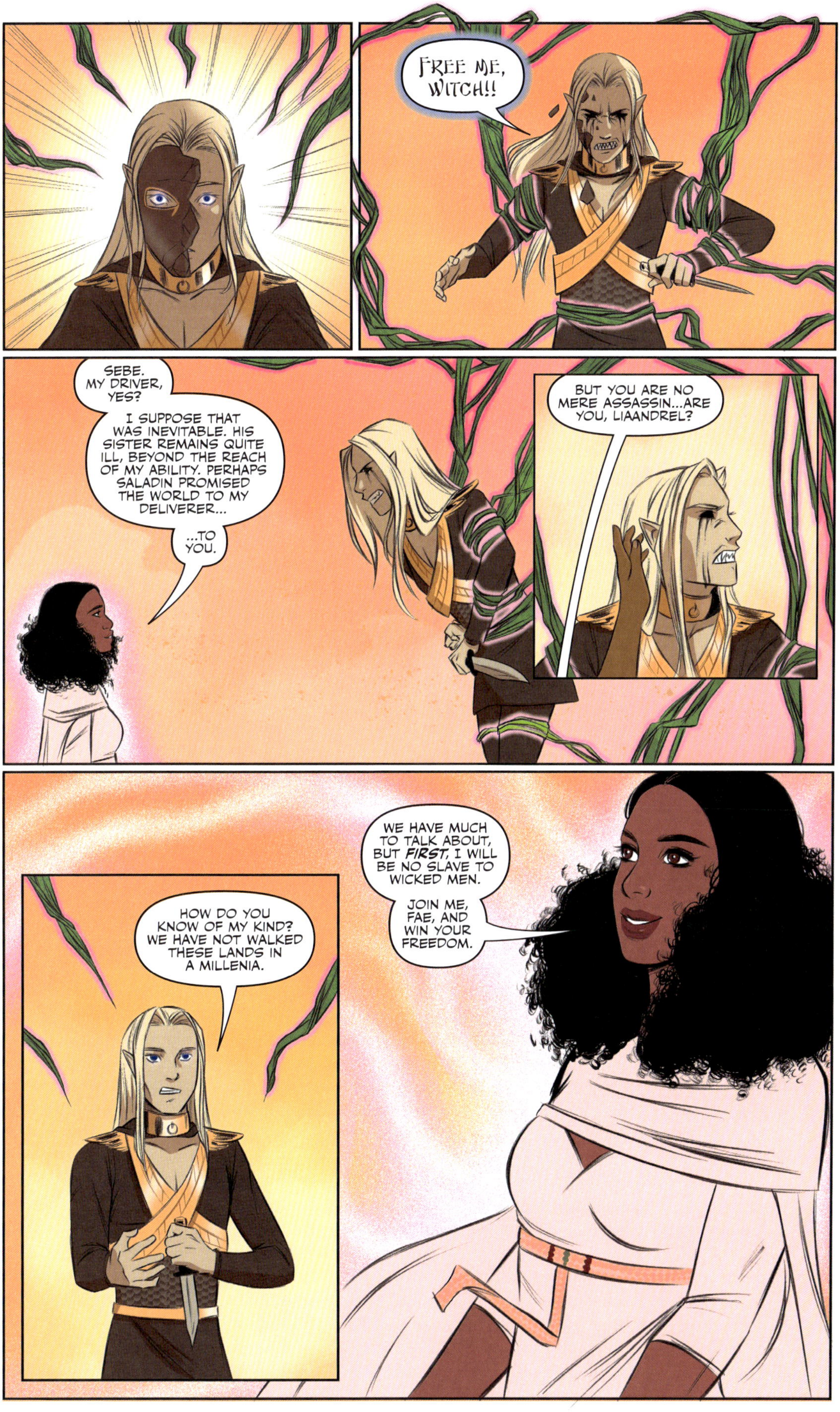
FREE ME, WITCH!!
SEBE. MY DRIVER, YES?
I SUPPOSE THAT WAS INEVITABLE. HIS SISTER REMAINS QUITE ILL, BEYOND THE REACH OF MY ABILITY. PERHAPS SALADIN PROMISED THE WORLD TO MY DELIVERER...
...TO YOU.
BUT YOU ARE NO MERE ASSASSIN...ARE YOU, LIAANDREL?
HOW DO YOU KNOW OF MY KIND? WE HAVE NOT WALKED THESE LANDS IN A MILLENIA.
WE HAVE MUCH TO TALK ABOUT, BUT *FIRST*, I WILL BE NO SLAVE TO WICKED MEN.
JOIN ME, FAE, AND WIN YOUR FREEDOM.

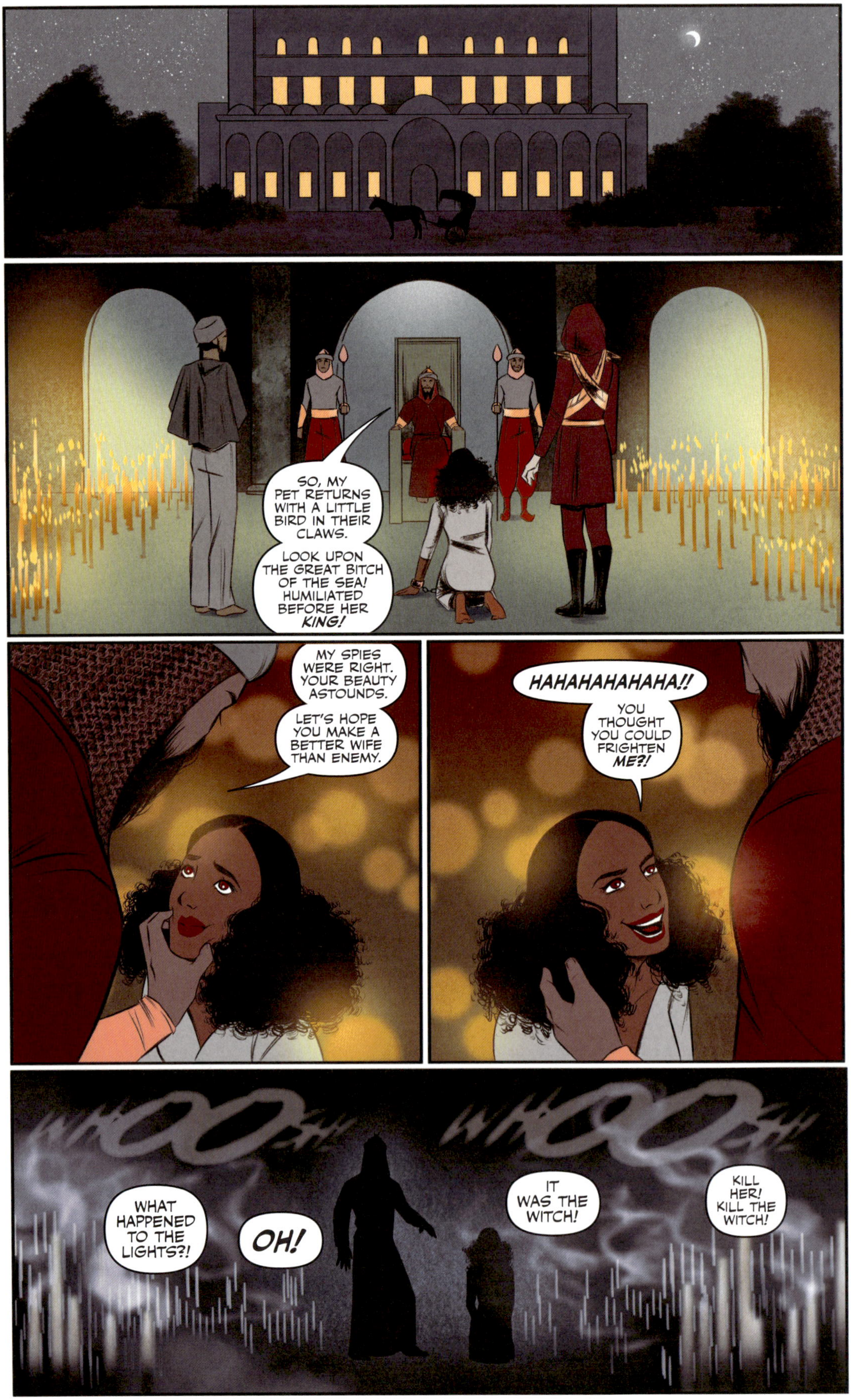
SO, MY PET RETURNS WITH A LITTLE BIRD IN THEIR CLAWS.
LOOK UPON THE GREAT BITCH OF THE SEA! HUMILIATED BEFORE HER *KING!*
MY SPIES WERE RIGHT. YOUR BEAUTY ASTOUNDS.
LET'S HOPE YOU MAKE A BETTER WIFE THAN ENEMY.
HAHAHAHAHAHA!!
YOU THOUGHT YOU COULD FRIGHTEN *ME?!*
WHAT HAPPENED TO THE LIGHTS?!
OH!
IT WAS THE WITCH!
KILL HER! KILL THE WITCH!

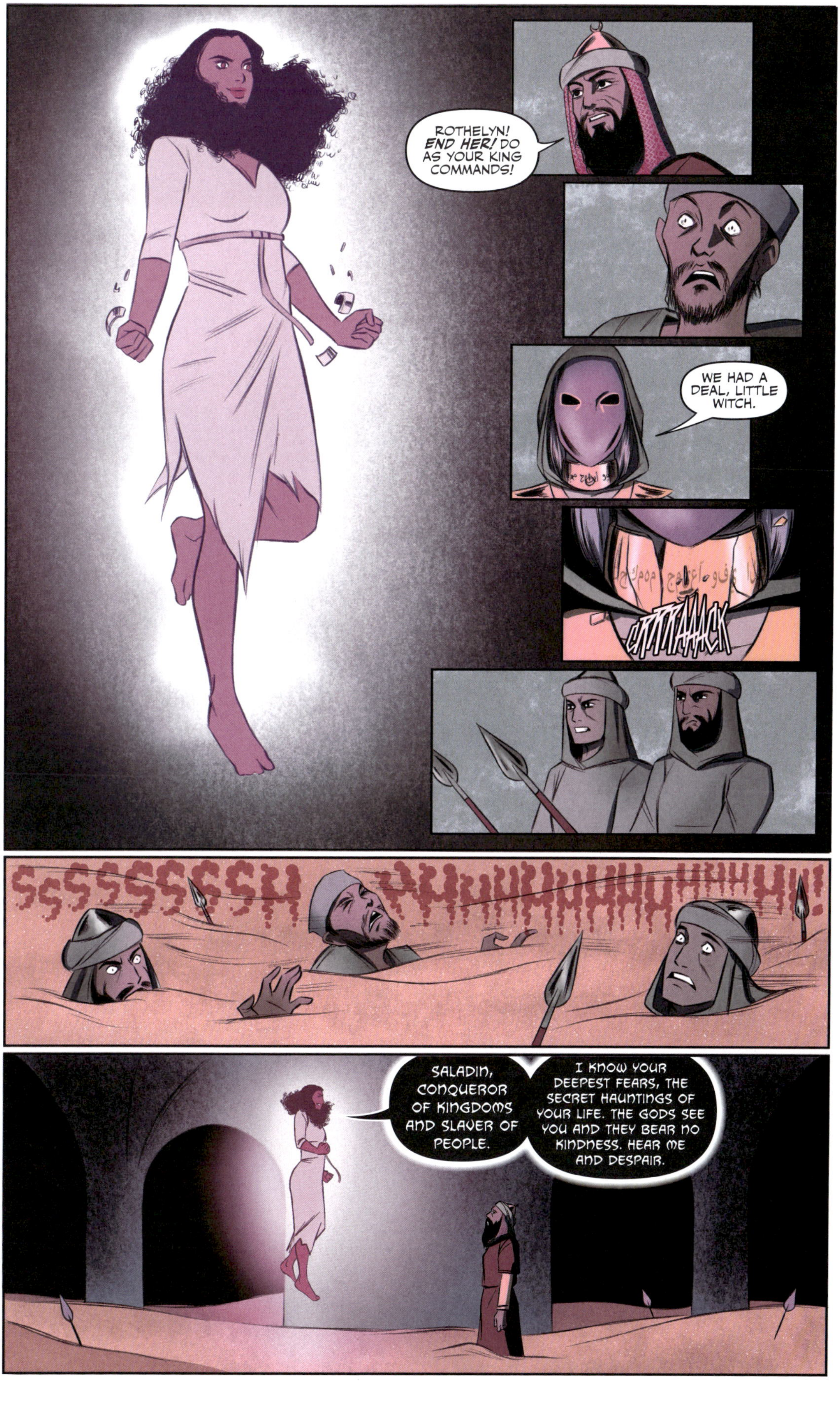
ROTHELYN! END HER! DO AS YOUR KING COMMANDS!
WE HAD A DEAL, LITTLE WITCH.
CRRRAAACK
SSSSSSSSH
VHHHHHHHHHHHHHHHH!
SALADIN, CONQUEROR OF KINGDOMS AND SLAYER OF PEOPLE.
I KNOW YOUR DEEPEST FEARS, THE SECRET HAUNTINGS OF YOUR LIFE. THE GODS SEE YOU AND THEY BEAR NO KINDNESS. HEAR ME AND DESPAIR.

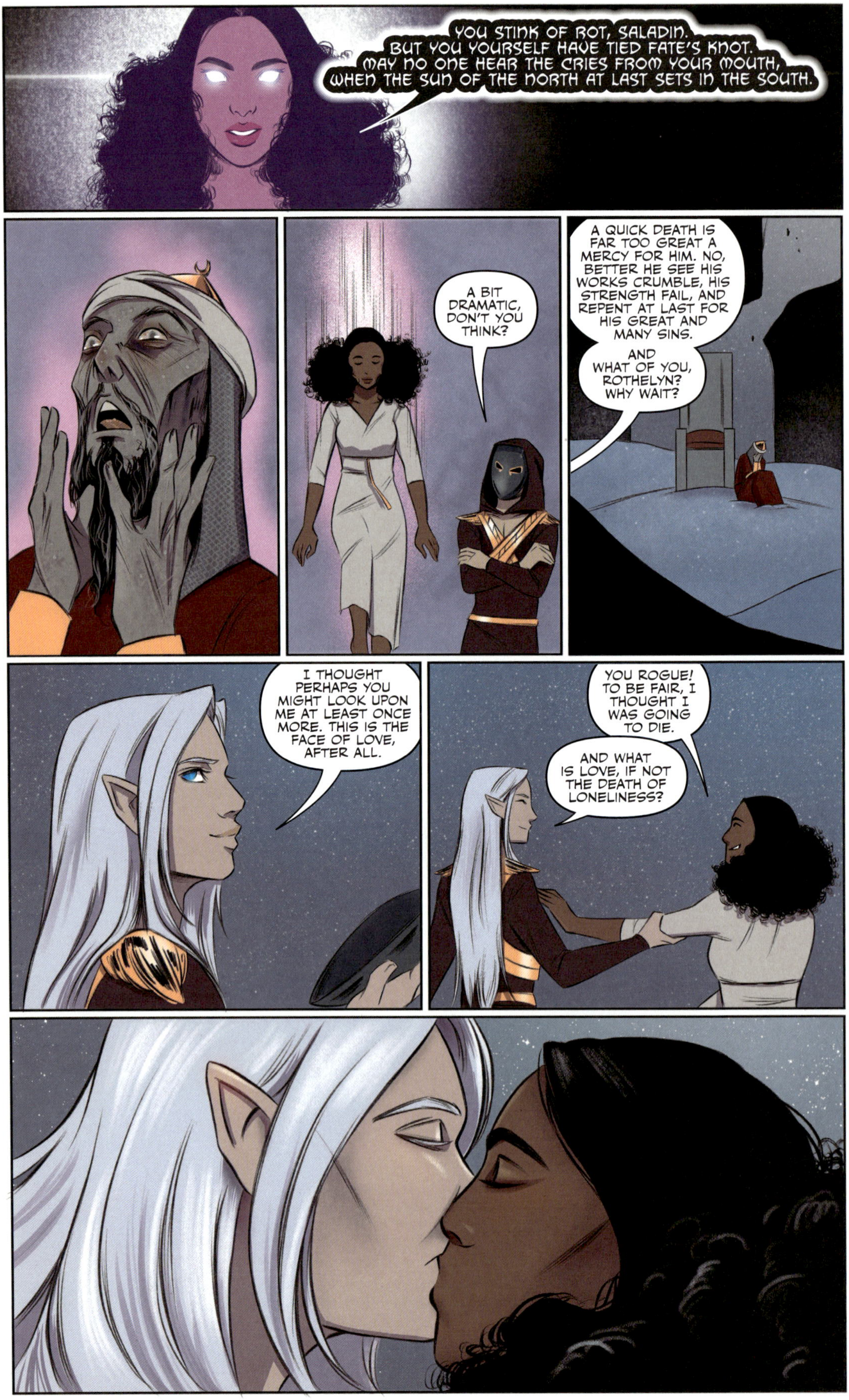
YOU STINK OF ROT, SALADIN. BUT YOU YOURSELF HAVE TIED FATE'S KNOT. MAY NO ONE HEAR THE CRIES FROM YOUR MOUTH, WHEN THE SUN OF THE NORTH AT LAST SETS IN THE SOUTH.
A BIT DRAMATIC, DON'T YOU THINK?
A QUICK DEATH IS FAR TOO GREAT A MERCY FOR HIM. NO, BETTER HE SEE HIS WORKS CRUMBLE, HIS STRENGTH FAIL, AND REPENT AT LAST FOR HIS GREAT AND MANY SINS.
AND WHAT OF YOU, ROTHELYN? WHY WAIT?
I THOUGHT PERHAPS YOU MIGHT LOOK UPON ME AT LEAST ONCE MORE. THIS IS THE FACE OF LOVE, AFTER ALL.
YOU ROGUE! TO BE FAIR, I THOUGHT I WAS GOING TO DIE.
AND WHAT IS LOVE, IF NOT THE DEATH OF LONELINESS?

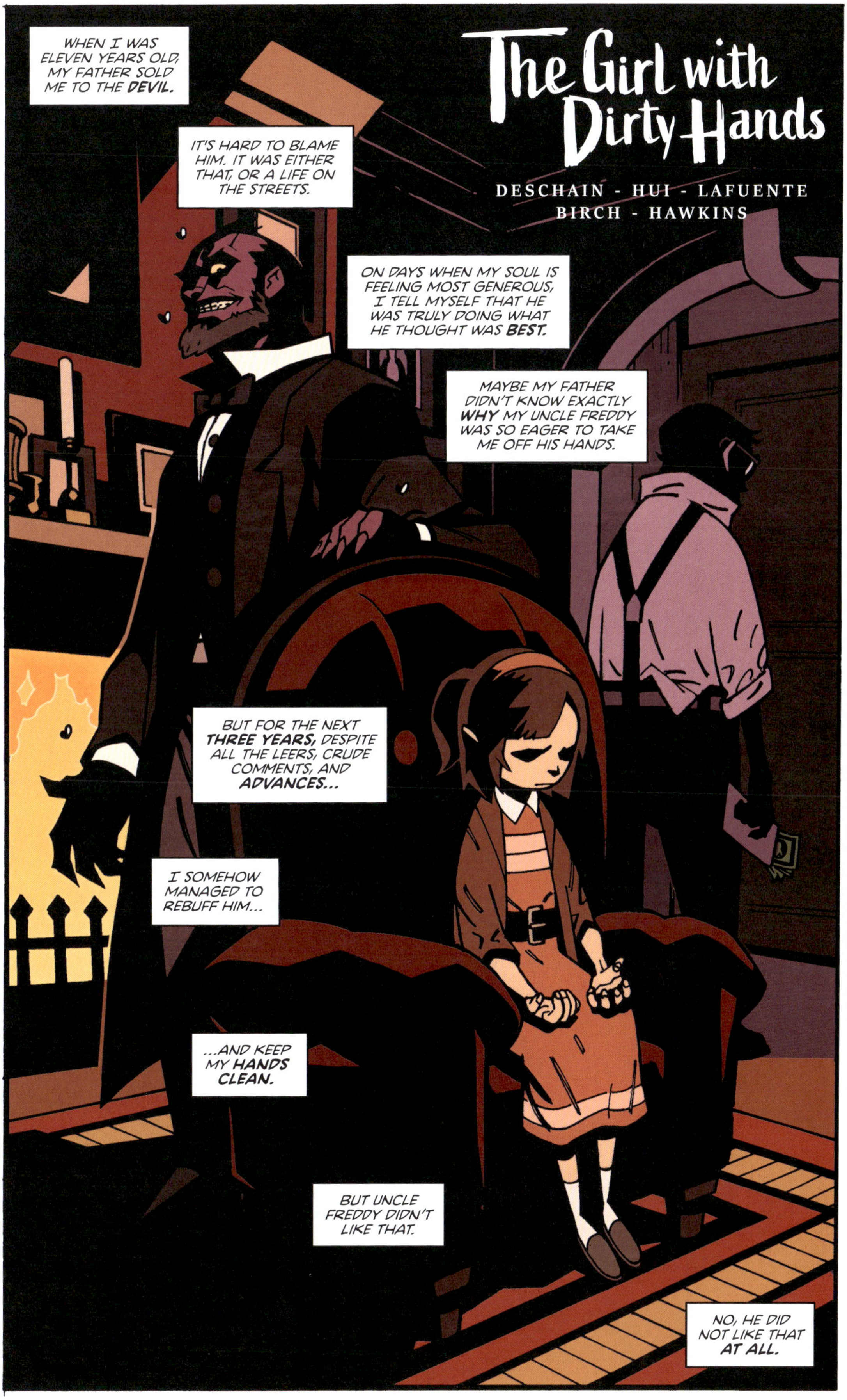

WHEN I WAS ELEVEN YEARS OLD, MY FATHER SOLD ME TO THE DEVIL.
The Girl with Dirty Hands
DESCHAIN - HUI - LAFUENTE
BIRCH - HAWKINS
IT'S HARD TO BLAME HIM. IT WAS EITHER THAT, OR A LIFE ON THE STREETS.
ON DAYS WHEN MY SOUL IS FEELING MOST GENEROUS, I TELL MYSELF THAT HE WAS TRULY DOING WHAT HE THOUGHT WAS BEST.
MAYBE MY FATHER DIDN'T KNOW EXACTLY WHY MY UNCLE FREDDY WAS SO EAGER TO TAKE ME OFF HIS HANDS.
BUT FOR THE NEXT THREE YEARS, DESPITE ALL THE LEERS, CRUDE COMMENTS, AND ADVANCES...
I SOMEHOW MANAGED TO REBUFF HIM...
...AND KEEP MY HANDS CLEAN.
BUT UNCLE FREDDY DIDN'T LIKE THAT.
NO, HE DID NOT LIKE THAT AT ALL.

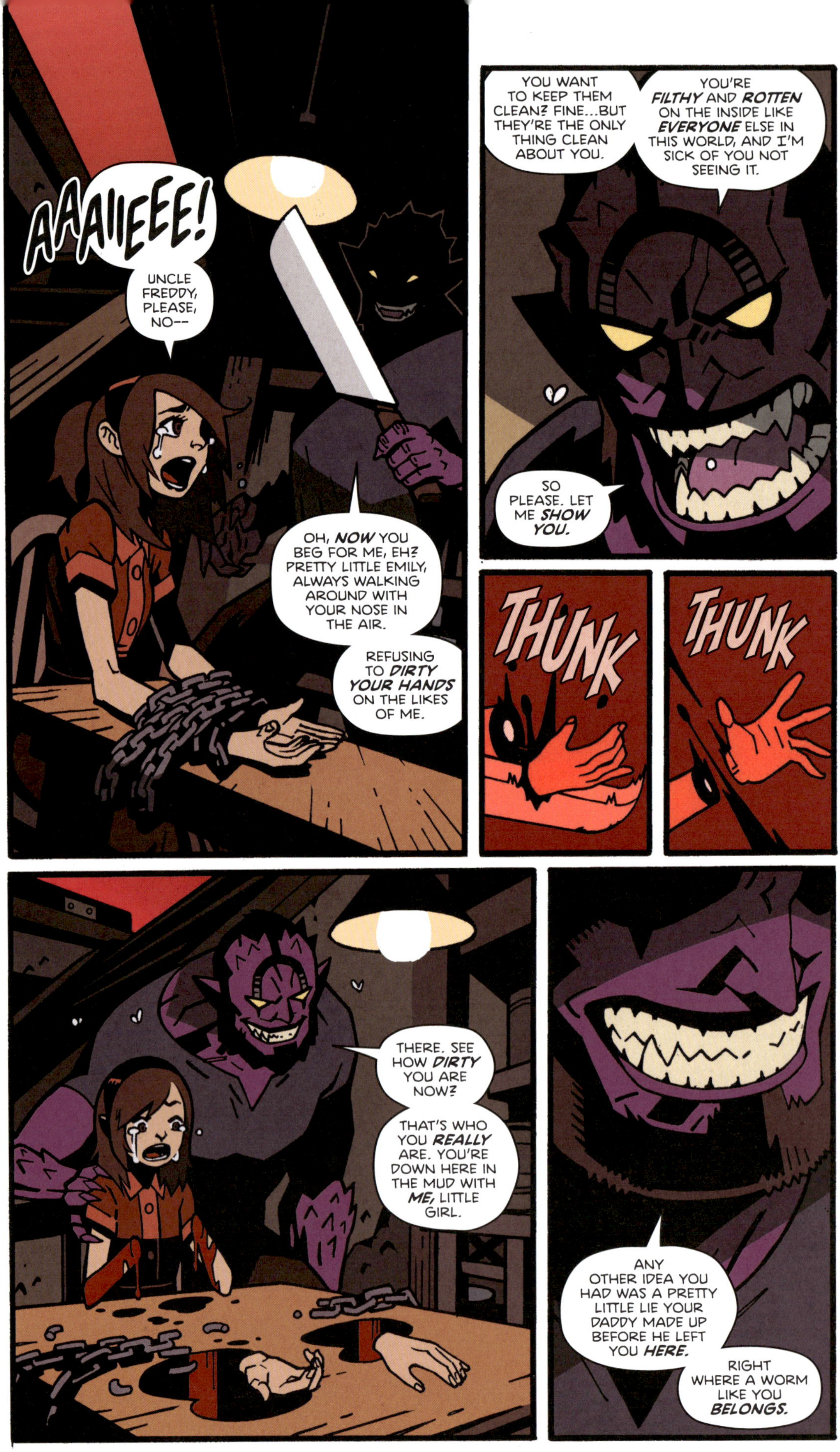
AAAIIEEE!
UNCLE FREDDY, PLEASE, NO--
OH, NOW YOU BEG FOR ME, EH? PRETTY LITTLE EMILY, ALWAYS WALKING AROUND WITH YOUR NOSE IN THE AIR.
REFUSING TO DIRTY YOUR HANDS ON THE LIKES OF ME.
YOU WANT TO KEEP THEM CLEAN? FINE...BUT THEY'RE THE ONLY THING CLEAN ABOUT YOU.
YOU'RE FILTHY AND ROTTEN ON THE INSIDE LIKE EVERYONE ELSE IN THIS WORLD, AND I'M SICK OF YOU NOT SEEING IT.
SO PLEASE. LET ME SHOW YOU.
THUNK
THUNK
THERE. SEE HOW DIRTY YOU ARE NOW?
THAT'S WHO YOU REALLY ARE. YOU'RE DOWN HERE IN THE MUD WITH ME, LITTLE GIRL.
ANY OTHER IDEA YOU HAD WAS A PRETTY LITTLE LIE YOUR DADDY MADE UP BEFORE HE LEFT YOU HERE.
RIGHT WHERE A WORM LIKE YOU BELONGS.

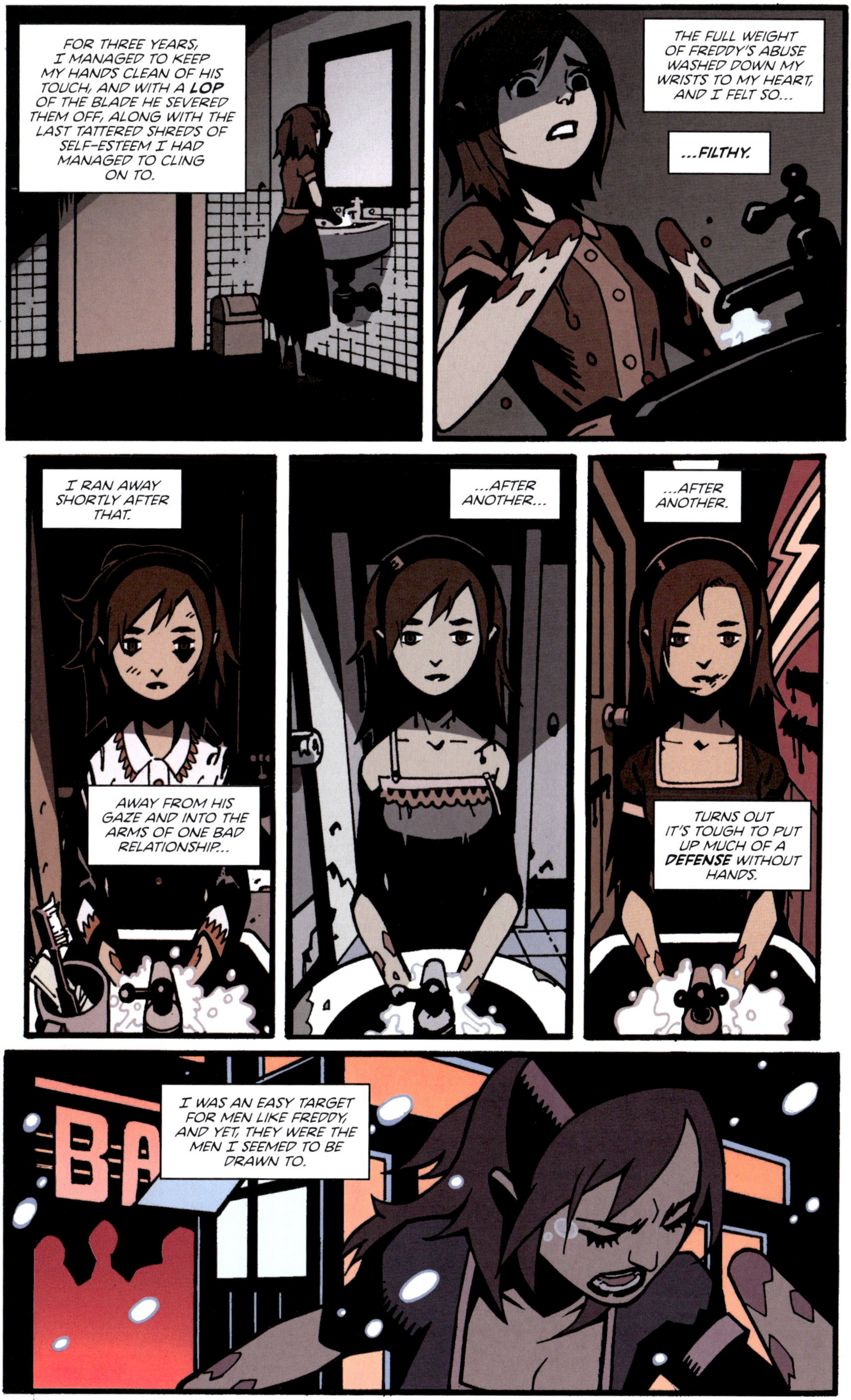
FOR THREE YEARS, I MANAGED TO KEEP MY HANDS CLEAN OF HIS TOUCH, AND WITH A **LOP** OF THE BLADE HE SEVERED THEM OFF, ALONG WITH THE LAST TATTERED SHREDS OF SELF-ESTEEM I HAD MANAGED TO CLING ON TO.
THE FULL WEIGHT OF FREDDY'S ABUSE WASHED DOWN MY WRISTS TO MY HEART, AND I FELT SO...
...FILTHY.
I RAN AWAY SHORTLY AFTER THAT.
AWAY FROM HIS GAZE AND INTO THE ARMS OF ONE BAD RELATIONSHIP...
...AFTER ANOTHER...
...AFTER ANOTHER.
TURNS OUT IT'S TOUGH TO PUT UP MUCH OF A **DEFENSE** WITHOUT HANDS.
I WAS AN EASY TARGET FOR MEN LIKE FREDDY, AND YET, THEY WERE THE MEN I SEEMED TO BE DRAWN TO.

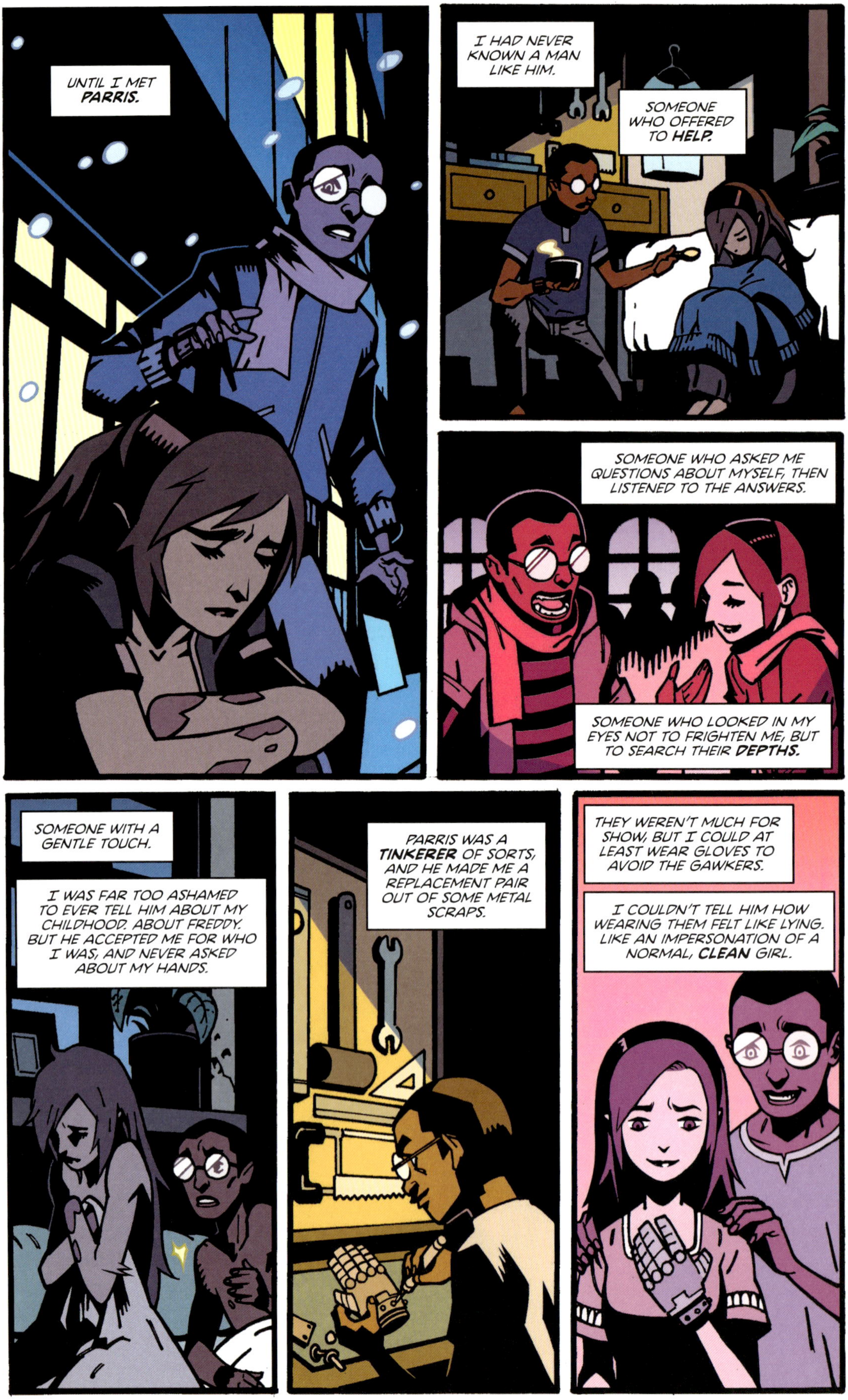
UNTIL I MET **PARRIS.**
I HAD NEVER KNOWN A MAN LIKE HIM.
SOMEONE WHO OFFERED TO **HELP.**
SOMEONE WHO ASKED ME QUESTIONS ABOUT MYSELF, THEN LISTENED TO THE ANSWERS.
SOMEONE WHO LOOKED IN MY EYES NOT TO FRIGHTEN ME, BUT TO SEARCH THEIR **DEPTHS.**
SOMEONE WITH A GENTLE TOUCH.
I WAS FAR TOO ASHAMED TO EVER TELL HIM ABOUT MY CHILDHOOD. ABOUT FREDDY. BUT HE ACCEPTED ME FOR WHO I WAS, AND NEVER ASKED ABOUT MY HANDS.
PARRIS WAS A **TINKERER** OF SORTS, AND HE MADE ME A REPLACEMENT PAIR OUT OF SOME METAL SCRAPS.
THEY WEREN'T MUCH FOR SHOW, BUT I COULD AT LEAST WEAR GLOVES TO AVOID THE GAWKERS.
I COULDN'T TELL HIM HOW WEARING THEM FELT LIKE LYING. LIKE AN IMPERSONATION OF A NORMAL, **CLEAN** GIRL.

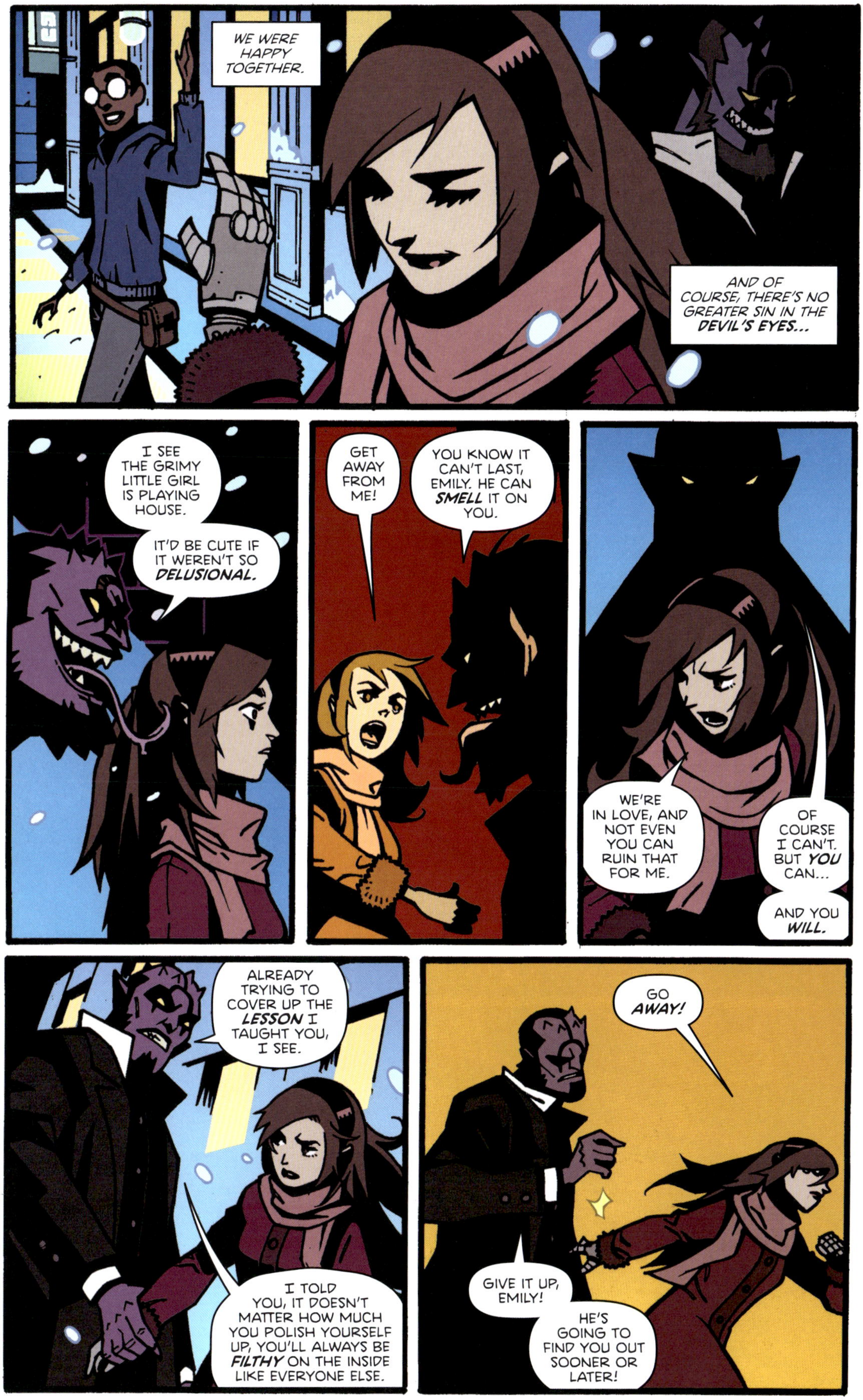
WE WERE HAPPY TOGETHER.
AND OF COURSE, THERE'S NO GREATER SIN IN THE DEVIL'S EYES...
I SEE THE GRIMY LITTLE GIRL IS PLAYING HOUSE.
IT'D BE CUTE IF IT WEREN'T SO DELUSIONAL.
GET AWAY FROM ME!
YOU KNOW IT CAN'T LAST, EMILY. HE CAN SMELL IT ON YOU.
WE'RE IN LOVE, AND NOT EVEN YOU CAN RUIN THAT FOR ME.
OF COURSE I CAN'T. BUT YOU CAN...
AND YOU WILL.
ALREADY TRYING TO COVER UP THE LESSON I TAUGHT YOU, I SEE.
I TOLD YOU, IT DOESN'T MATTER HOW MUCH YOU POLISH YOURSELF UP, YOU'LL ALWAYS BE FILTHY ON THE INSIDE LIKE EVERYONE ELSE.
GO AWAY!
GIVE IT UP, EMILY!
HE'S GOING TO FIND YOU OUT SOONER OR LATER!

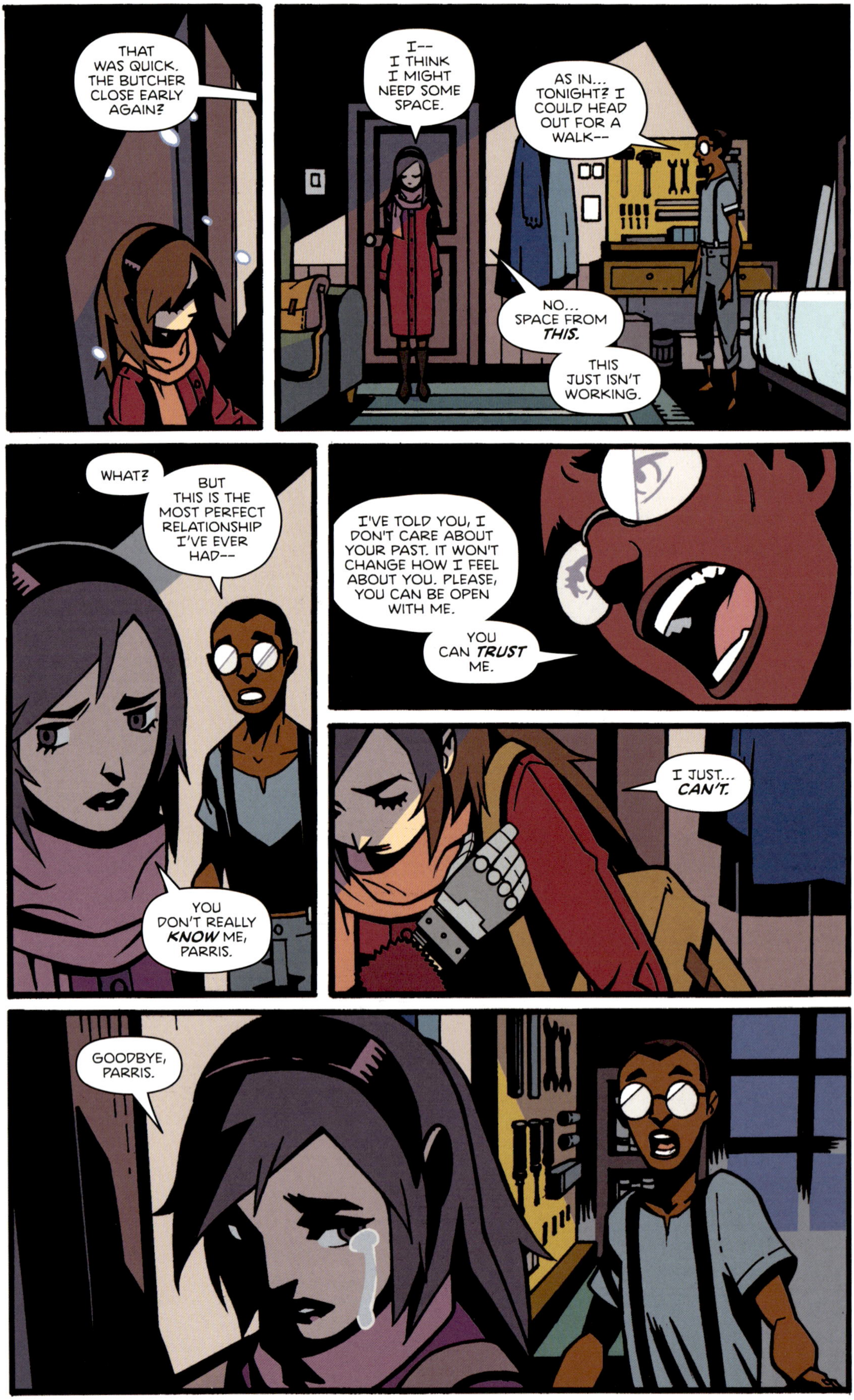
THAT WAS QUICK. THE BUTCHER CLOSE EARLY AGAIN?
I-- I THINK I MIGHT NEED SOME SPACE.
AS IN... TONIGHT? I COULD HEAD OUT FOR A WALK--
NO... SPACE FROM *THIS.*
THIS JUST ISN'T WORKING.
WHAT?
BUT THIS IS THE MOST PERFECT RELATIONSHIP I'VE EVER HAD--
YOU DON'T REALLY *KNOW* ME, PARRIS.
I'VE TOLD YOU, I DON'T CARE ABOUT YOUR PAST. IT WON'T CHANGE HOW I FEEL ABOUT YOU. PLEASE, YOU CAN BE OPEN WITH ME.
YOU CAN *TRUST* ME.
I JUST... *CAN'T.*
GOODBYE, PARRIS.

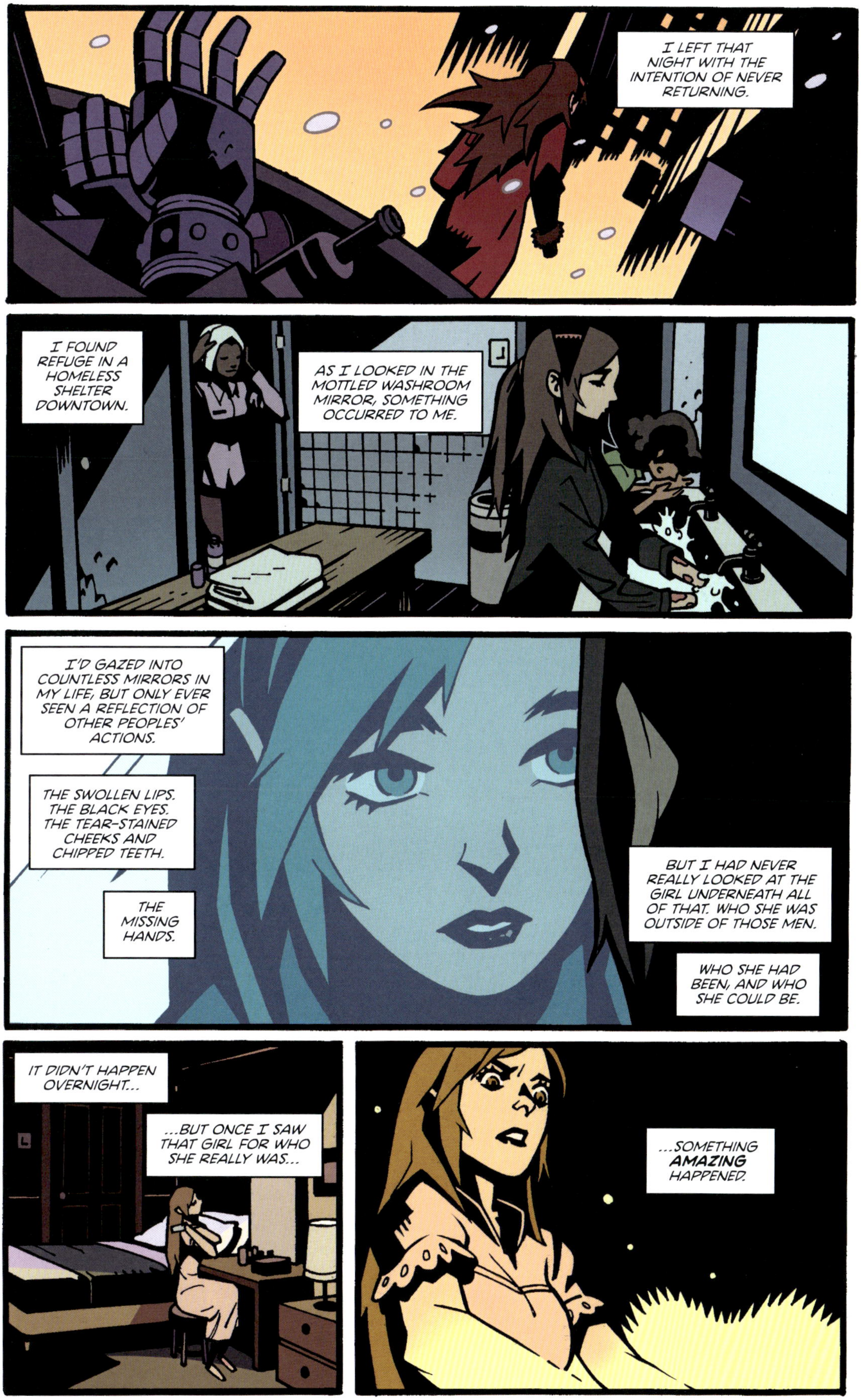
I LEFT THAT NIGHT WITH THE INTENTION OF NEVER RETURNING.
I FOUND REFUGE IN A HOMELESS SHELTER DOWNTOWN.
AS I LOOKED IN THE MOTTLED WASHROOM MIRROR, SOMETHING OCCURRED TO ME.
I'D GAZED INTO COUNTLESS MIRRORS IN MY LIFE, BUT ONLY EVER SEEN A REFLECTION OF OTHER PEOPLES' ACTIONS.
THE SWOLLEN LIPS. THE BLACK EYES. THE TEAR-STAINED CHEEKS AND CHIPPED TEETH.
THE MISSING HANDS.
BUT I HAD NEVER REALLY LOOKED AT THE GIRL UNDERNEATH ALL OF THAT. WHO SHE WAS OUTSIDE OF THOSE MEN.
WHO SHE HAD BEEN, AND WHO SHE COULD BE.
IT DIDN'T HAPPEN OVERNIGHT...
...BUT ONCE I SAW THAT GIRL FOR WHO SHE REALLY WAS...
...SOMETHING **AMAZING** HAPPENED.

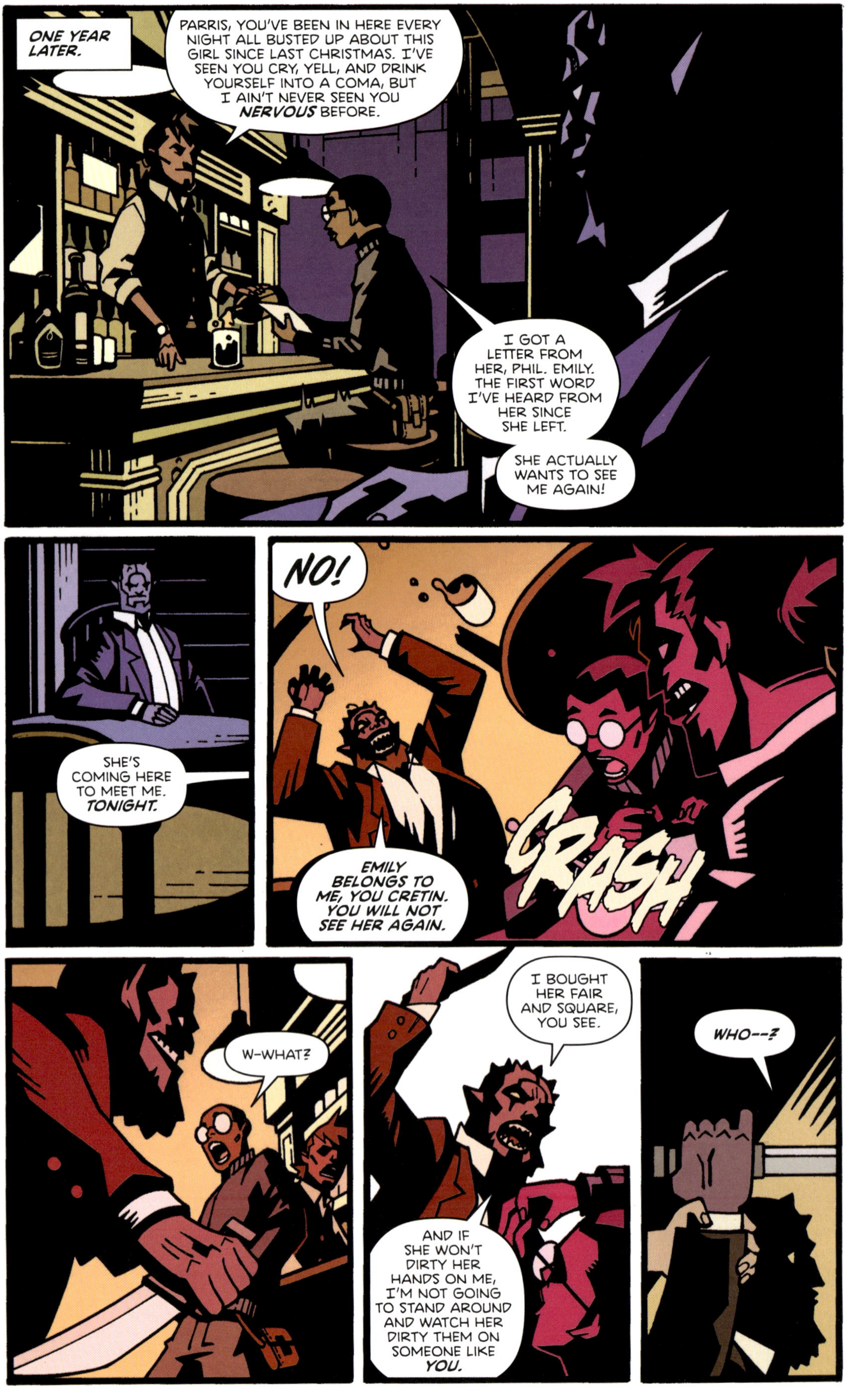

ONE YEAR LATER.
PARRIS, YOU'VE BEEN IN HERE EVERY NIGHT ALL BUSTED UP ABOUT THIS GIRL SINCE LAST CHRISTMAS. I'VE SEEN YOU CRY, YELL, AND DRINK YOURSELF INTO A COMA, BUT I AIN'T NEVER SEEN YOU *NERVOUS* BEFORE.
I GOT A LETTER FROM HER, PHIL. EMILY. THE FIRST WORD I'VE HEARD FROM HER SINCE SHE LEFT.
SHE ACTUALLY WANTS TO SEE ME AGAIN!
SHE'S COMING HERE TO MEET ME. *TONIGHT.*
NO!
EMILY BELONGS TO ME, YOU CRETIN. YOU WILL NOT SEE HER AGAIN.
CRASH
W-WHAT?
I BOUGHT HER FAIR AND SQUARE, YOU SEE.
AND IF SHE WON'T DIRTY HER HANDS ON ME, I'M NOT GOING TO STAND AROUND AND WATCH HER DIRTY THEM ON SOMEONE LIKE *YOU.*
WHO--?

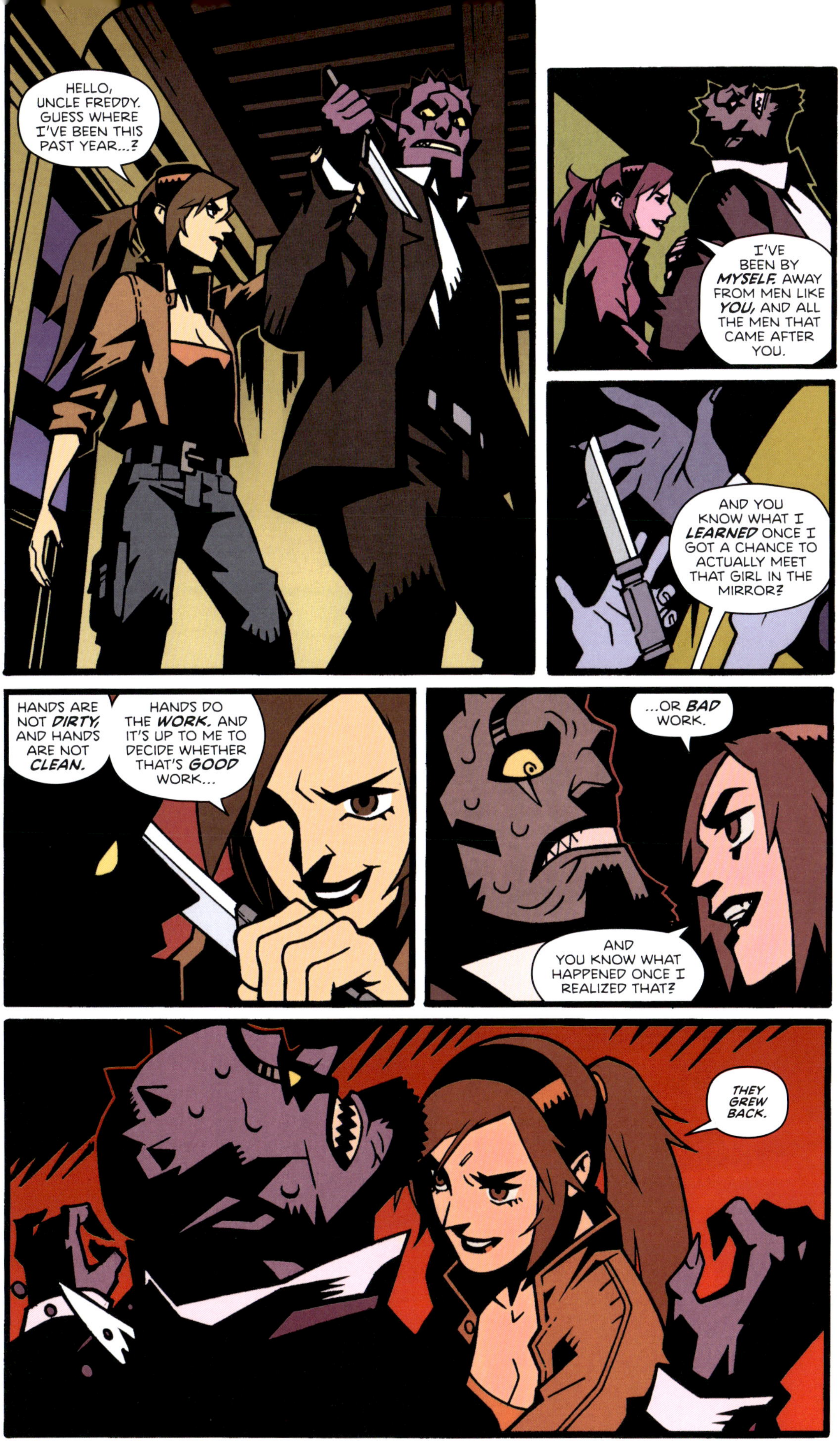
HELLO, UNCLE FREDDY. GUESS WHERE I'VE BEEN THIS PAST YEAR...?
I'VE BEEN BY MYSELF. AWAY FROM MEN LIKE YOU, AND ALL THE MEN THAT CAME AFTER YOU.
AND YOU KNOW WHAT I LEARNED ONCE I GOT A CHANCE TO ACTUALLY MEET THAT GIRL IN THE MIRROR?
HANDS ARE NOT DIRTY, AND HANDS ARE NOT CLEAN.
HANDS DO THE WORK. AND IT'S UP TO ME TO DECIDE WHETHER THAT'S GOOD WORK...
...OR BAD WORK.
AND YOU KNOW WHAT HAPPENED ONCE I REALIZED THAT?
THEY GREW BACK.

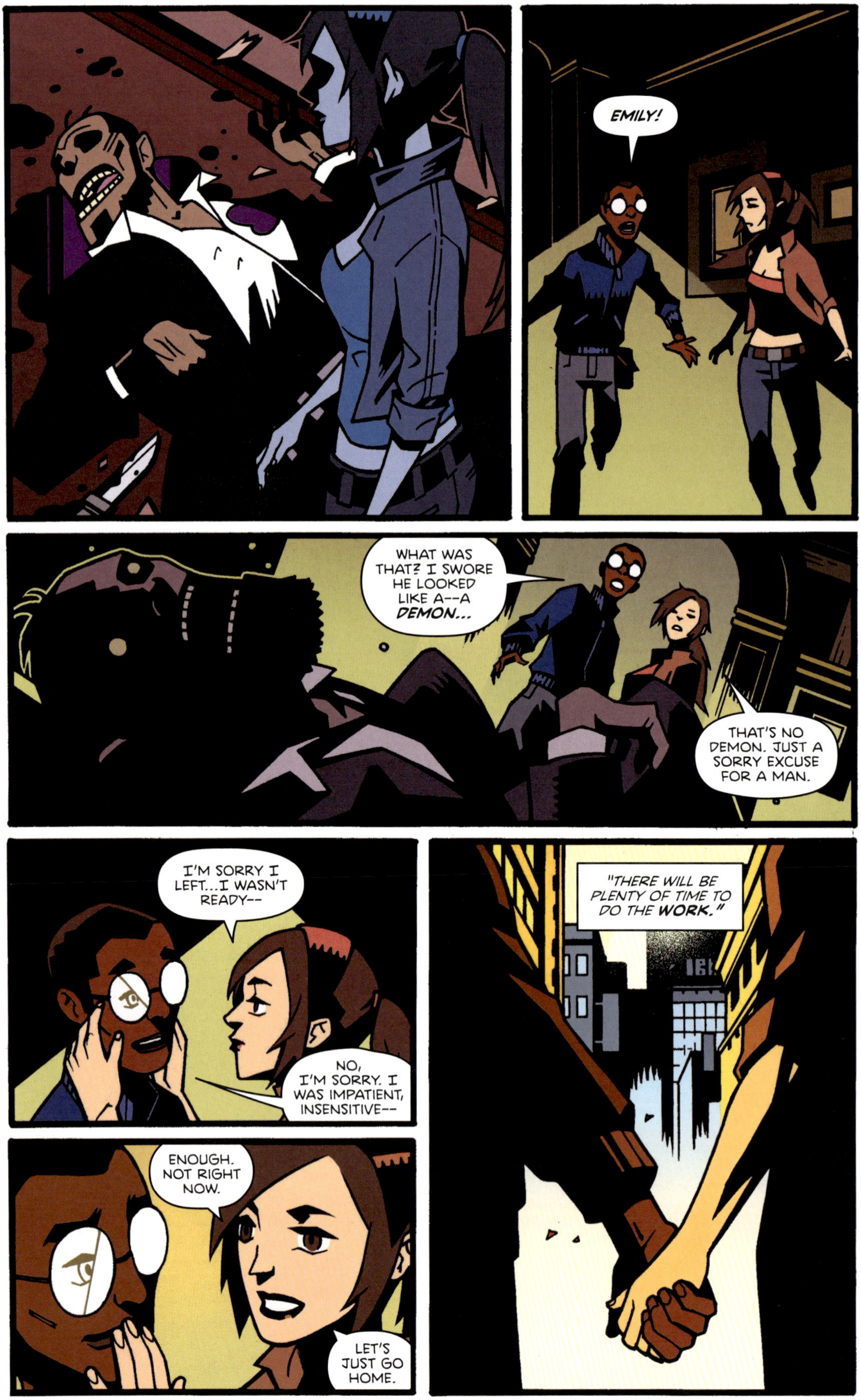
EMILY!
WHAT WAS THAT? I SWORE HE LOOKED LIKE A--A DEMON...
THAT'S NO DEMON. JUST A SORRY EXCUSE FOR A MAN.
I'M SORRY I LEFT...I WASN'T READY--
NO, I'M SORRY. I WAS IMPATIENT, INSENSITIVE--
ENOUGH. NOT RIGHT NOW.
LET'S JUST GO HOME.
"THERE WILL BE PLENTY OF TIME TO DO THE WORK."

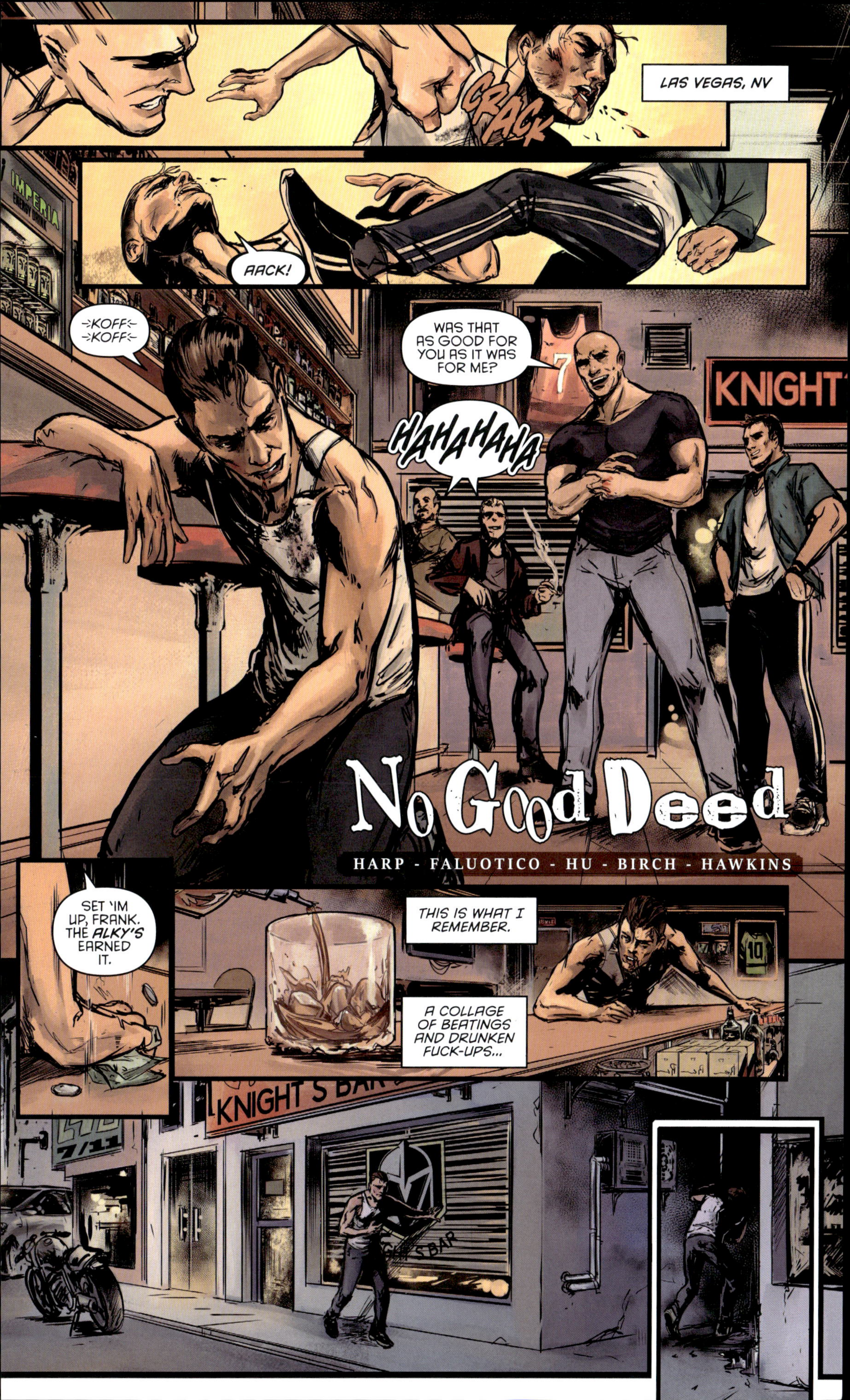
LAS VEGAS, NV
CRACK
AACK!
-KOFF-
-KOFF-
WAS THAT AS GOOD FOR YOU AS IT WAS FOR ME?
HAHAHAHA
KNIGHT
No Good Deed
HARP - FALUOTICO - HU - BIRCH - HAWKINS
SET 'IM UP, FRANK. THE ALKY'S EARNED IT.
THIS IS WHAT I REMEMBER.
A COLLAGE OF BEATINGS AND DRUNKEN FUCK-UPS...
KNIGHT S BAR
7/11

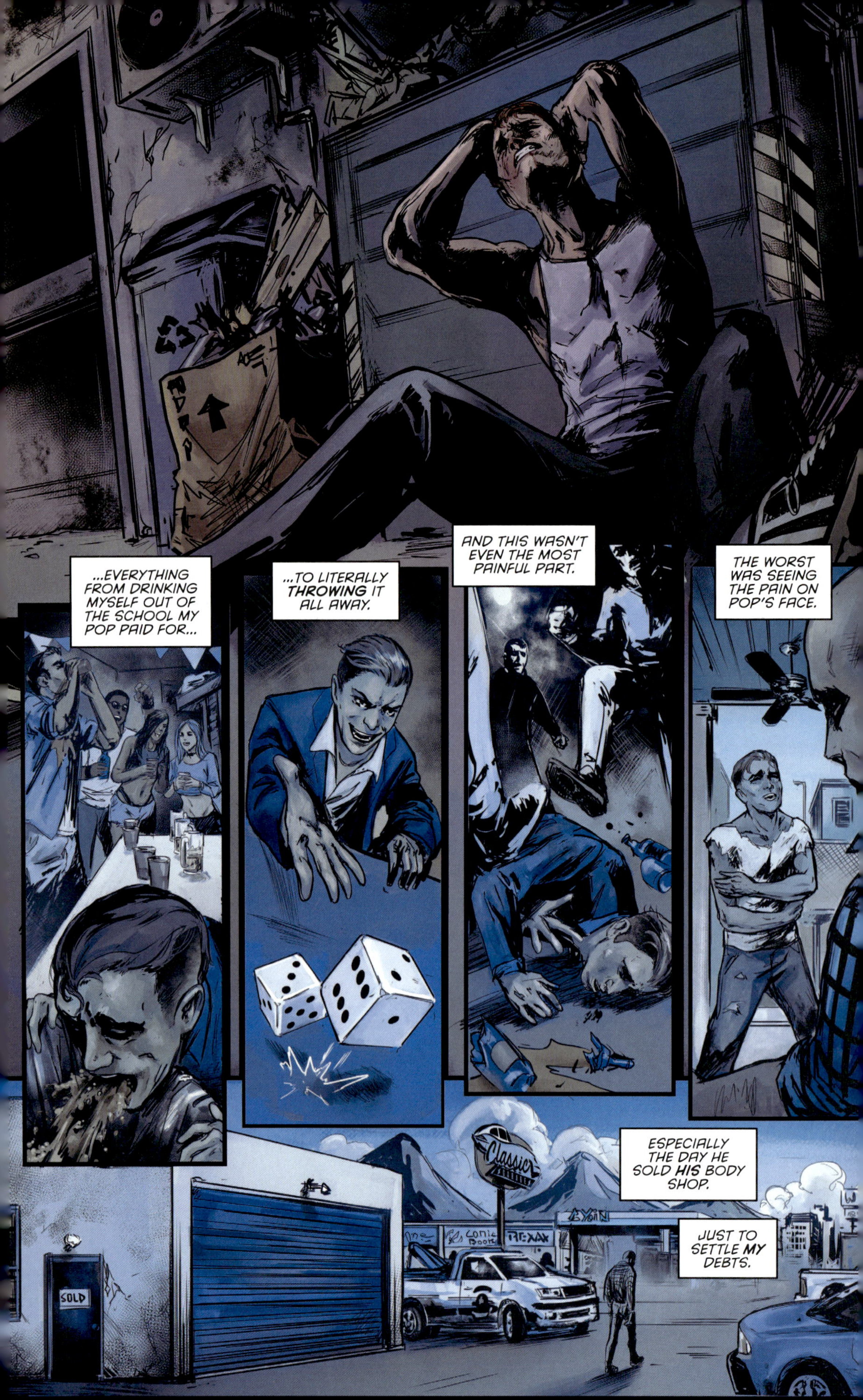
...EVERYTHING FROM DRINKING MYSELF OUT OF THE SCHOOL MY POP PAID FOR...
...TO LITERALLY THROWING IT ALL AWAY.
AND THIS WASN'T EVEN THE MOST PAINFUL PART.
THE WORST WAS SEEING THE PAIN ON POP'S FACE.
ESPECIALLY THE DAY HE SOLD HIS BODY SHOP.
JUST TO SETTLE MY DEBTS.
SOLD
Classic

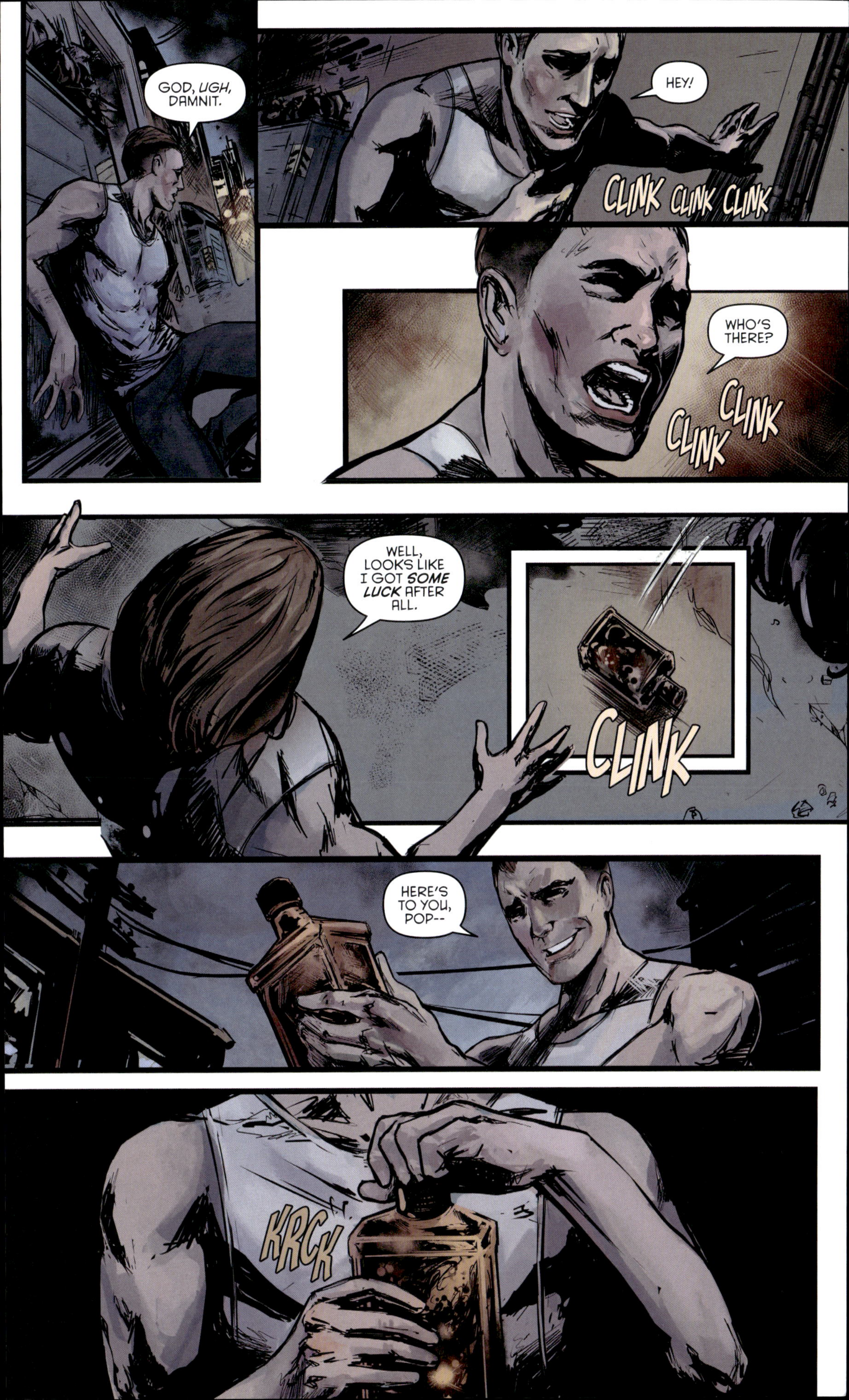
GOD, *UGH*, DAMNIT.
HEY!
CLINK CLINK CLINK
WHO'S THERE?
CLINK CLINK
WELL, LOOKS LIKE I GOT ***SOME LUCK*** AFTER ALL.
CLINK
HERE'S TO YOU, POP--
KRCK

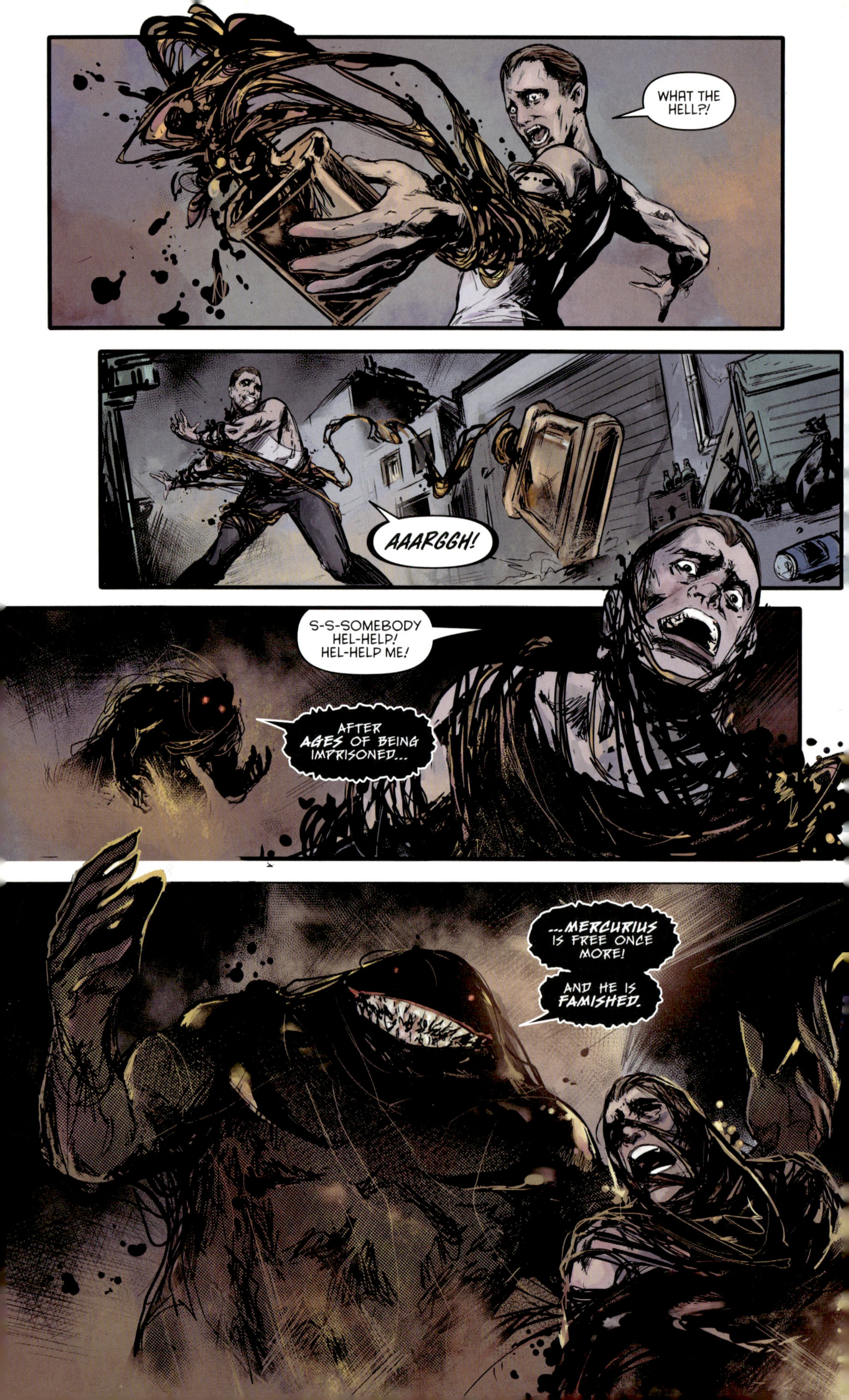
WHAT THE HELL?!
AAARGGH!
S-S-SOMEBODY HEL-HELP! HEL-HELP ME!
AFTER AGES OF BEING IMPRISONED...
...MERCURIUS IS FREE ONCE MORE!
AND HE IS FAMISHED.

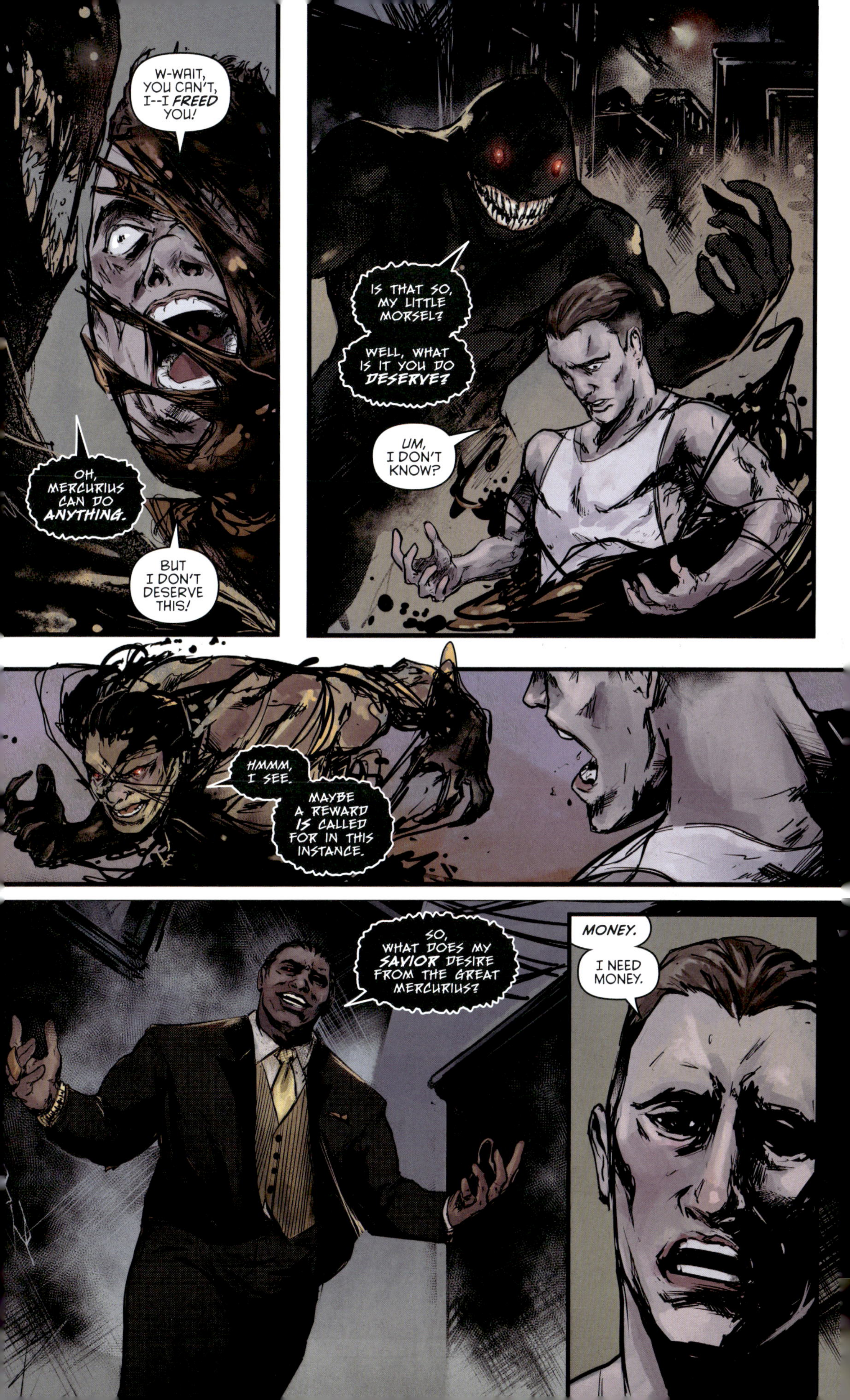
W-WAIT, YOU CAN'T, I--I FREED YOU!
OH, MERCURIUS CAN DO ANYTHING.
BUT I DON'T DESERVE THIS!
IS THAT SO, MY LITTLE MORSEL?
WELL, WHAT IS IT YOU DO DESERVE?
UM, I DON'T KNOW?
HMMM, I SEE.
MAYBE A REWARD IS CALLED FOR IN THIS INSTANCE.
SO, WHAT DOES MY SAVIOR DESIRE FROM THE GREAT MERCURIUS?
MONEY.
I NEED MONEY.

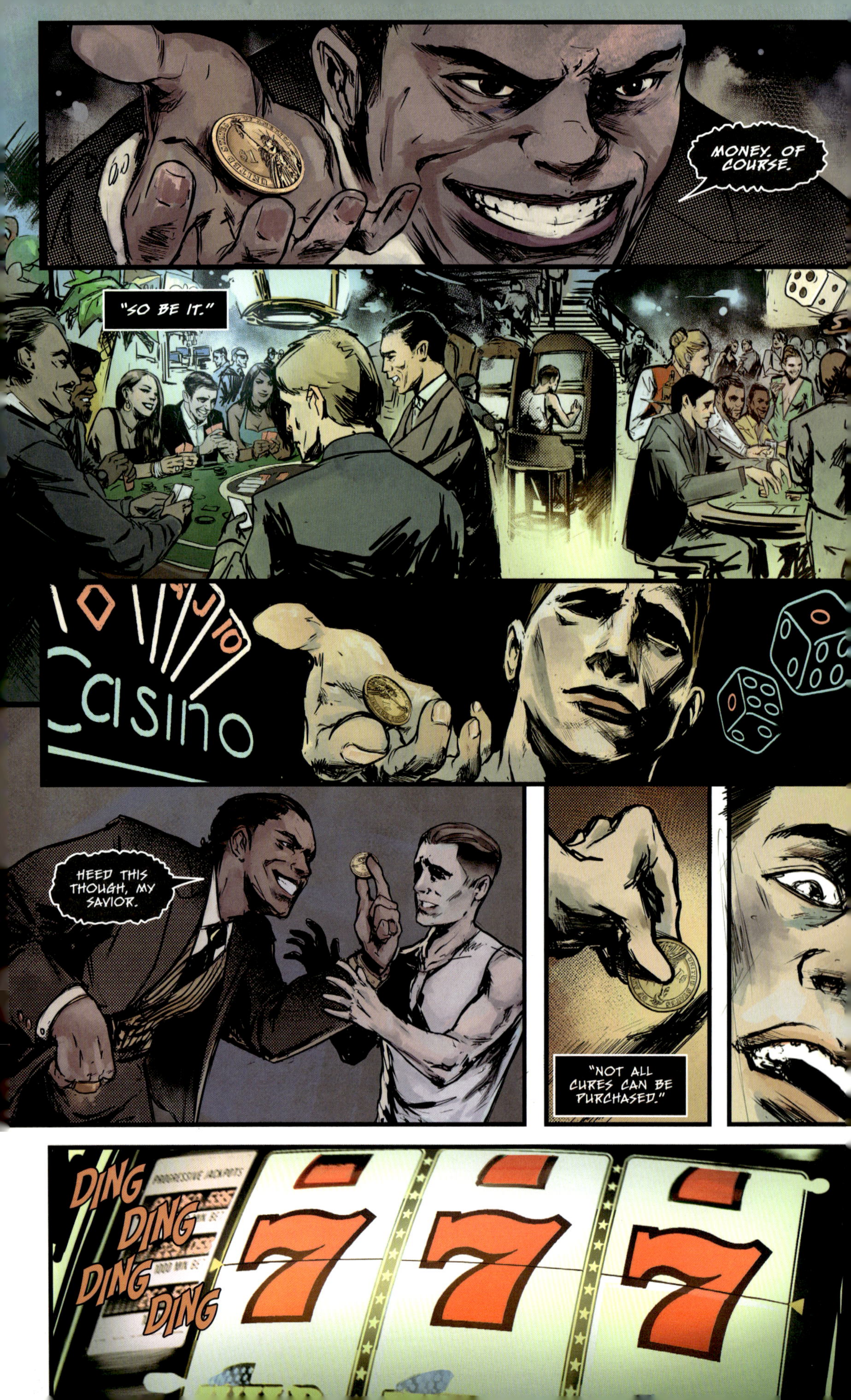
MONEY. OF COURSE.
"SO BE IT."
Casino
HEED THIS THOUGH, MY SAVIOR.
"NOT ALL CURES CAN BE PURCHASED."
PROGRESSIVE JACKPOTS
DING DING DING DING

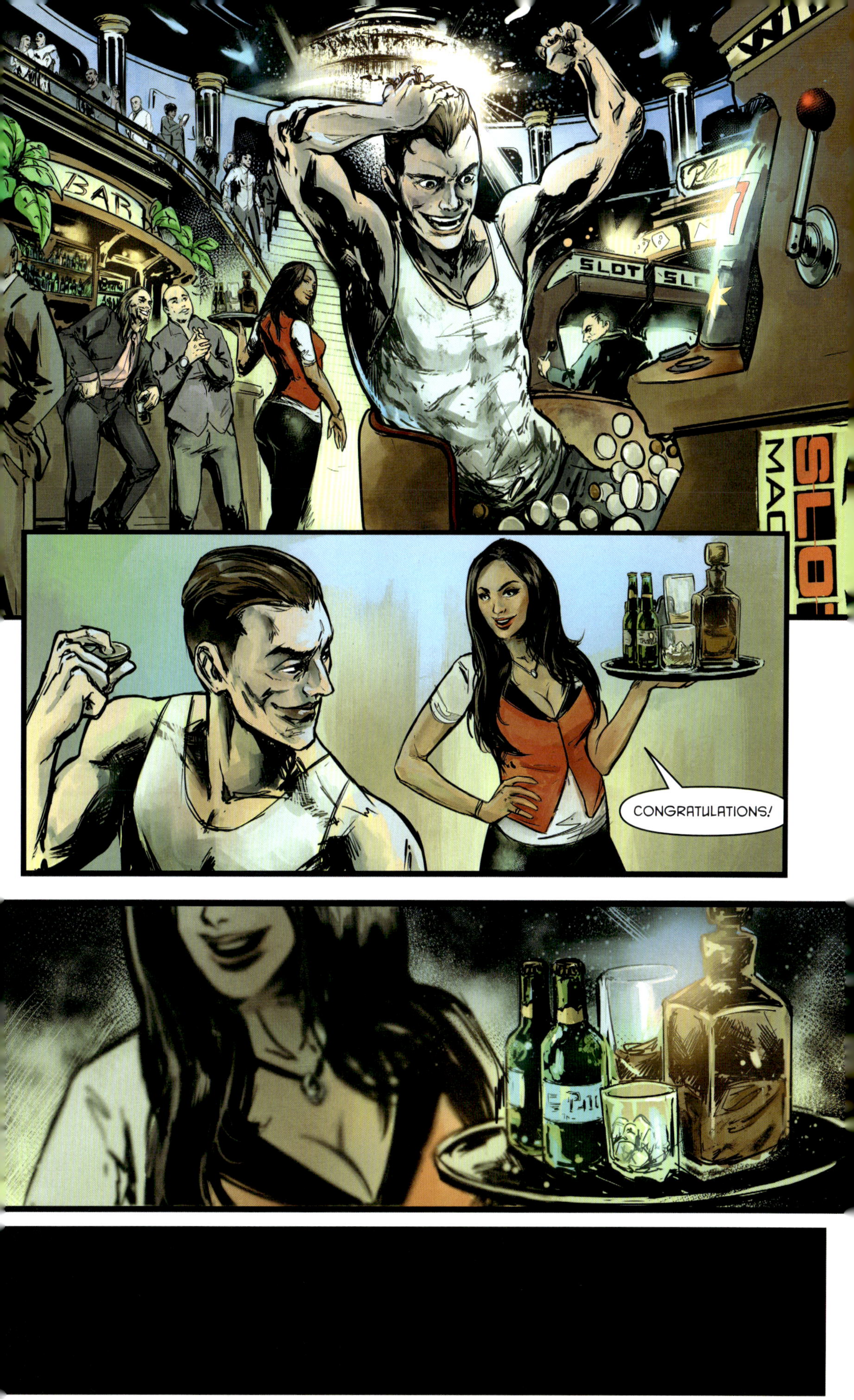
BAR
SLOT
CONGRATULATIONS!

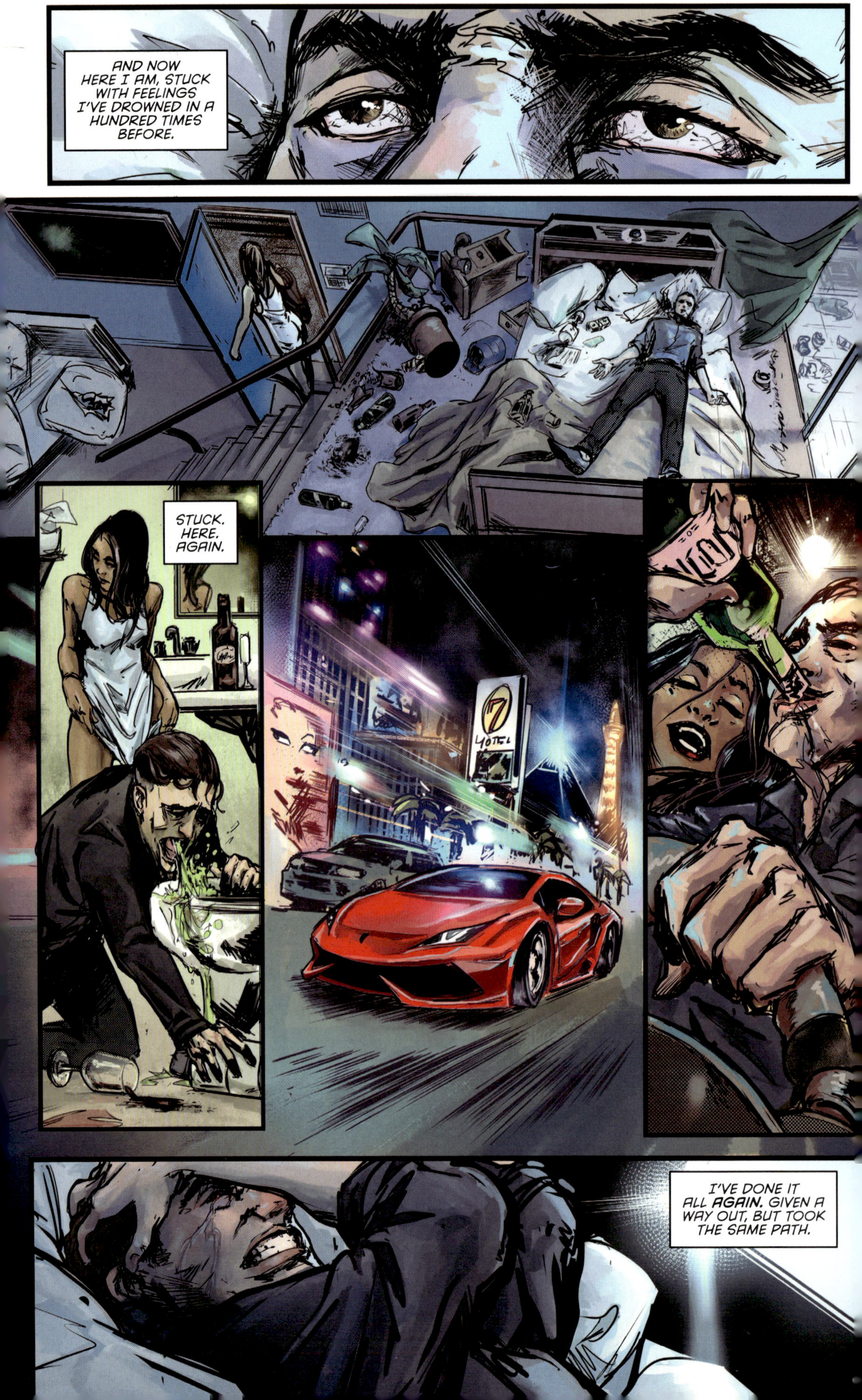
AND NOW HERE I AM, STUCK WITH FEELINGS I'VE DROWNED IN A HUNDRED TIMES BEFORE.
STUCK. HERE. AGAIN.
HOTEL
I'VE DONE IT ALL **AGAIN.** GIVEN A WAY OUT, BUT TOOK THE SAME PATH.

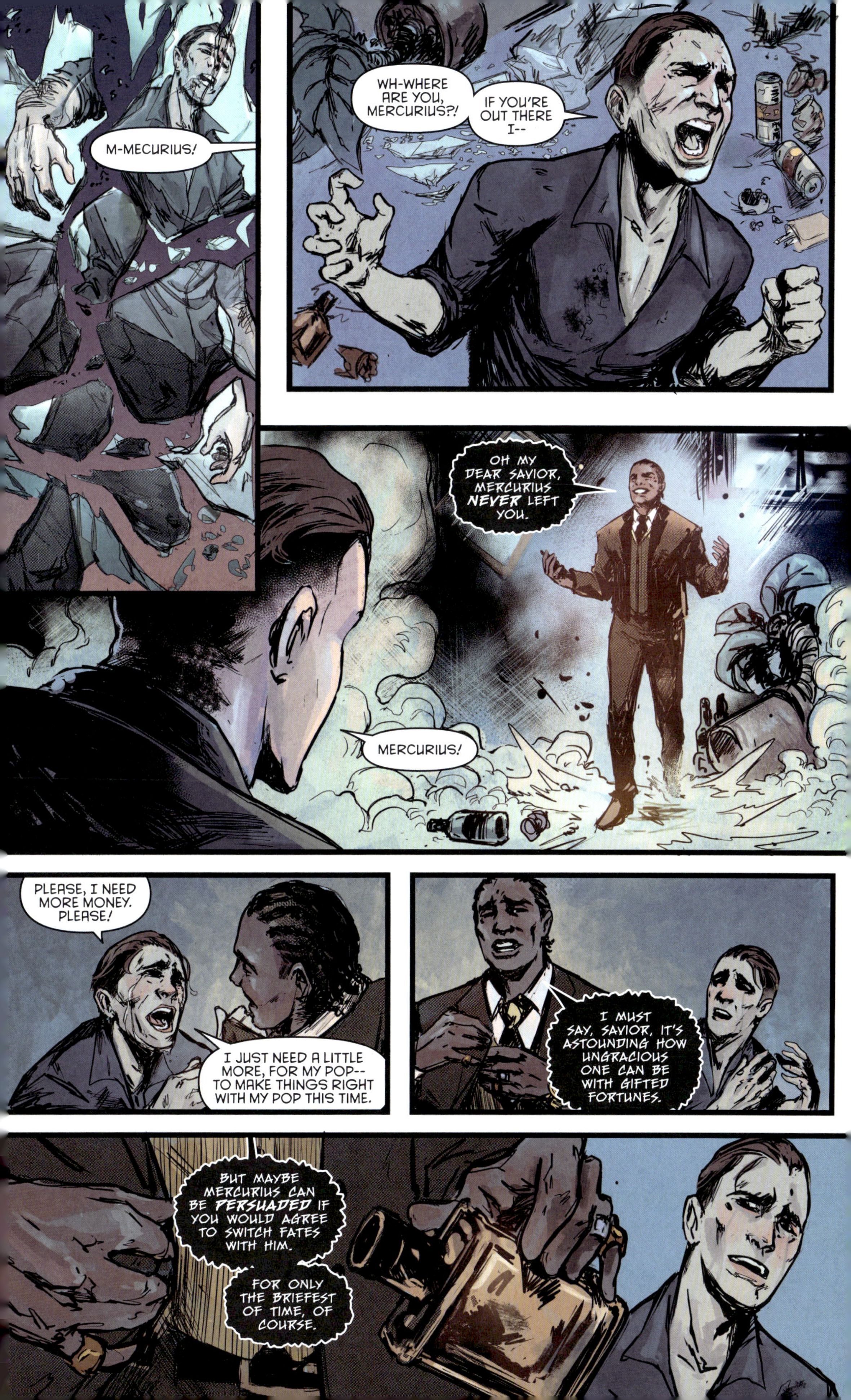
M-MECURIUS!
WH-WHERE ARE YOU, MERCURIUS?!
IF YOU'RE OUT THERE I--
OH MY DEAR SAVIOR, MERCURIUS NEVER LEFT YOU.
MERCURIUS!
PLEASE, I NEED MORE MONEY. PLEASE!
I JUST NEED A LITTLE MORE, FOR MY POP-- TO MAKE THINGS RIGHT WITH MY POP THIS TIME.
I MUST SAY, SAVIOR, IT'S ASTOUNDING HOW UNGRACIOUS ONE CAN BE WITH GIFTED FORTUNES.
BUT MAYBE MERCURIUS CAN BE PERSUADED IF YOU WOULD AGREE TO SWITCH FATES WITH HIM.
FOR ONLY THE BRIEFEST OF TIME, OF COURSE.

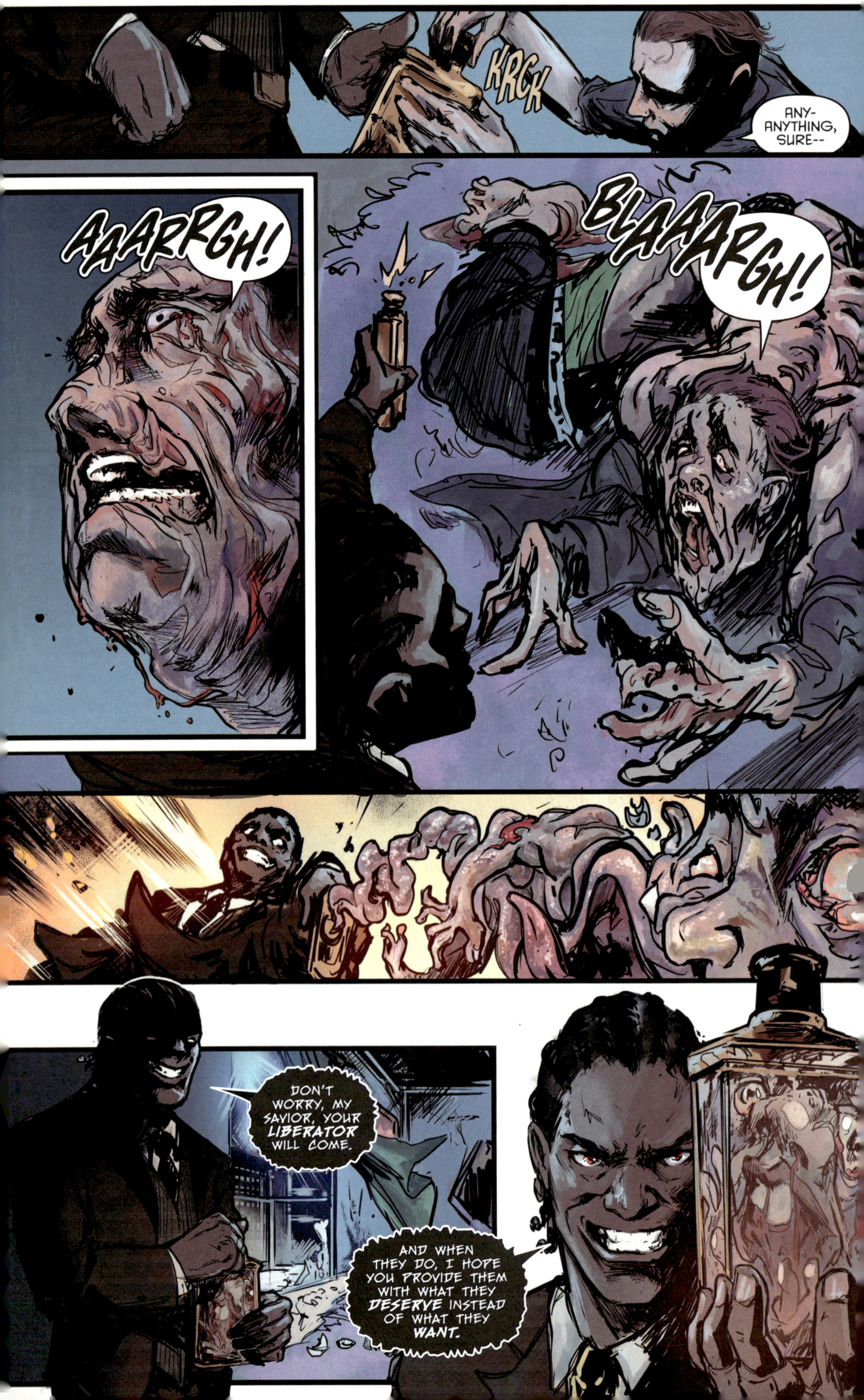
KRCK
ANY- ANYTHING, SURE--
AAARRGH!
BLAAAARGH!
DON'T WORRY, MY SAVIOR, YOUR LIBERATOR WILL COME.
AND WHEN THEY DO, I HOPE YOU PROVIDE THEM WITH WHAT THEY DESERVE INSTEAD OF WHAT THEY WANT.

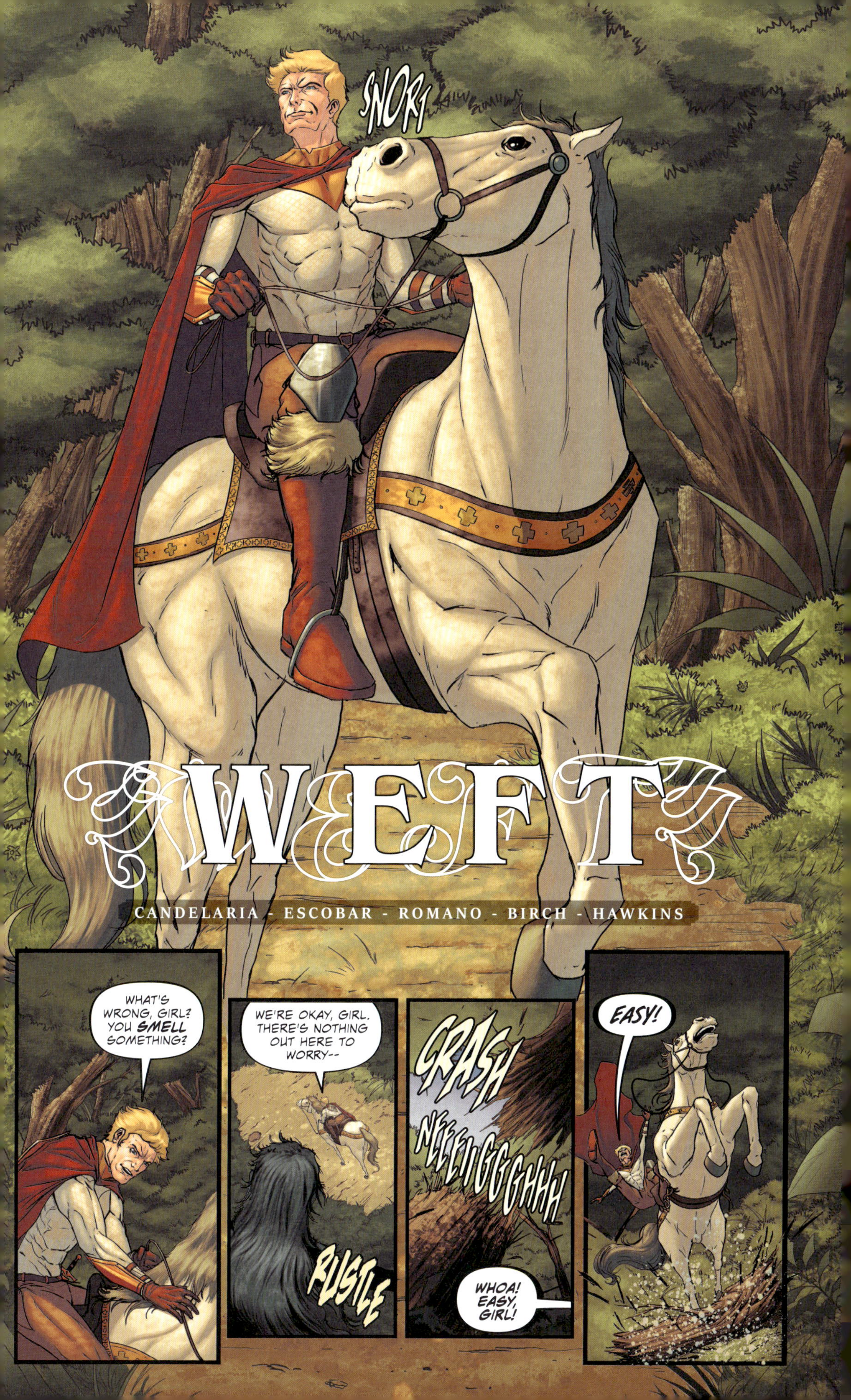
SNORT
WEFT
CANDELARIA - ESCOBAR - ROMANO - BIRCH - HAWKINS
WHAT'S WRONG, GIRL? YOU SMELL SOMETHING?
WE'RE OKAY, GIRL. THERE'S NOTHING OUT HERE TO WORRY--
RUSTLE
CRASH
NEEEIIGGGHHH
WHOA! EASY, GIRL!
EASY!

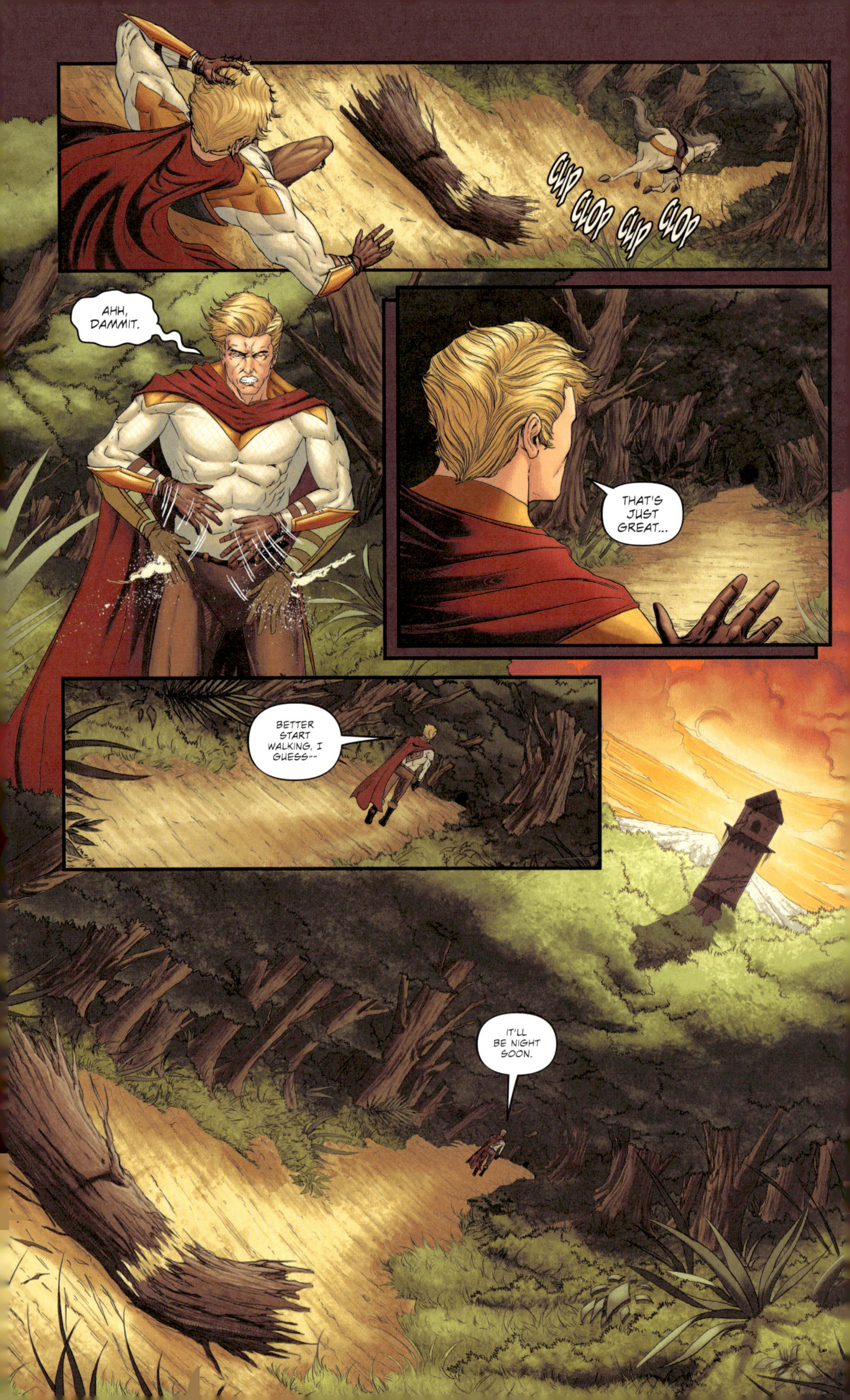
CLIP CLOP CLIP CLOP
AHH, DAMMIT.
THAT'S JUST GREAT...
BETTER START WALKING, I GUESS--
IT'LL BE NIGHT SOON.

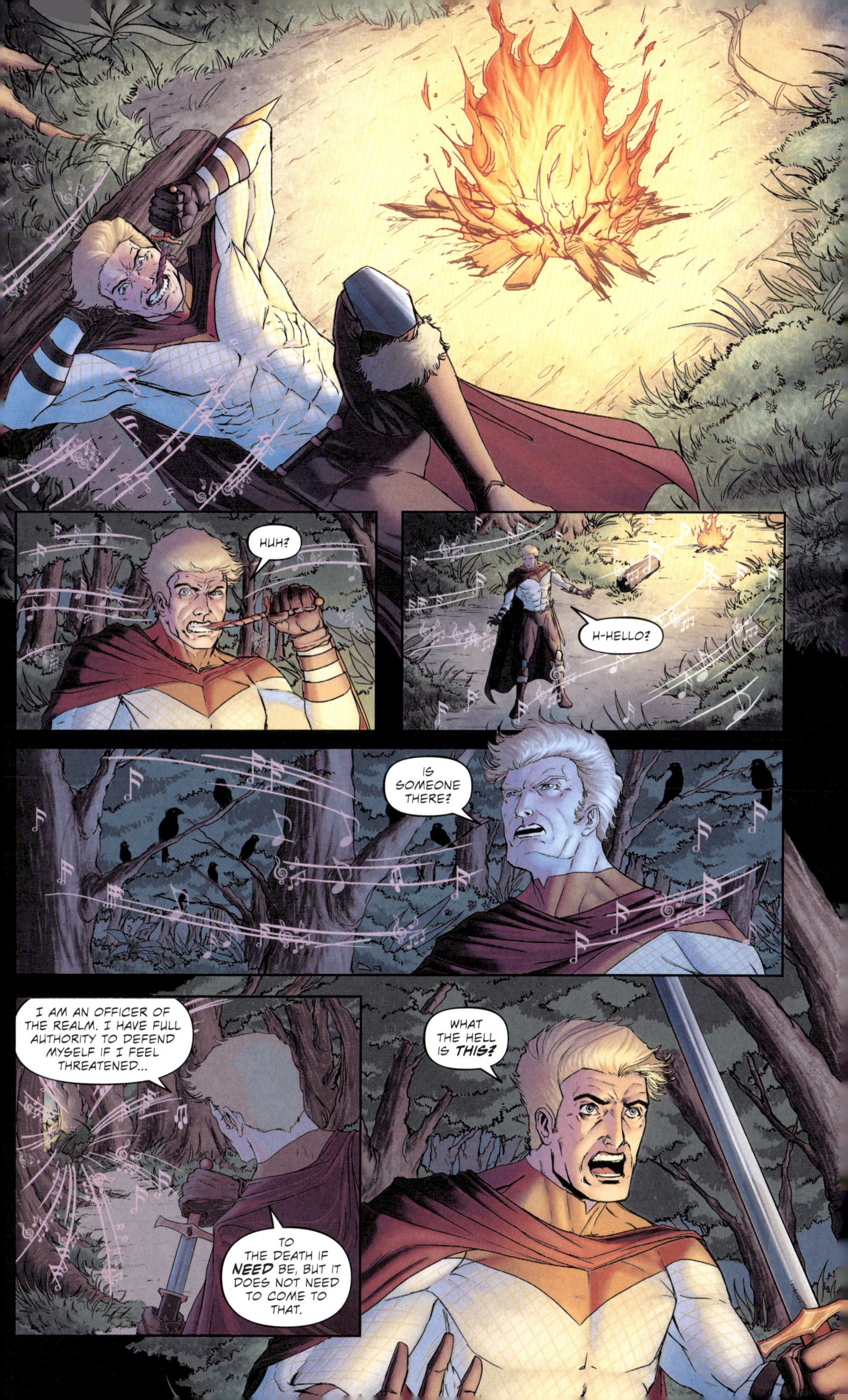
HUH?
H-HELLO?
IS SOMEONE THERE?
I AM AN OFFICER OF THE REALM. I HAVE FULL AUTHORITY TO DEFEND MYSELF IF I FEEL THREATENED...
TO THE DEATH IF NEED BE, BUT IT DOES NOT NEED TO COME TO THAT.
WHAT THE HELL IS THIS?

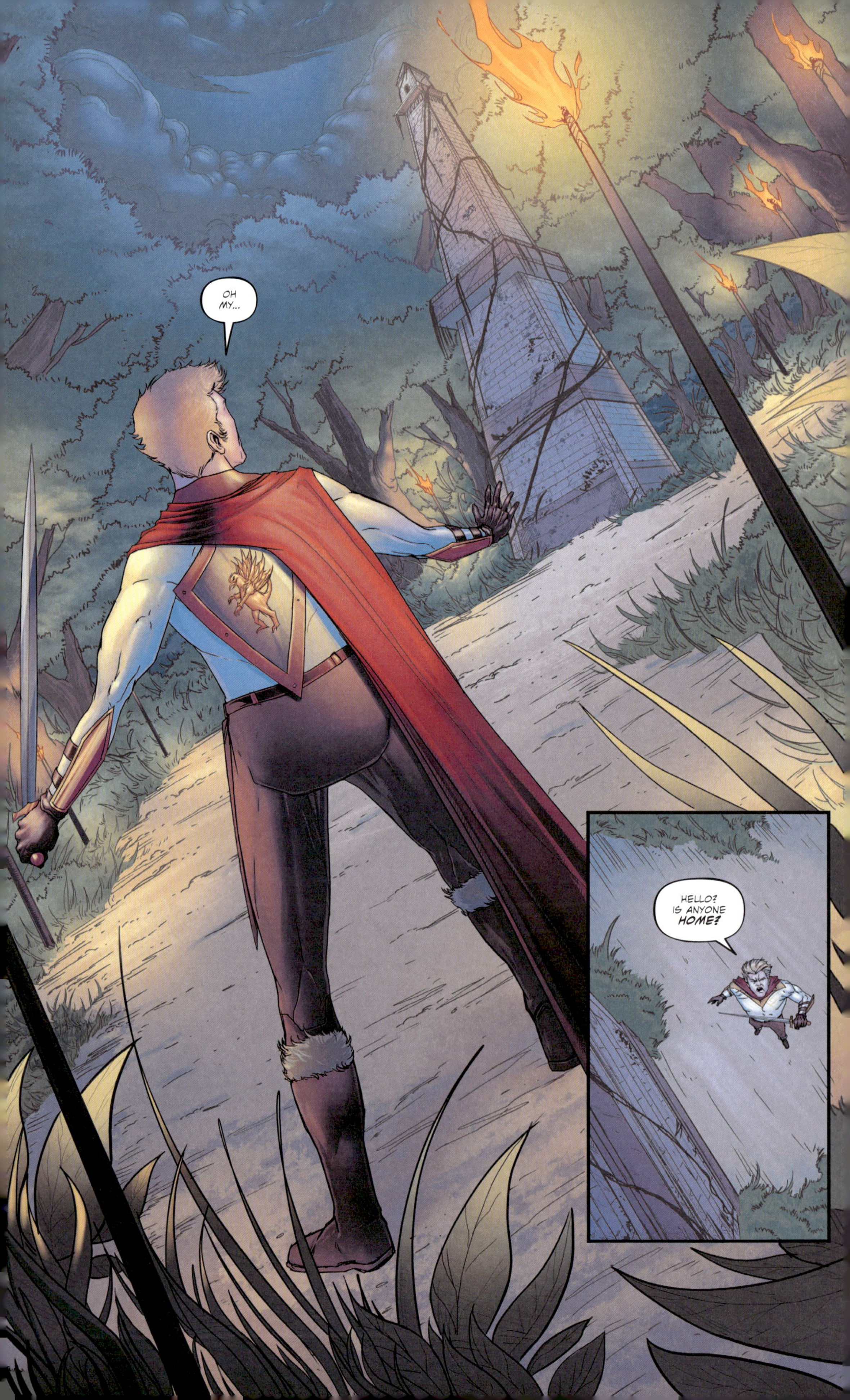
OH MY...
HELLO? IS ANYONE HOME?

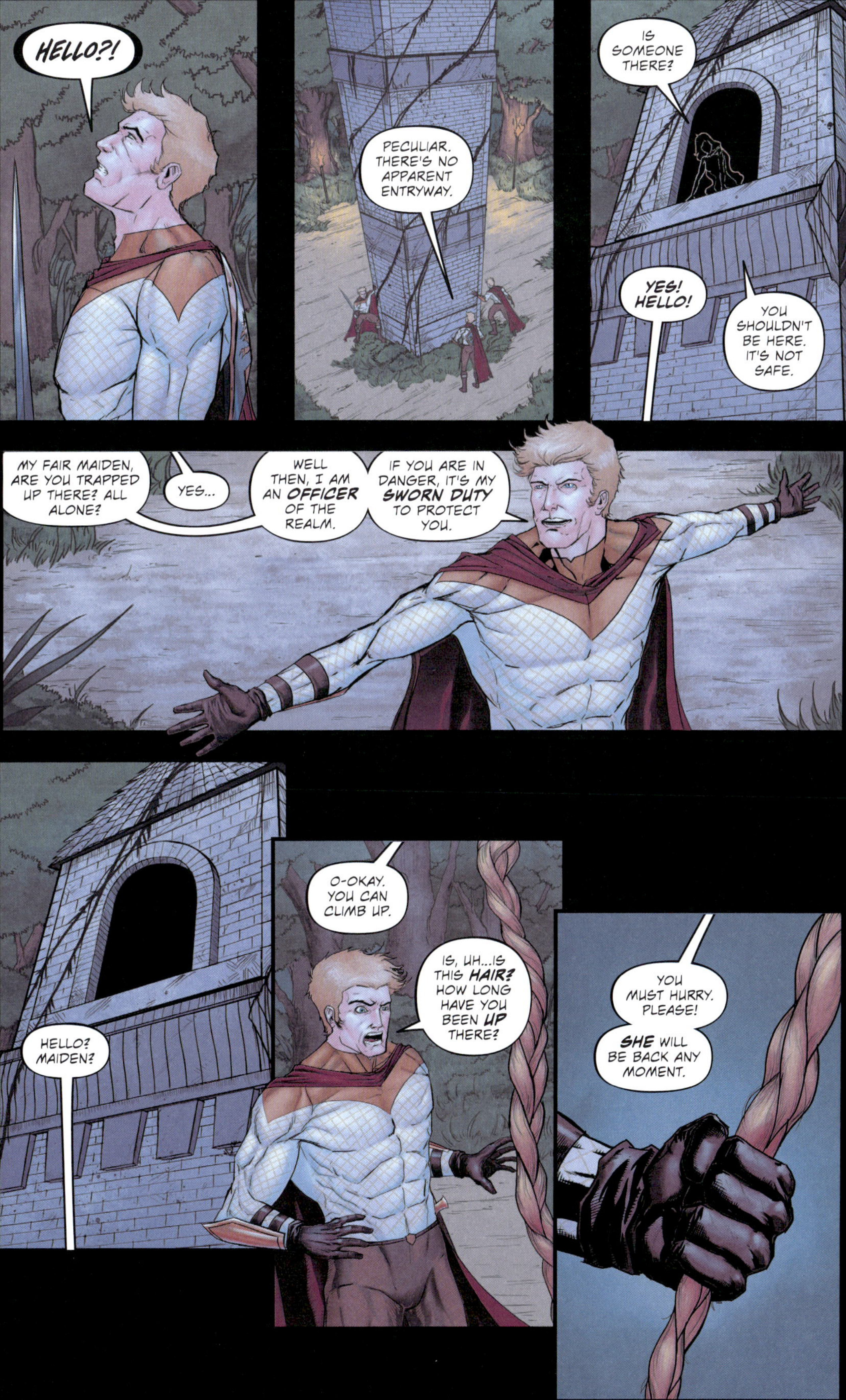
HELLO?!
PECULIAR. THERE'S NO APPARENT ENTRYWAY.
IS SOMEONE THERE?
YES! HELLO!
YOU SHOULDN'T BE HERE. IT'S NOT SAFE.
MY FAIR MAIDEN, ARE YOU TRAPPED UP THERE? ALL ALONE?
YES...
WELL THEN, I AM AN OFFICER OF THE REALM.
IF YOU ARE IN DANGER, IT'S MY SWORN DUTY TO PROTECT YOU.
HELLO? MAIDEN?
O-OKAY. YOU CAN CLIMB UP.
IS, UH...IS THIS HAIR? HOW LONG HAVE YOU BEEN UP THERE?
YOU MUST HURRY. PLEASE!
SHE WILL BE BACK ANY MOMENT.

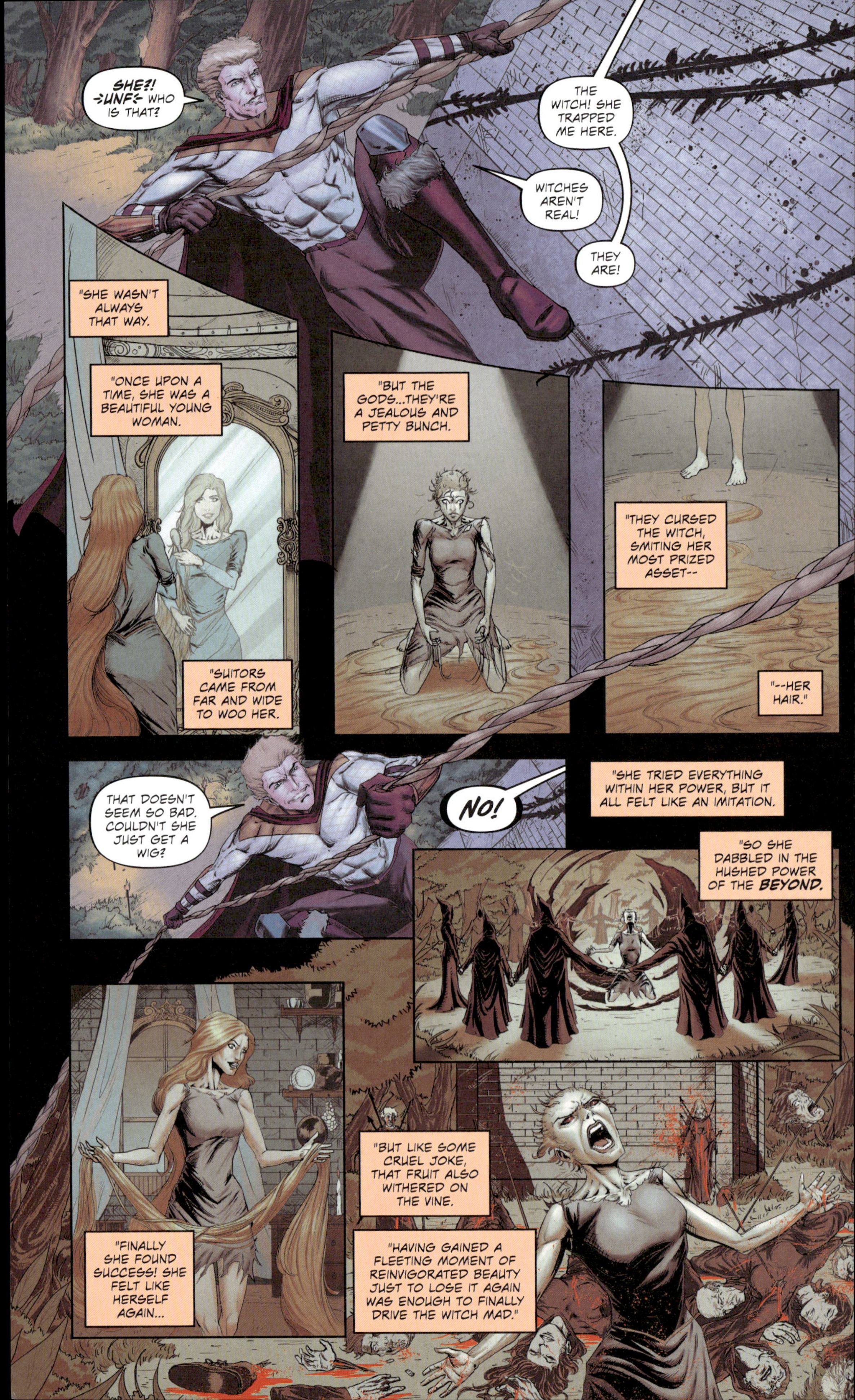
SHE?! -UNF- WHO IS THAT?
THE WITCH! SHE TRAPPED ME HERE.
WITCHES AREN'T REAL!
THEY ARE!
"SHE WASN'T ALWAYS THAT WAY.
"ONCE UPON A TIME, SHE WAS A BEAUTIFUL YOUNG WOMAN.
"SUITORS CAME FROM FAR AND WIDE TO WOO HER.
"BUT THE GODS...THEY'RE A JEALOUS AND PETTY BUNCH.
"THEY CURSED THE WITCH, SMITING HER MOST PRIZED ASSET--
"--HER HAIR."
THAT DOESN'T SEEM SO BAD. COULDN'T SHE JUST GET A WIG?
NO!
"SHE TRIED EVERYTHING WITHIN HER POWER, BUT IT ALL FELT LIKE AN IMITATION.
"SO SHE DABBLED IN THE HUSHED POWER OF THE BEYOND.
"FINALLY SHE FOUND SUCCESS! SHE FELT LIKE HERSELF AGAIN...
"BUT LIKE SOME CRUEL JOKE, THAT FRUIT ALSO WITHERED ON THE VINE.
"HAVING GAINED A FLEETING MOMENT OF REINVIGORATED BEAUTY JUST TO LOSE IT AGAIN WAS ENOUGH TO FINALLY DRIVE THE WITCH MAD."

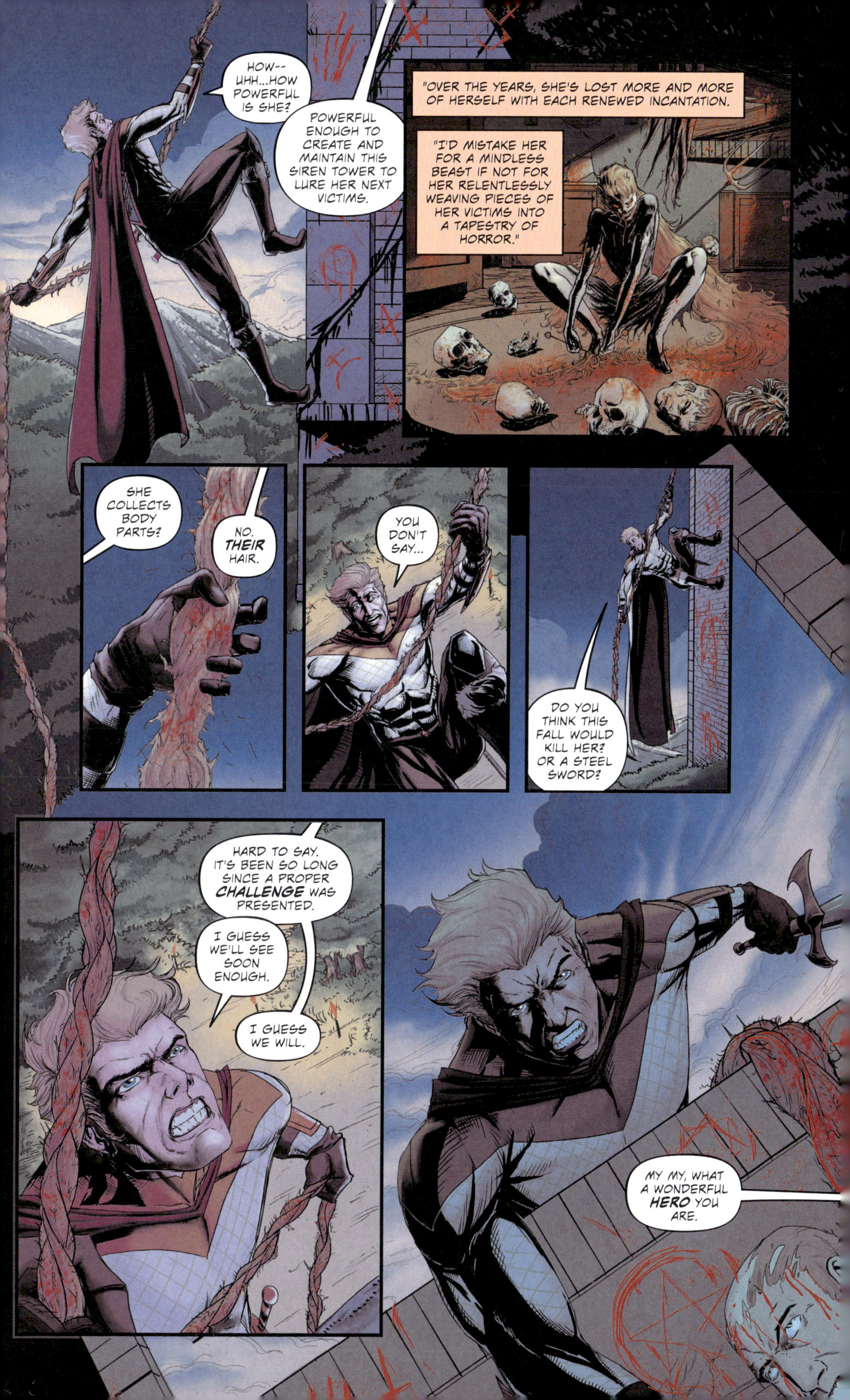
HOW-- UHH...HOW POWERFUL IS SHE?
POWERFUL ENOUGH TO CREATE AND MAINTAIN THIS SIREN TOWER TO LURE HER NEXT VICTIMS.
"OVER THE YEARS, SHE'S LOST MORE AND MORE OF HERSELF WITH EACH RENEWED INCANTATION.
"I'D MISTAKE HER FOR A MINDLESS BEAST IF NOT FOR HER RELENTLESSLY WEAVING PIECES OF HER VICTIMS INTO A TAPESTRY OF HORROR."
SHE COLLECTS BODY PARTS?
NO. **THEIR** HAIR.
YOU DON'T SAY...
DO YOU THINK THIS FALL WOULD KILL HER? OR A STEEL SWORD?
HARD TO SAY. IT'S BEEN SO LONG SINCE A PROPER **CHALLENGE** WAS PRESENTED.
I GUESS WE'LL SEE SOON ENOUGH.
I GUESS WE WILL.
MY MY, WHAT A WONDERFUL **HERO** YOU ARE.

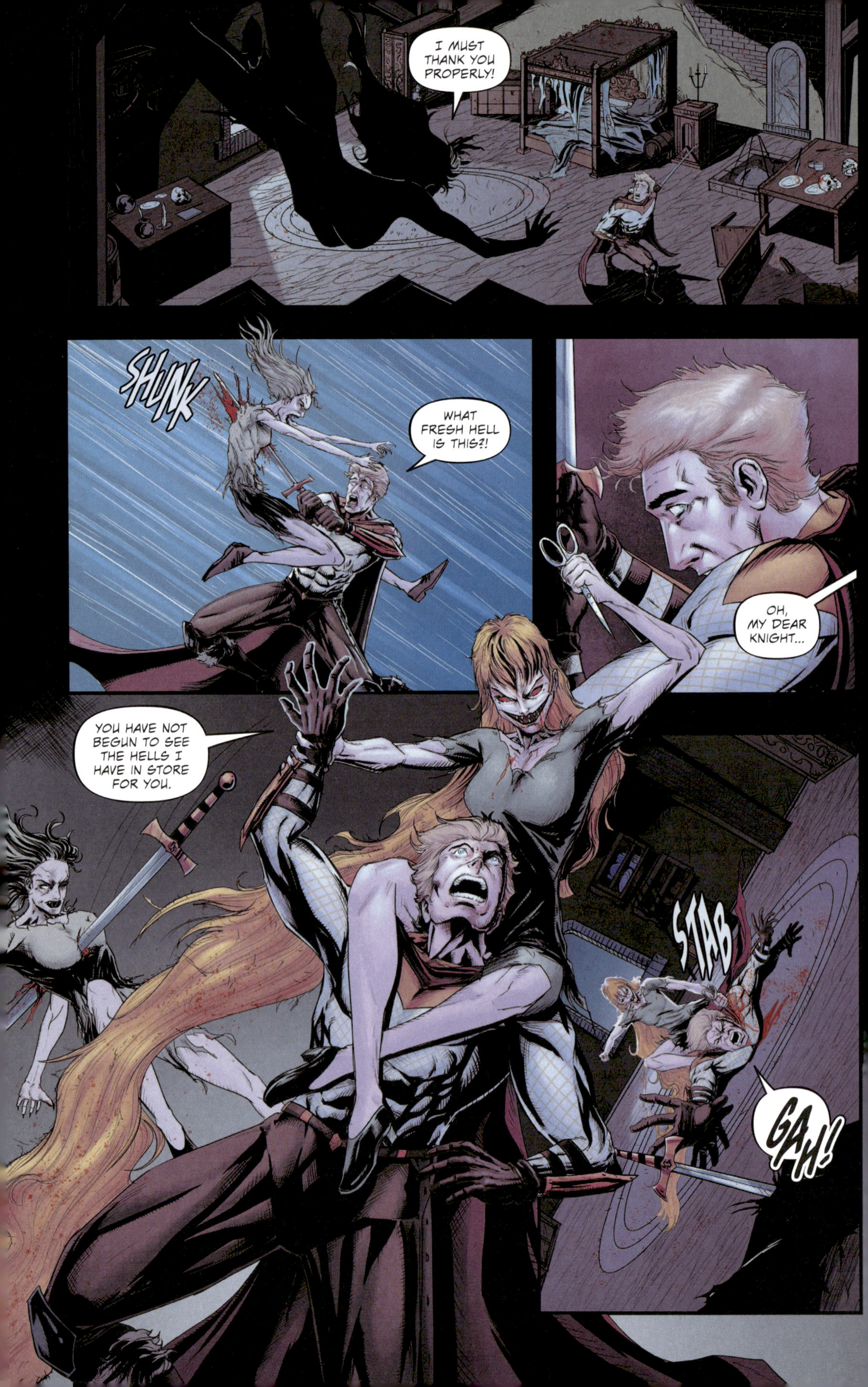
I MUST THANK YOU PROPERLY!
SHUNK
WHAT FRESH HELL IS THIS?!
OH, MY DEAR KNIGHT...
YOU HAVE NOT BEGUN TO SEE THE HELLS I HAVE IN STORE FOR YOU.
STAB
GAH!

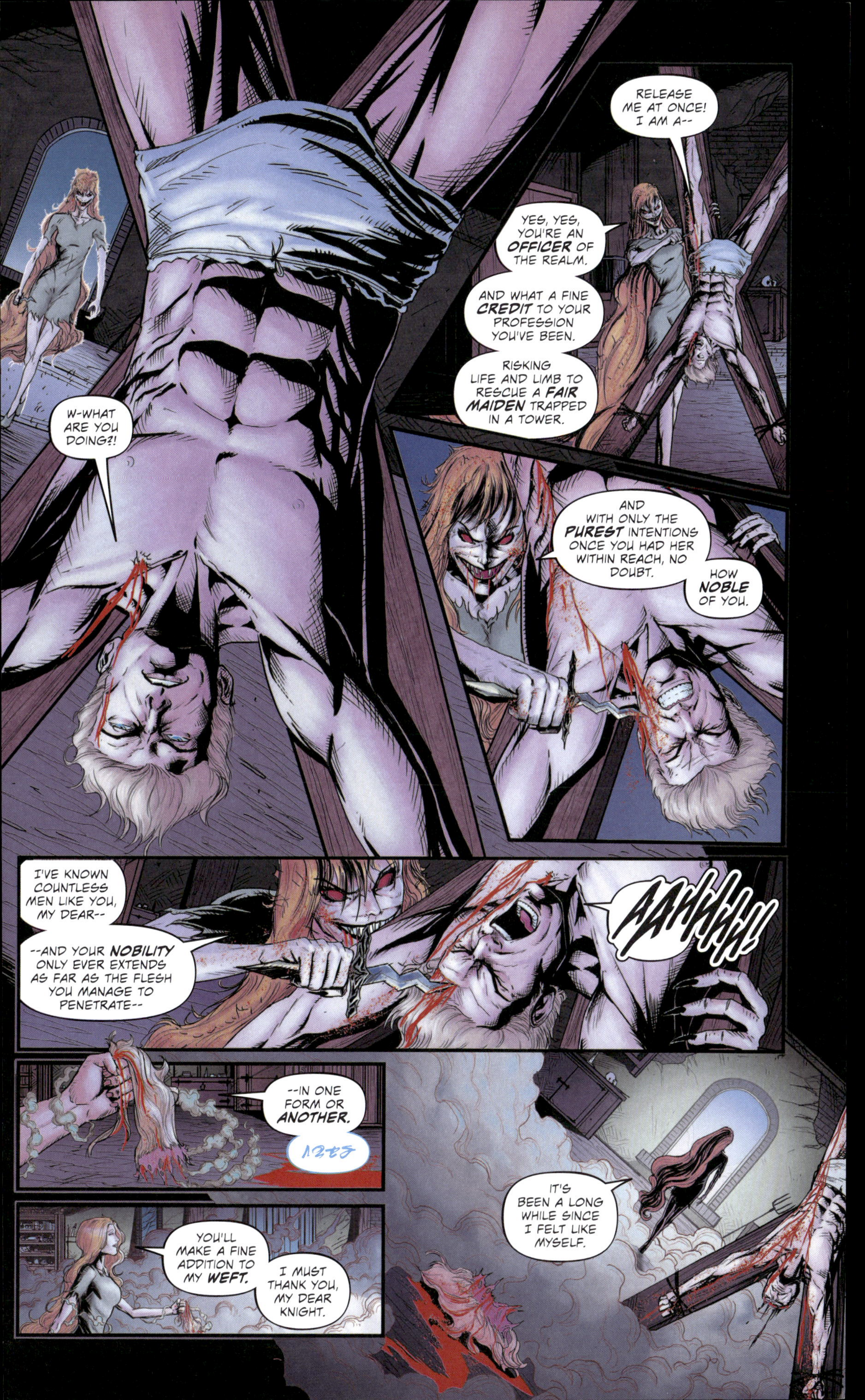
RELEASE ME AT ONCE! I AM A--
W-WHAT ARE YOU DOING?!
YES, YES, YOU'RE AN OFFICER OF THE REALM.
AND WHAT A FINE CREDIT TO YOUR PROFESSION YOU'VE BEEN.
RISKING LIFE AND LIMB TO RESCUE A FAIR MAIDEN TRAPPED IN A TOWER.
AND WITH ONLY THE PUREST INTENTIONS ONCE YOU HAD HER WITHIN REACH, NO DOUBT.
HOW NOBLE OF YOU.
I'VE KNOWN COUNTLESS MEN LIKE YOU, MY DEAR--
--AND YOUR NOBILITY ONLY EVER EXTENDS AS FAR AS THE FLESH YOU MANAGE TO PENETRATE--
AAHHHH!!
--IN ONE FORM OR ANOTHER.
YOU'LL MAKE A FINE ADDITION TO MY WEFT.
I MUST THANK YOU, MY DEAR KNIGHT.
IT'S BEEN A LONG WHILE SINCE I FELT LIKE MYSELF.

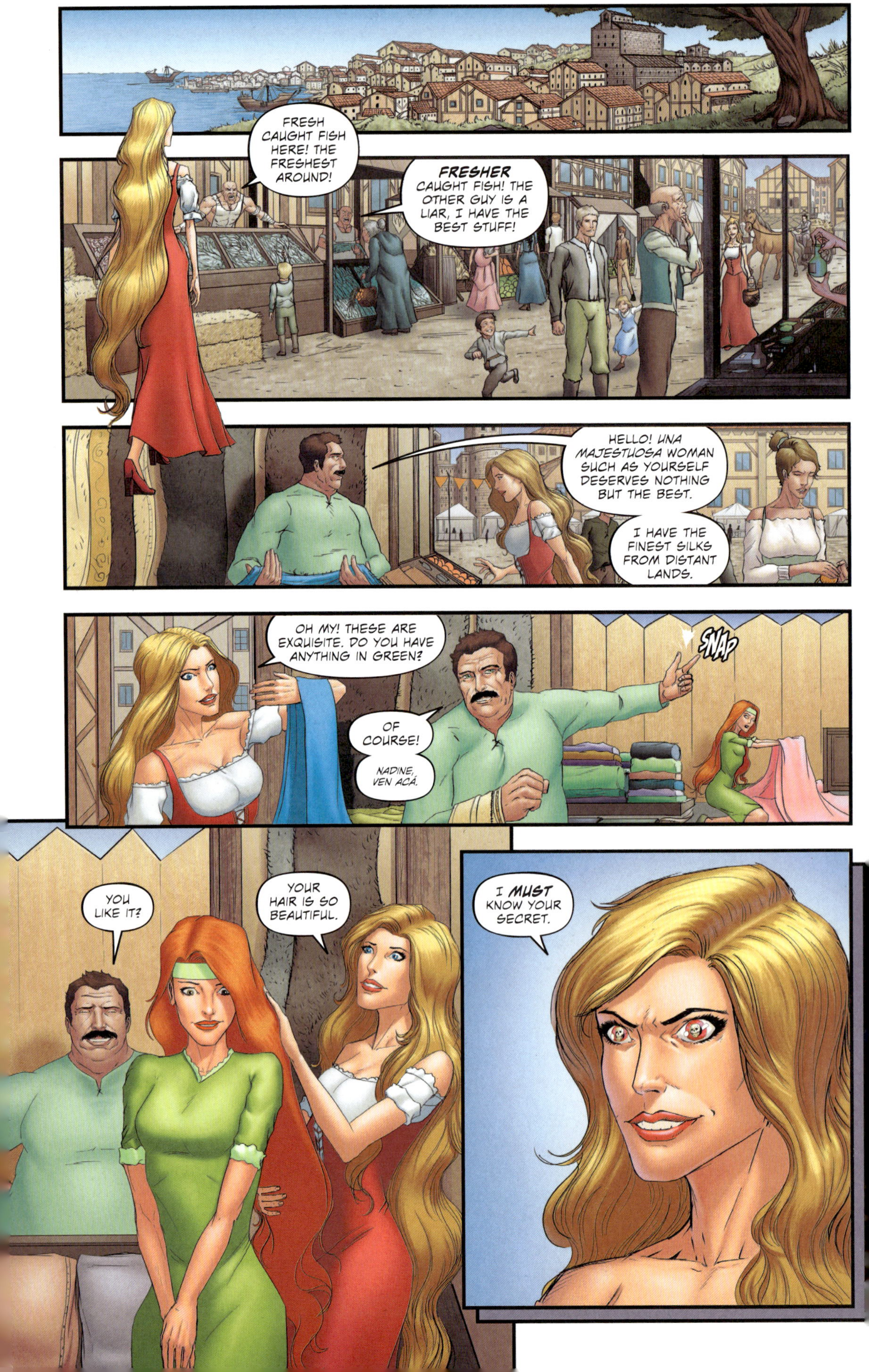
FRESH CAUGHT FISH HERE! THE FRESHEST AROUND!
FRESHER CAUGHT FISH! THE OTHER GUY IS A LIAR, I HAVE THE BEST STUFF!
HELLO! UNA MAJESTUOSA WOMAN SUCH AS YOURSELF DESERVES NOTHING BUT THE BEST.
I HAVE THE FINEST SILKS FROM DISTANT LANDS.
OH MY! THESE ARE EXQUISITE. DO YOU HAVE ANYTHING IN GREEN?
SNAP
OF COURSE!
NADINE, VEN ACÁ.
YOU LIKE IT?
YOUR HAIR IS SO BEAUTIFUL.
I MUST KNOW YOUR SECRET.

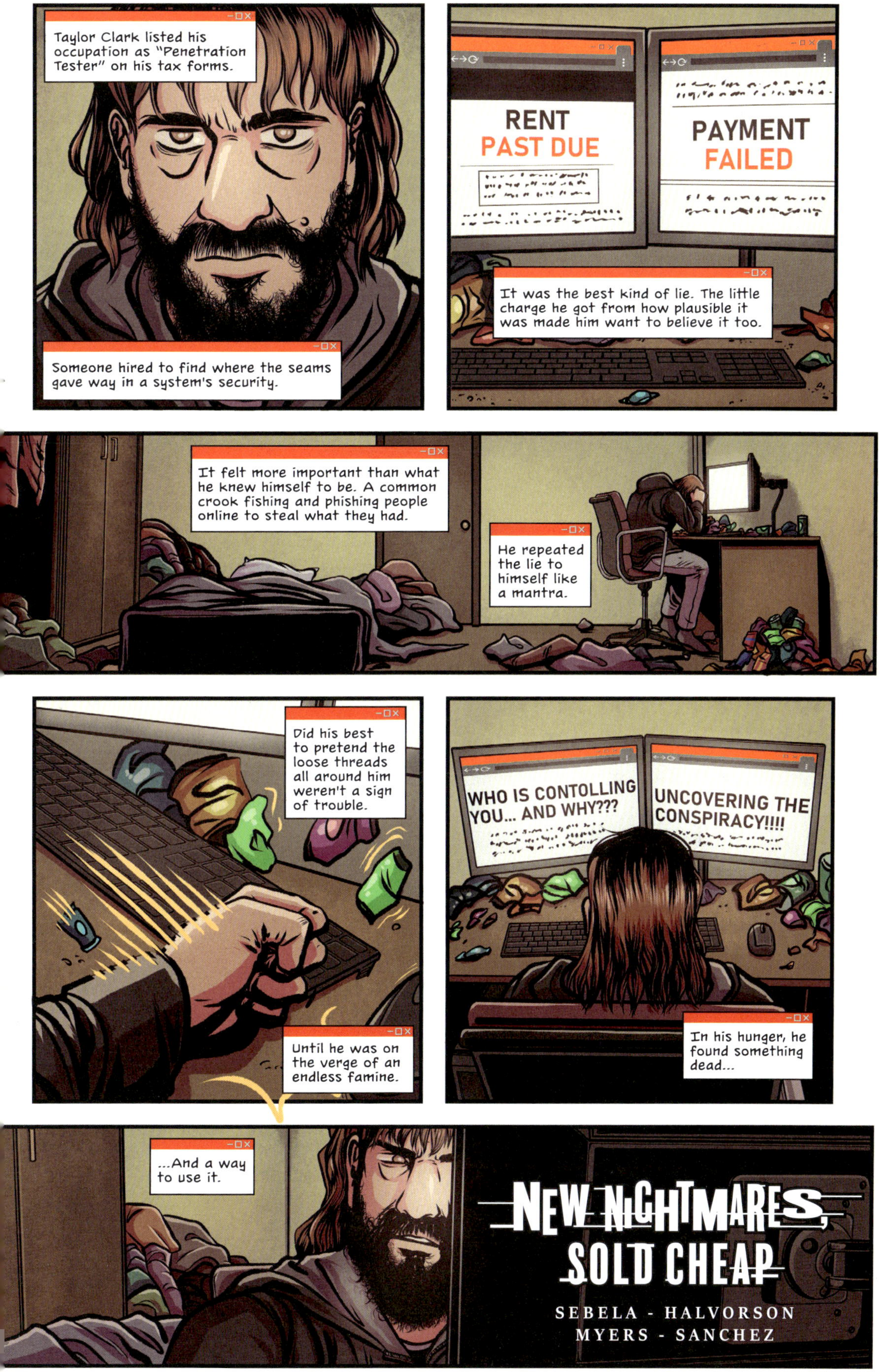

Taylor Clark listed his occupation as "Penetration Tester" on his tax forms.
Someone hired to find where the seams gave way in a system's security.
RENT
PAST DUE
PAYMENT
FAILED
It was the best kind of lie. The little charge he got from how plausible it was made him want to believe it too.
It felt more important than what he knew himself to be. A common crook fishing and phishing people online to steal what they had.
He repeated the lie to himself like a mantra.
Did his best to pretend the loose threads all around him weren't a sign of trouble.
Until he was on the verge of an endless famine.
WHO IS CONTOLLING YOU... AND WHY???
UNCOVERING THE CONSPIRACY!!!!
In his hunger, he found something dead...
...And a way to use it.
NEW NIGHTMARES, SOLD CHEAP
SEBELA - HALVORSON
MYERS - SANCHEZ

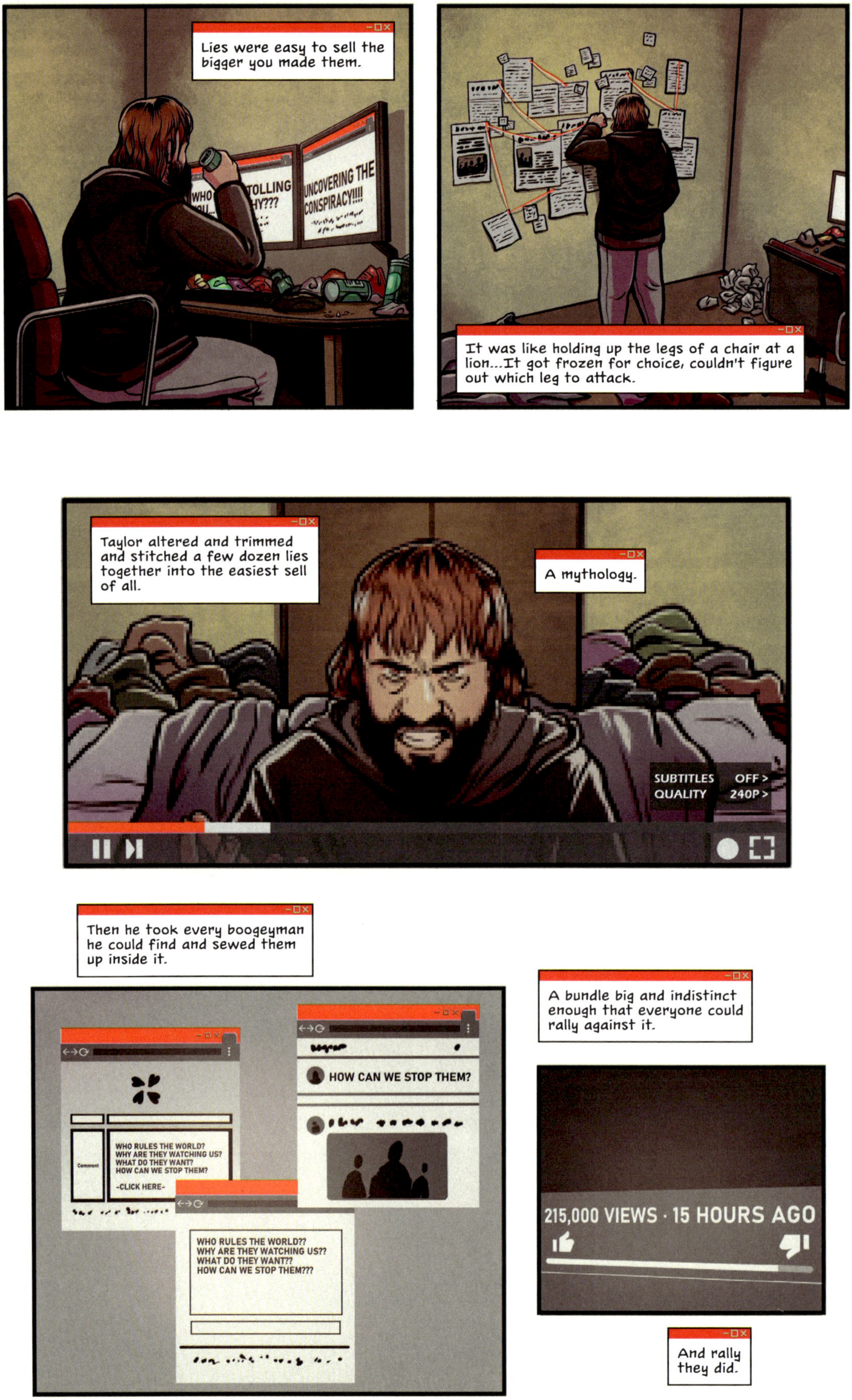
Lies were easy to sell the bigger you made them.
UNCOVERING THE CONSPIRACY!!!!
It was like holding up the legs of a chair at a lion...It got frozen for choice, couldn't figure out which leg to attack.
Taylor altered and trimmed and stitched a few dozen lies together into the easiest sell of all.
A mythology.
SUBTITLES OFF >
QUALITY 240P >
Then he took every boogeyman he could find and sewed them up inside it.
WHO RULES THE WORLD?
WHY ARE THEY WATCHING US?
WHAT DO THEY WANT?
HOW CAN WE STOP THEM?
-CLICK HERE-
HOW CAN WE STOP THEM?
WHO RULES THE WORLD??
WHY ARE THEY WATCHING US??
WHAT DO THEY WANT??
HOW CAN WE STOP THEM???
A bundle big and indistinct enough that everyone could rally against it.
215,000 VIEWS · 15 HOURS AGO
And rally they did.

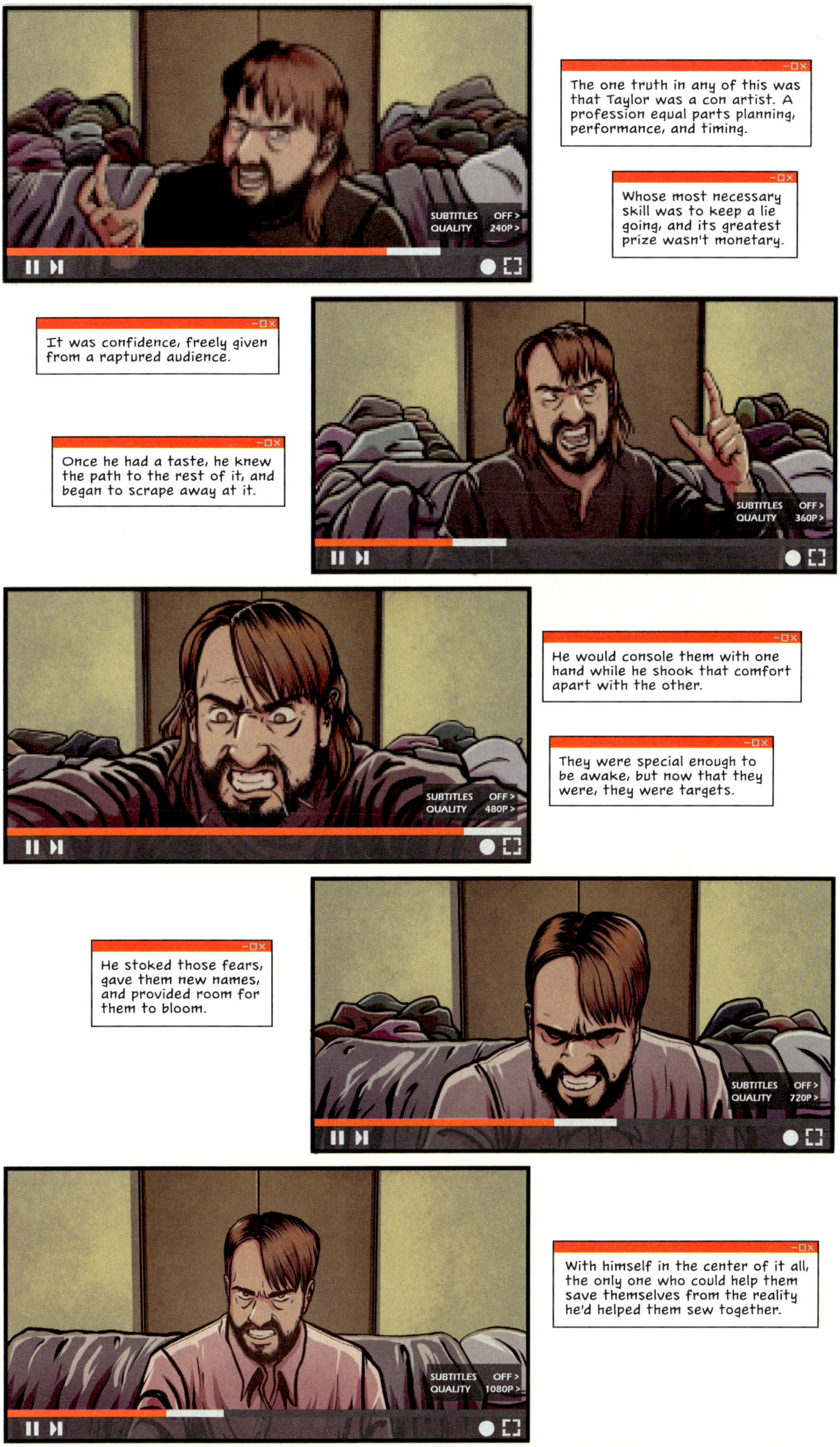
SUBTITLES OFF >
QUALITY 240P >
The one truth in any of this was that Taylor was a con artist. A profession equal parts planning, performance, and timing.
Whose most necessary skill was to keep a lie going, and its greatest prize wasn't monetary.
It was confidence, freely given from a raptured audience.
Once he had a taste, he knew the path to the rest of it, and began to scrape away at it.
SUBTITLES OFF >
QUALITY 360P >
SUBTITLES OFF >
QUALITY 480P >
He would console them with one hand while he shook that comfort apart with the other.
They were special enough to be awake, but now that they were, they were targets.
He stoked those fears, gave them new names, and provided room for them to bloom.
SUBTITLES OFF >
QUALITY 720P >
SUBTITLES OFF >
QUALITY 1080P >
With himself in the center of it all, the only one who could help them save themselves from the reality he'd helped them sew together.

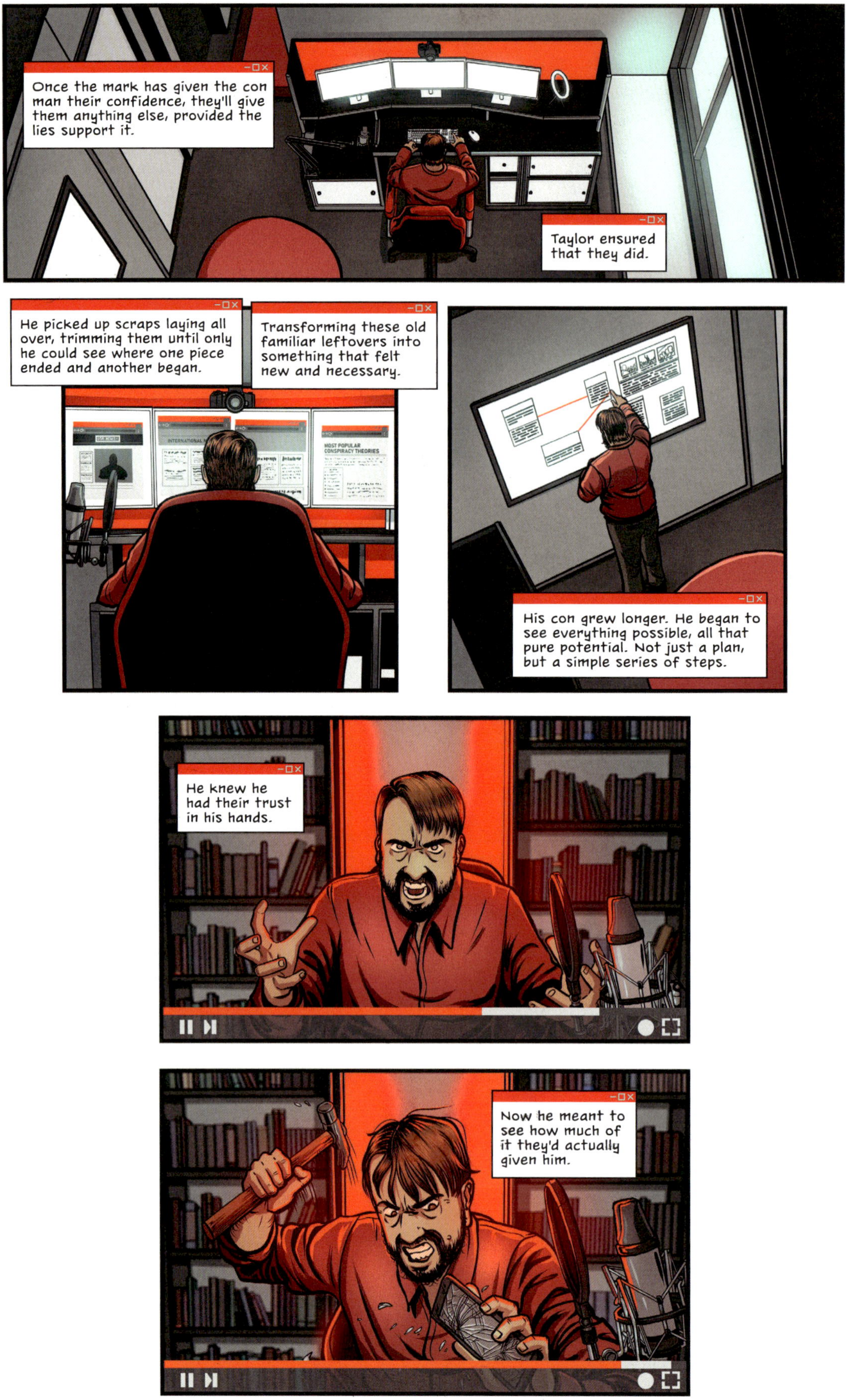
Once the mark has given the con man their confidence, they'll give them anything else, provided the lies support it.
Taylor ensured that they did.
He picked up scraps laying all over, trimming them until only he could see where one piece ended and another began.
Transforming these old familiar leftovers into something that felt new and necessary.
MOST POPULAR CONSPIRACY THEORIES
His con grew longer. He began to see everything possible, all that pure potential. Not just a plan, but a simple series of steps.
He knew he had their trust in his hands.
Now he meant to see how much of it they'd actually given him.

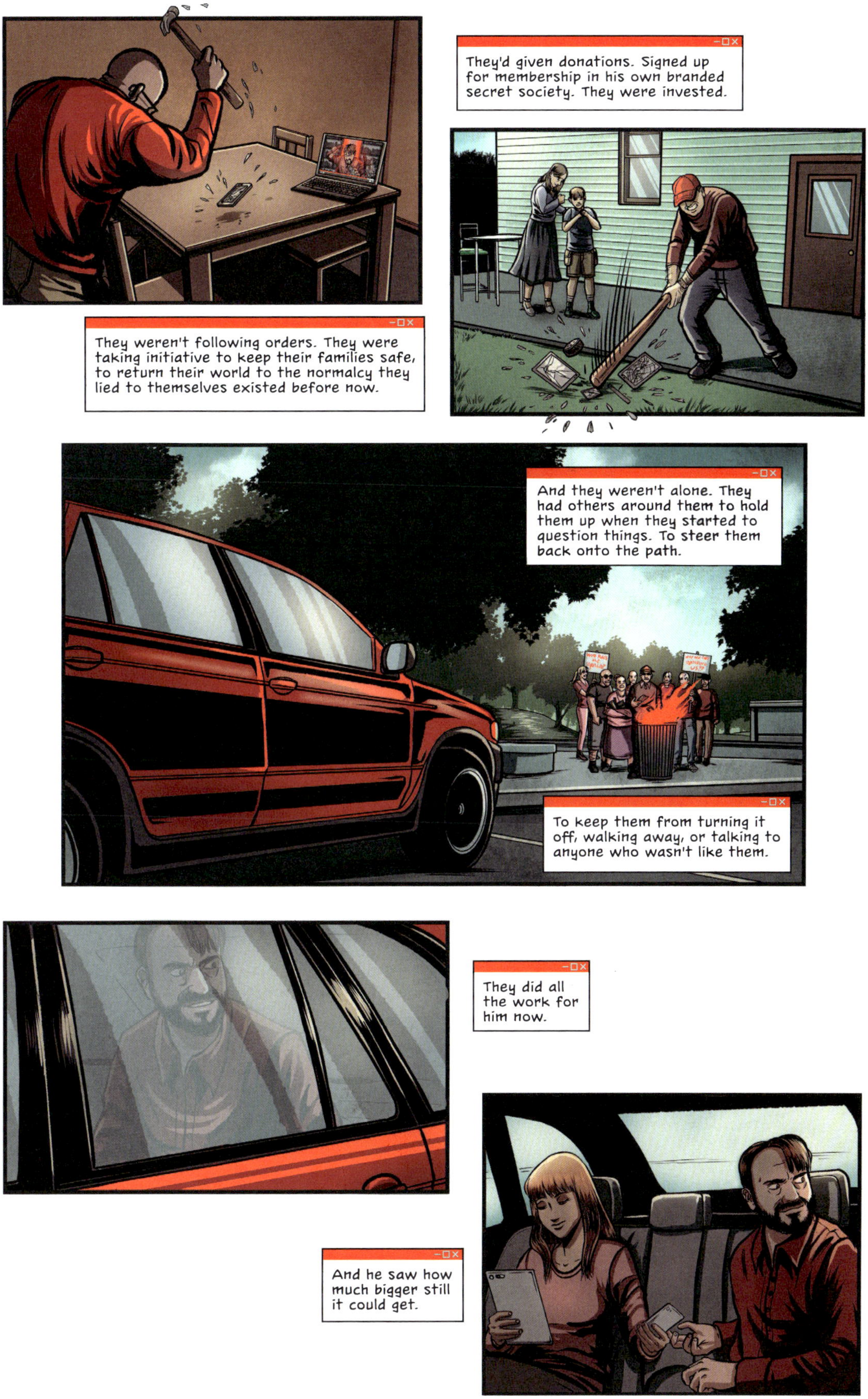
They'd given donations. Signed up for membership in his own branded secret society. They were invested.
They weren't following orders. They were taking initiative to keep their families safe, to return their world to the normalcy they lied to themselves existed before now.
And they weren't alone. They had others around them to hold them up when they started to question things. To steer them back onto the path.
To keep them from turning it off, walking away, or talking to anyone who wasn't like them.
They did all the work for him now.
And he saw how much bigger still it could get.

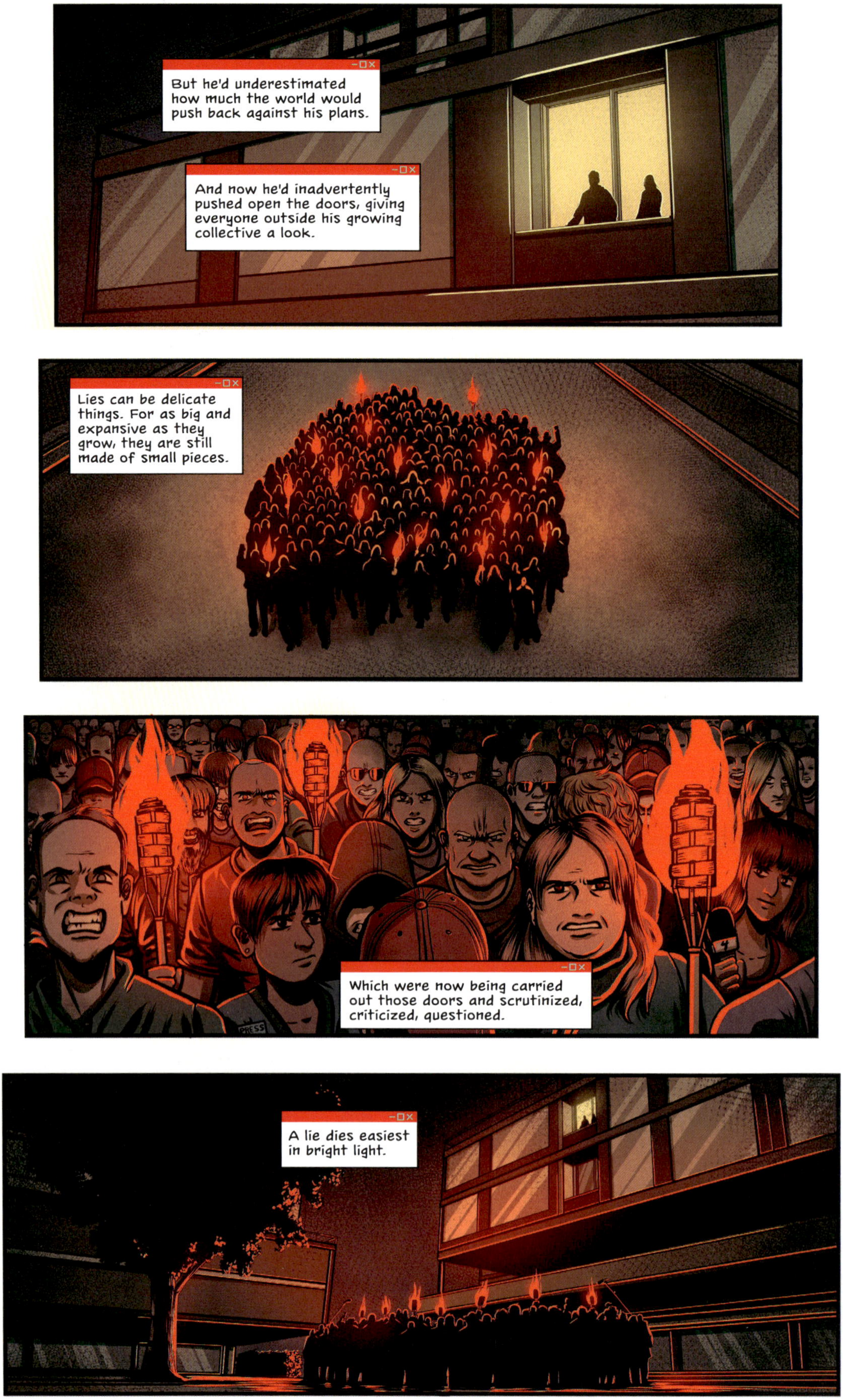
But he'd underestimated how much the world would push back against his plans.
And now he'd inadvertently pushed open the doors, giving everyone outside his growing collective a look.
Lies can be delicate things. For as big and expansive as they grow, they are still made of small pieces.
PRESS
Which were now being carried out those doors and scrutinized, criticized, questioned.
A lie dies easiest in bright light.

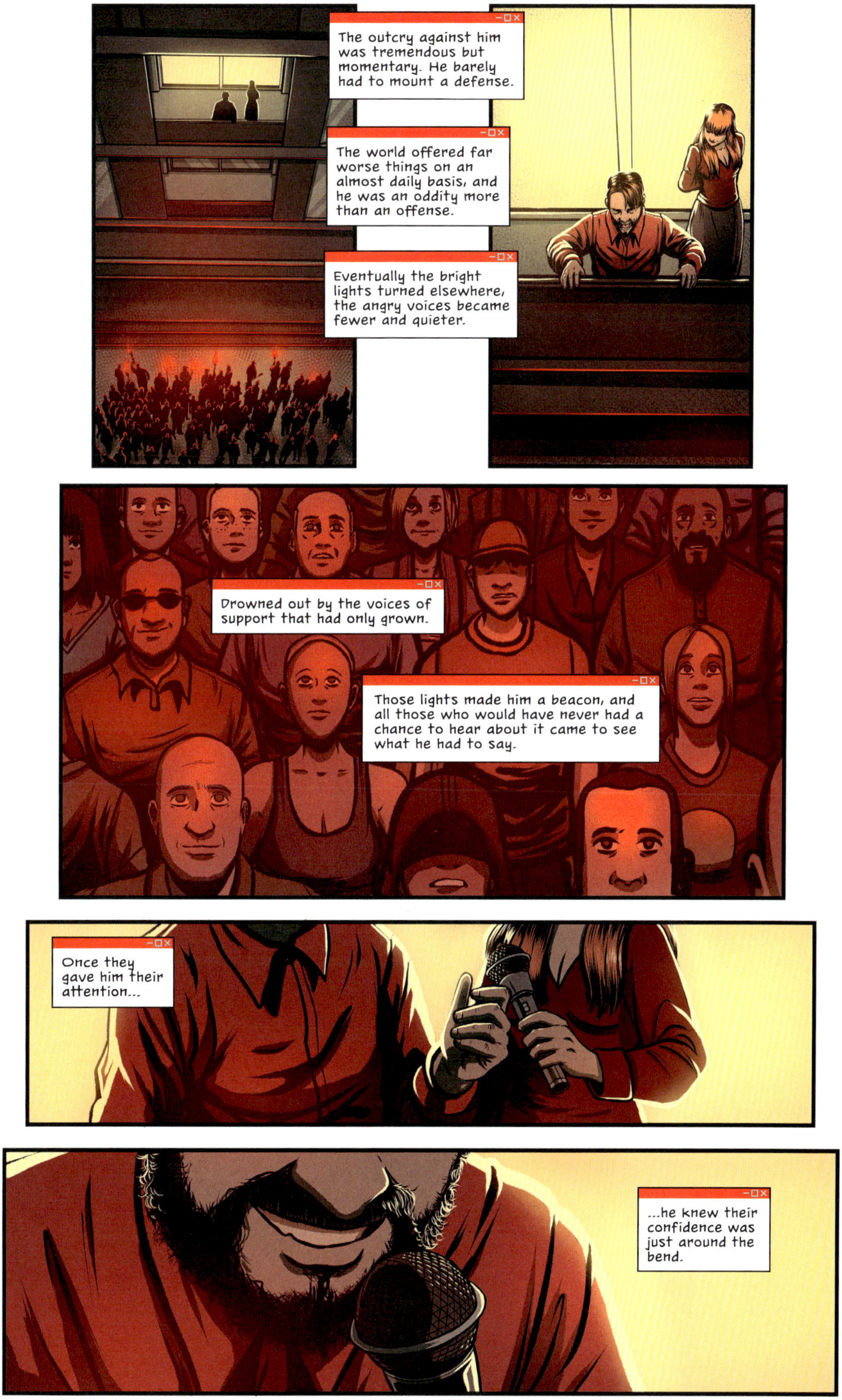
The outcry against him was tremendous but momentary. He barely had to mount a defense.
The world offered far worse things on an almost daily basis, and he was an oddity more than an offense.
Eventually the bright lights turned elsewhere, the angry voices became fewer and quieter.
Drowned out by the voices of support that had only grown.
Those lights made him a beacon, and all those who would have never had a chance to hear about it came to see what he had to say.
Once they gave him their attention...
...he knew their confidence was just around the bend.

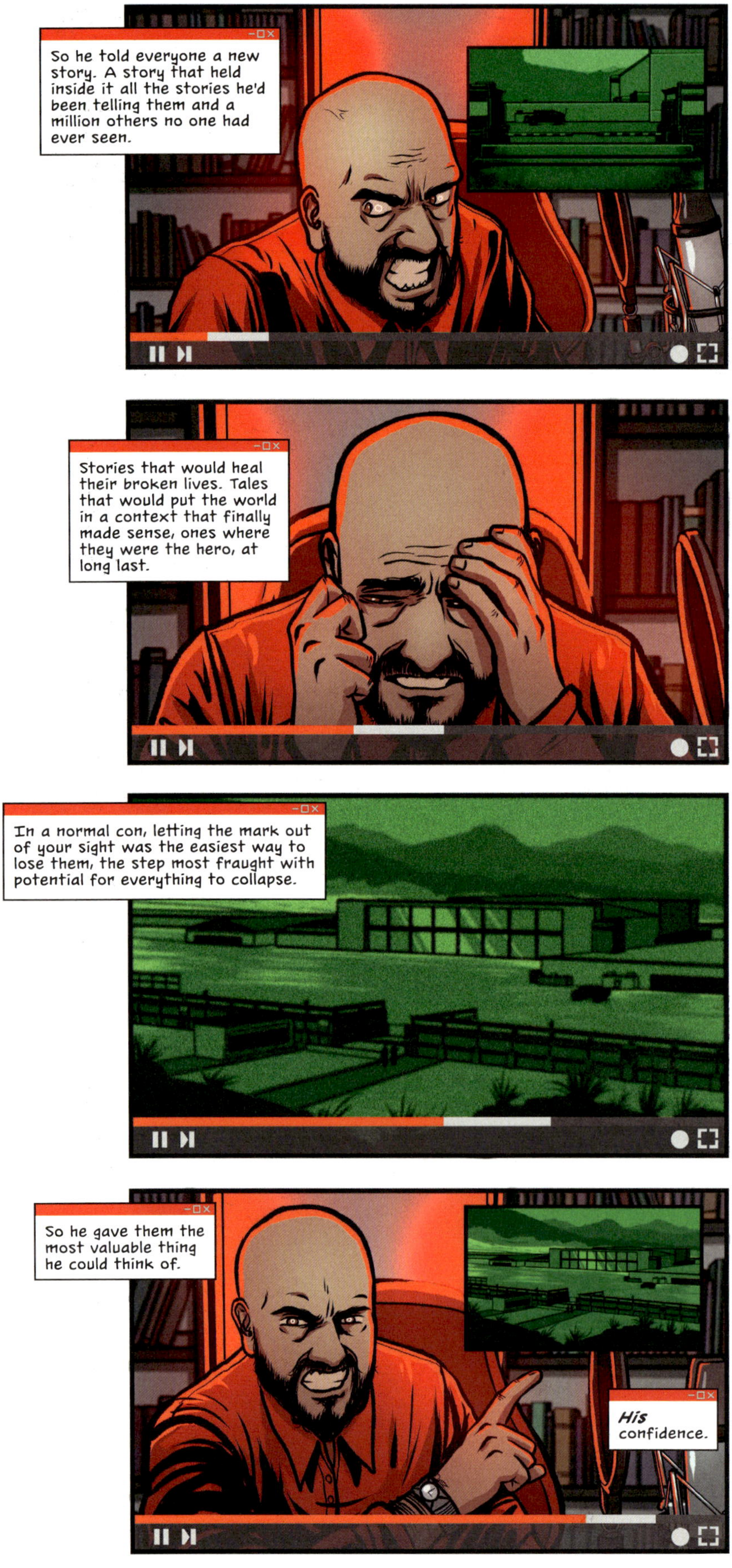
So he told everyone a new story. A story that held inside it all the stories he'd been telling them and a million others no one had ever seen.
Stories that would heal their broken lives. Tales that would put the world in a context that finally made sense, ones where they were the hero, at long last.
In a normal con, letting the mark out of your sight was the easiest way to lose them, the step most fraught with potential for everything to collapse.
So he gave them the most valuable thing he could think of.
His confidence.

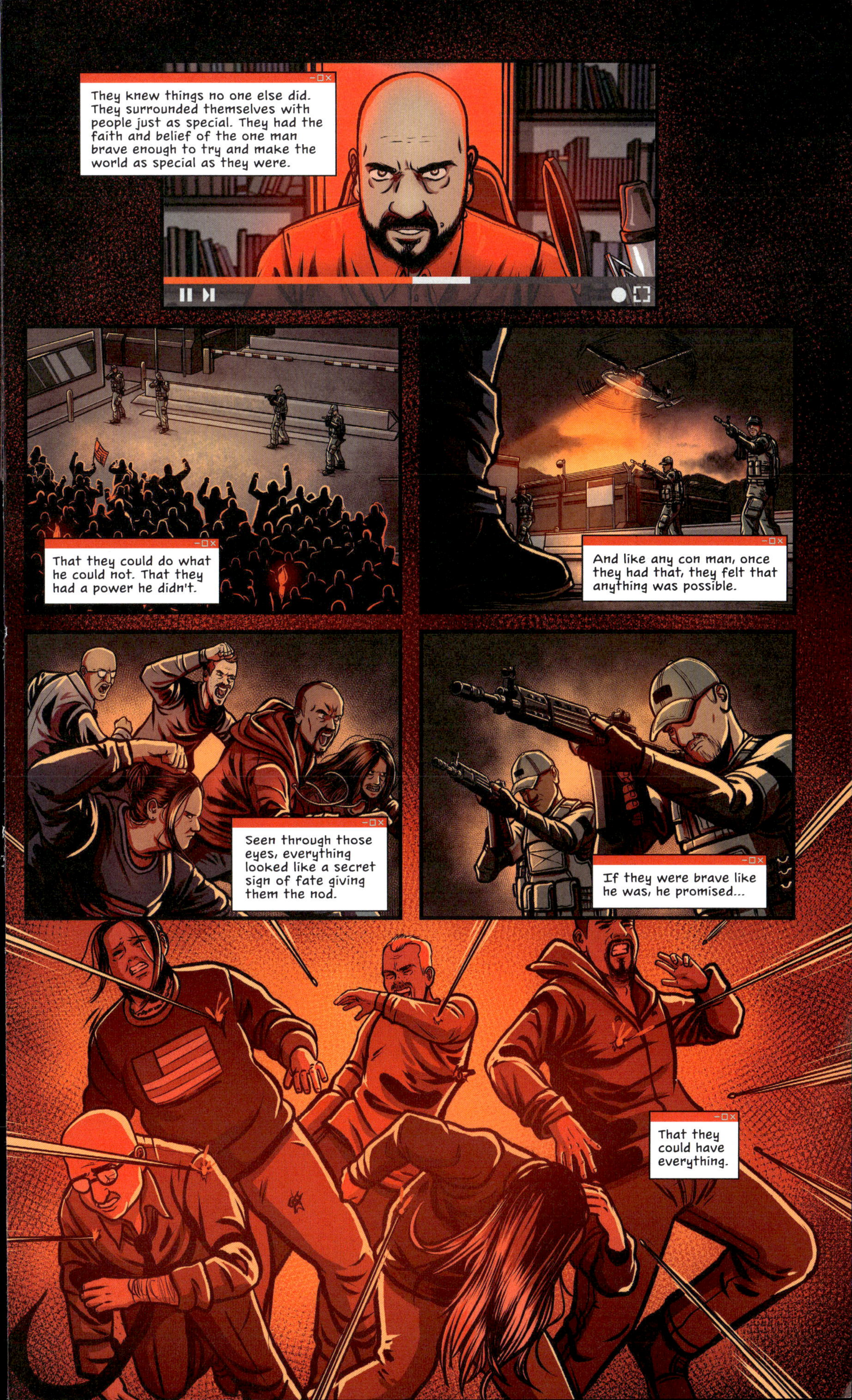
They knew things no one else did. They surrounded themselves with people just as special. They had the faith and belief of the one man brave enough to try and make the world as special as they were.
That they could do what he could not. That they had a power he didn't.
And like any con man, once they had that, they felt that anything was possible.
Seen through those eyes, everything looked like a secret sign of fate giving them the nod.
If they were brave like he was, he promised...
That they could have everything.

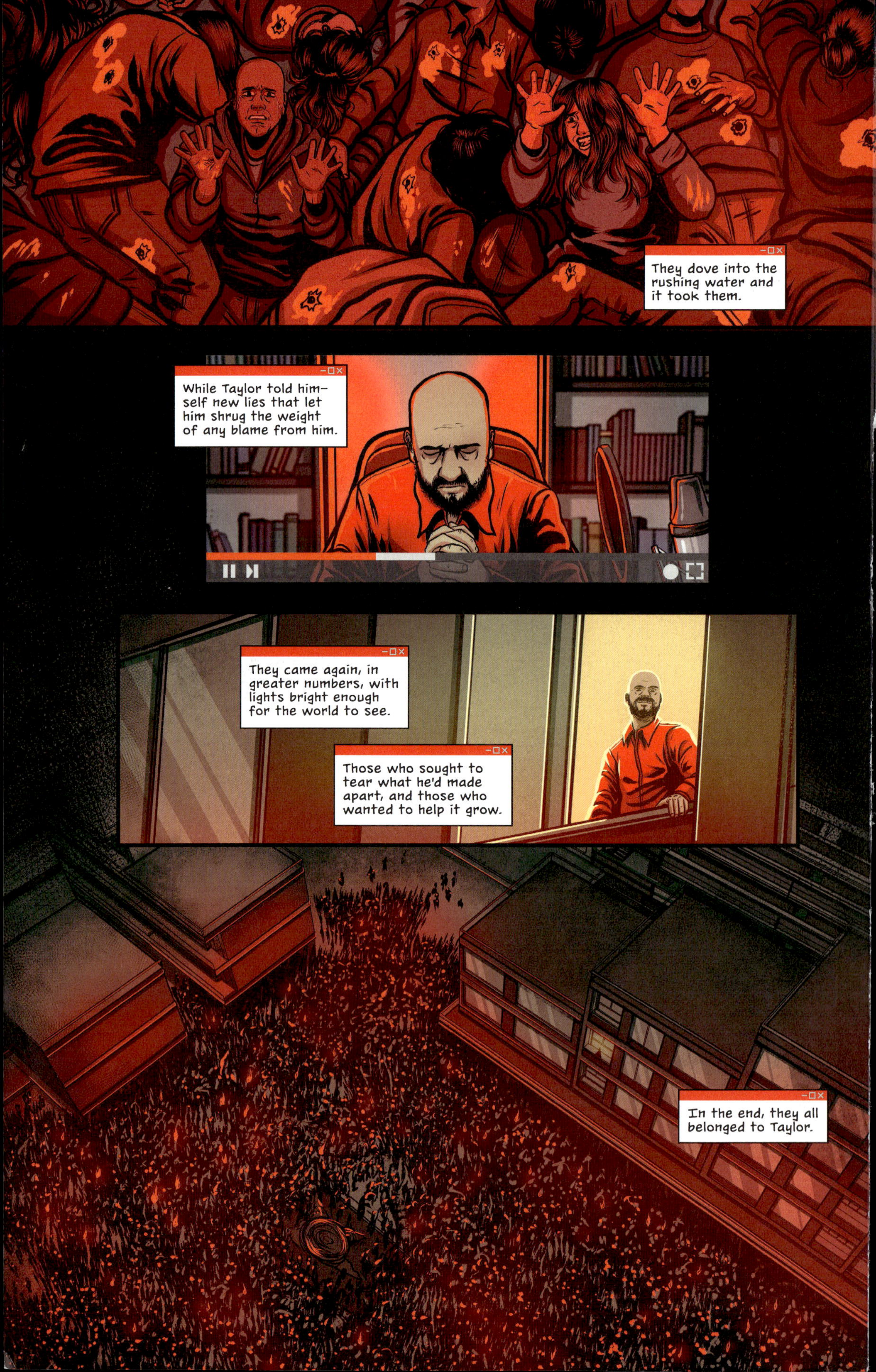
They dove into the rushing water and it took them.
While Taylor told himself new lies that let him shrug the weight of any blame from him.
They came again, in greater numbers, with lights bright enough for the world to see.
Those who sought to tear what he'd made apart, and those who wanted to help it grow.
In the end, they all belonged to Taylor.

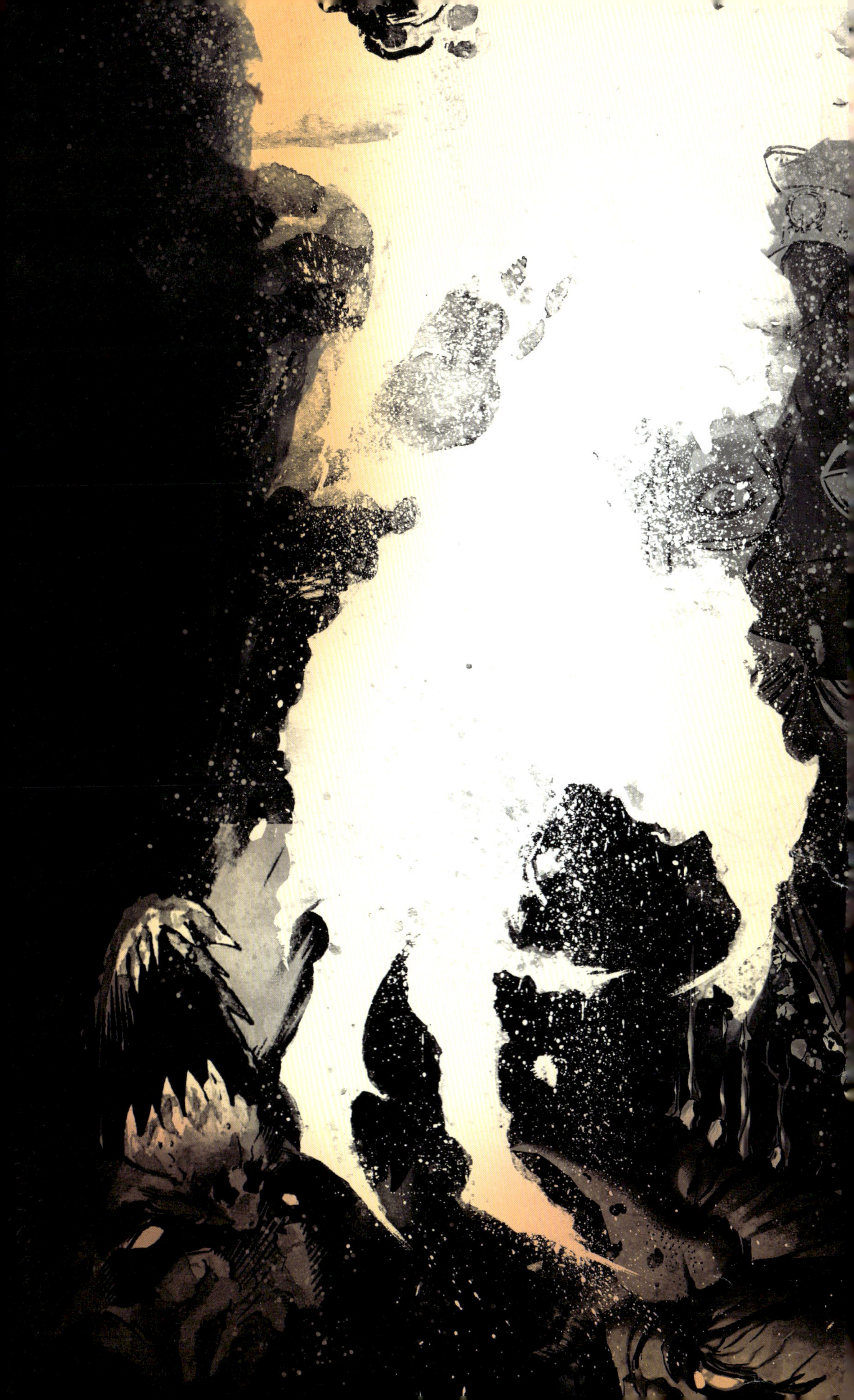